CW00794266

NARRATIVE OF

THE FIELD OPERATIONS

CONNECTED WITH

THE ZULU WAR OF 1879

PREPARED IN THE INTELLIGENCE BRANCH OF THE QUARTERMASTER-GENERAL'S DEPARTMENT, HORSE GUARDS, WAR OFFICE

The Naval & Military Press Ltd

published in association with

FIREPOWER
The Royal Artillery Museum
Woolwich

Published by
The Naval & Military Press Ltd
Unit 10 Ridgewood Industrial Park,
Uckfield, East Sussex,
TN22 5QE England
Tel: +44 (0) 1825 749494
Fax: +44 (0) 1825 765701
www.naval-military-press.com

in association with

FIREPOWER
The Royal Artillery Museum, Woolwich
www.firepower.org.uk

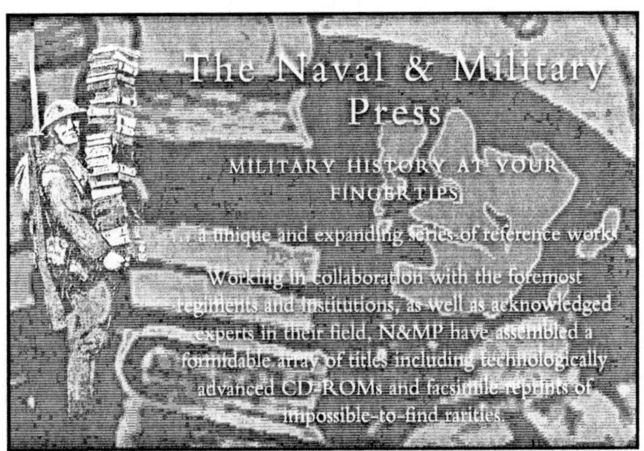

In reprinting in facsimile from the original, any imperfections are inevitably reproduced and the quality may fall short of modern type and cartographic standards.

CONTENTS.

PAGE

I. Introduction and Operations against Sekukuni, February to October, 1878 5
II. The Events which preceded the outbreak of hostilities, August, 1878, to 10th January, 1879 11
III. Operations of the Right Column, 11th to 23rd January, 1879 .. 22
IV. Operations of the Centre Column, 11th to 23rd January, 1879 .. 26
V. Operations of the Left Column, 11th to 23rd January, 1879 .. 50
VI. Blockade of Etshowe, 24th January to 3rd April 53
VII. Proceedings in Natal from 24th January to 3rd April, and Relief of Etshowe 59
VIII. Operations of the Left Column, 24th January to 3rd April .. 67
IX. Arrival of Reinforcements and General Situation, 4th to 15th April 82
X. Operations of the I Division, 16th April to 17th June 86
XI. Operations of the II Division, 16th April to 17th June 89
XII. Operations of Brigadier-General Wood's Flying Column, 16th April to 17th June 99
XIII. Operations of the I Division, 18th June to 8th July 104
XIV. Combined Operations of the II Division and Wood's Flying Column, 18th June to 8th July 109
XV. Operations of the I Division, 9th to 23rd July 119
XVI. Operations of Wood's Flying Column, 9th to 31st July 122
XVII. Operations of the II Division, 9th to 27th July 124
XVIII. Operations of Lieutenant-Colonel Clarke's Column, 24th July to 12th August 126
XIX. Operations of Lieutenant-Colonel Baker Russell's Column, 26th July to 2nd September 129
XX. Pursuit and Capture of Ketchwayo, 13th August to 2nd September 132

APPENDICES.

PLATES.

I. Map of Zululand.
II. Map of Sekukuni's Territory.
III. Survey of Country around Isandhlwana.
IV. Survey of Battle Field of Isandhlwana.
V. Plan of Fort Etshowe.
VI. Survey of Battle Field of Ulundi.

THE ZULU WAR OF 1879.

I. Introduction; and Operations against Sekukuni, February to October, 1878.

In the history of South Africa it has rarely happened that peaceful relations have subsisted for a lengthened period between the small community of European descent and the great masses of the native race among whom they dwell, and the sixth of those periodical struggles which have become familiar under the name of Kaffir Wars was in progress when the command of the troops in South Africa was handed over by General Sir A. T. Cunynghame to Lieutenant-General* the Honorable F. A. Thesiger.

This took place at King William's Town, British Kaffraria, on the 4th March, 1878, when the Imperial troops in the command consisted of two batteries R. A. (N | 5 and 11 | 7), the 7th Company R.E., and the 1 | 24th, 88th, and 90th Regiments in the Cape Colony, with the 2 | 3rd and 80th in Natal, and the 1 | 13th in the Transvaal, amounting in all to about 5,000 men.

It is not proposed here to follow the course of this Kaffir War, which was practically terminated at the beginning of June, 1878, by the death of the great chief Sandilli, and was formally concluded by the proclamation of an amnesty on the 28th of the same month.

A very wide-spread feeling of restlessness and hatred towards the white races had for some time been known to exist among the natives of South Africa, and at the date when this war on the eastern frontier of the Cape Colony was ended, disturbances claiming serious attention had occurred in remote districts. The area over which they extended was large. While a war with the Zulus could hardly be regarded as improbable, hostilities were actually in progress in Griqualand West, in the country on the north-west of that territory, and in two districts of the Transvaal, one near Bloemhof, and the other near Lydenburg, this latter being known as Sekukuni's country.

Sekukuni, who with his tribe is of Basuto descent, was the most powerful chief acknowledging the supremacy of the Zulu King Ketchwayo†, and had in 1876 taken up arms against the

---

* Local rank.

† This name is also spelt Cetewayo, Cetywayo, and Cetshwayo.

Boers when the Government of the Transvaal Republic attempted to exercise rights of possession over certain lands on the left bank of the Blood river, claimed by the Zulus, and generally known as "the Disputed Territory." On that occasion Sekukuni and his tribe had made active and tolerably successful efforts on behalf of their suzerain. Though the Dutch forces, aided by Swazie allies, had at first gained certain advantages, yet on their attempting on the 2nd August, 1876, to storm Sekukuni's main stronghold, they had been repulsed with loss, and, being short of provisions, had been obliged to abandon the enterprise and retire.

No further operations had been then attempted, as this failure had resulted in the disorganisation and dispersion of the Boers, and Sekukuni, on promising to pay a fine of cattle, had been left in undisturbed possession of his mountain fortress.

It may here be remarked, that at the date of these operations the limits of the Transvaal were very imperfectly defined, and that while the Republican Government regarded this war as "undertaken in self-defence against an insubordinate chief living far within the boundaries of the Republic," the view taken by the British Government was that Sekukuni was not a rebel against the Transvaal Republic, inasmuch as his territory had never formed part of their dominions, and that the war carried on against him was an unjustifiable aggression against an independent ruler.

In April, 1877, the annexation of the Transvaal took place, and Sekukuni's country appears to have been included without question in the territory which was thus added to the British possessions.

The relations of Sekukuni with the new rulers of the Transvaal were not unfriendly. The fine of cattle remained unpaid, and the settlement of this claim, though demanded, was not pressed.

In February, 1878, however, Sekukuni, acting under the influence of messengers from Ketchwayo, despatched a small force, in conjunction with the retainers of his sister Legolwana, to make a raid on a neighbouring chief named Pokwana, who was friendly to the English, and a somewhat severe struggle occurred, which resulted in the defeat of the assailants.

Early in March, on receiving a message of remonstrance from Captain Clarke, British Commissioner for the district, Sekukuni, who was fortified by the presence of some fresh envoys from Ketchwayo, replied that the English were afraid to fight, that the country was his, and the white people must leave, and that he was quite ready for war.

At this time the force available for the maintenance of order in the Lydenberg district consisted of a small number of police, and the only Imperial troops within reach were three companies of the 1 | 13th Regiment, which formed the garrison of Pretoria. These, however, could not be spared from the capital, as their presence there was necessary to keep in check a portion of the population, who, disapproving of the annexation, took the occasion of the return from England of certain commissioners to express their discontent openly about this time.

Under these circumstances, Sir T. Shepstone, the Administrator of the Transvaal, appealed to Sir H. Bulwer, Lieutenant-Governor of Natal, and to Sir Bartle Frere, Governor of the Cape Colony, requesting that additional Imperial troops might be sent to his assistance.

In compliance with this request, three companies of the 90th Regiment, recently landed in Natal, marched from Pietermaritzburg for Utrecht on the 12th March, and about the same time **12th March, 1878.** three companies of the 1 | 13th were moved from Utrecht to Standerton and Pretoria.

Local efforts were also made, and a force of fifty Volunteers proceeded from Pretoria to Fort Weeber, a post on the borders of the mountainous district ruled by Sekukuni, and on the 5th **5th April.** April this force, aided by some native contingents furnished by Pokwana and other friendly chiefs, attacked Masselaroon, the stronghold of Legolwana.

Masselaroon, like most other Basuto towns, had considerable capabilities for offering a strong resistance. Round a rocky conical hill, whose sides were more or less covered with thorn bush, clusters of native huts had been built on platforms artificially levelled. Each of these clusters of huts was surrounded by a stockade and hedge of prickly pear, while the hillside was in places scarped, and the approaches leading from one platform to another were stockaded and flanked from rifle pits. Such a fastness could not be easily carried by assault, and as on this occasion the native contingents proved useless for offensive operations, the Volunteers and police were only able to attain a modified success. They cleared the northern end of the hill, however, and carried off a certain amount of cattle.

Matters still remaining unsettled in this part of the Transvaal, two companies of the 1 | 13th left Pretoria on the 16th **16th April.** April for Lydenburg, while another company marched for Middleburg.

Towards the end of April Legolwana's tribe submitted, but Sekukuni continued in open revolt, and during the month of May, the small force opposed to him remained in fortified posts established near the Lulu mountains, in which his stronghold is situated. These posts, however, were insufficient to restrain the marauders of his tribe, who early in June made a successful raid on a farmer near Pilgrim's Rest. On the 3rd July the **3rd July.** Volunteers assumed the offensive, and attacked the Magnet heights, which form the southern end of the Lulu mountains, but they were repulsed with a loss of 7 killed and 9 wounded. On the 26th July some horses and cattle were carried off from **26th July.** a post named Fort Faugh-a-ballagh, one Volunteer being killed; and on the 7th August a party belonging to the Diamond Fields **7th August.** Horse were surprised on the Dwars river, and lost 52 horses and 48 oxen. This force, about 83 strong, had been raised in

Griqualand West, and had arrived at Lydenburg on the 8th June. By the loss of its horses it was now rendered almost useless, and as many of the Volunteers, finding the discipline irksome, began to withdraw about the same time, while the native police had to be disarmed for mutiny, it became evident that the local forces could not cope unaided with the revolted chief.

It was therefore decided by General Thesiger, whose Head-quarters were established at Pietermaritzburg on the 9th
9th August, 1878. August, that the Imperial troops in the Transvaal should be at once increased by one battalion of infantry, and on the 13th
13th August. August the command of all the troops in that territory, Colonial as well as Imperial, was placed in the hands of Colonel Rowlands, V.C.

The 80th Regiment, which had been stationed in Natal, was now ordered to the Transvaal to take the place of the 1 | 13th, which was in garrison at Pretoria, Lydenburg, Middleburg, and Standerton, and was now to take the field against Sekukuni The force in Natal was maintained by the arrival of the 2 | 24th Regiment from the Cape, set free by the termination of hostilities there. This battalion had landed at Durban on the 28th July.

The Frontier Light Horse, a colonial force of about 200 strong, raised in the Cape Colony, had also become available for service in the Transvaal, and received orders to march to Lydenberg. This corps was at this time in Kaffraria, and left
19th August. Kokstadt on the 19th August, marching by way of Pietermaritzburg and Newcastle.

28th August. On the 28th August the Head-quarter column of Colonel Rowlands' force left Pretoria and marched by the Eland river
6th Sept. into the valley of the Oliphant, where on the 6th September a consultation was held between its commander and Captain Clarke, who had come out from Fort Weeber to meet him.

It had been originally intended that Colonel Rowlands' column should follow the Oliphant river down to its junction with the Steelpoort, and then ascend the valley of the latter to Fort Burghers, a post at this time abandoned, which was to be re-occupied and formed into an advanced depôt for the operations against the stronghold.

It was now, however, recognised that there were serious objections to this plan, and it was decided to move on Fort Burghers by the more direct route past Fort Weeber, abandoning the line of communications by the Oliphant river, and making Lydenburg the base of operations.

8th Sept. On the 8th September, therefore, Colonel Rowlands moved his force across the Oliphant, near an old Dutch fort, and having detached one company of the 1 | 13th to occupy an entrenched camp about 10 miles lower down the river, proceeded to Fort
10th Sept. Weeber, which was reached on the 10th September. Here the force halted for two days, and starting again on the 13th, en-
19th Sept. camped on the Speckboom river on the 19th September, having had various slight skirmishes with the enemy, who occupied the rugged hills on either side of the track.

Fort Burghers is situated at the junction of the Steelpoort 19th Sept.,
and Speckboom rivers, and at this point the troops were concen- 1878.
trated about the end of September. On the 3rd October Colonel Rowlands marched out with a force of 130 men of the 1/13th Regiment, 338 mounted men belonging to the Frontier Light Horse and Mounted Infantry, and two 7-pr. Krupp guns.* The object of the expedition was not to make an immediate attack on Sekukuni's stronghold, which lies in the northern part of the Lulu mountains some 25 miles west of Fort Burghers, but to occupy a position near it, from which raids might be made on the cattle of the tribe, and from which further operations might be undertaken.

On the 3rd October the distance traversed by the force was 3rd October.
about 8 miles, and a halt was made at a watercourse, where
there were a few pools of water. Starting at 5 A.M. on the 4th, 4th October.
the column proceeded up a valley in a north-easterly direction, and after marching about 7 miles through a very rugged country where some opposition was met with, crossed the watershed separating the affluents of the Steelpoort from those of the Oliphant, and at 3.30 P.M. bivouacked near a large dry watercourse. By digging in its sandy bed, sufficient water for the men was obtained; but both horses and cattle fared badly, as there was little water for them, and the country around was totally denuded of pasture. At 8 P.M. the enemy attacked this bivouack on three sides, but were driven back and silenced in about half-an-hour. The firing caused a stampede of some of the horses and of the slaughter oxen, and the latter were not recovered.

On the 5th October the column again advanced, the first 5th October.
part of the route lying in the bed of a deep ravine with precipitous sides. When clear of this, the advance was continued into a sort of natural amphitheatre of hills, near the centre of which it was ascertained that water was obtainable. The water, which was only sufficient for the men and the horses, was in two pools, entirely commanded by a koppie or isolated hill, and this was occupied after a little resistance by men of the Volunteers and Frontier Light Horse, who held it while the column halted. After about three hours the march was resumed, the advanced party having reported that a camping-ground existed some 3 miles distant, in a northerly direction. On arriving at this camping-ground, however, it was found that the water was insufficient, as the advanced party had already quite exhausted the supply. Holes were dug in the sand, and about one-third of the horses of the column were watered, the remainder of the animals having to do without any.

Recognising that the exceptional dryness of the season rendered an advance impossible, Colonel Rowlands on the evening of the 5th issued orders for a retreat to Fort Burghers. This
was commenced at 6 A.M. on the 6th, but on arriving at the pools 6th October.

* These guns had belonged to the Transvaal Republic.

6th October, 1878. of water where the column had halted the day before, it was found that the isolated hill, already referred to, was held in force by the enemy. Although the want of water was very severely felt, Colonel Rowlands did not consider it advisable to incur the delay which the capture of this position would have involved, and the retreat was accordingly continued. At 4.30 P.M., after marching about 15 miles, the troops arrived at the pools of water where they had bivouacked on the night of the 3rd, men, horses, and oxen thoroughly exhausted by this trying march, made under a burning sun*, when they had already been without water for many hours.

7th October. On the 7th October the column reached Fort Burghers, the casualties having been as follows:—One man wounded, 15 horses killed or died of horse sickness, 4 horses and 1 mule wounded.

27th October. No further attempt was now made against Sekukuni, but on the 27th October Colonel Rowlands attacked a kraal belonging to one of his dependants, situated at a distance of about 5 miles from the British camp on the Speckboom river. The position was strong, rocks and caves affording a considerable amount of cover to the defenders, but the attack was successful, a loss of 16 killed being inflicted on the enemy, the kraal burnt, and a certain number of cattle being captured. The casualties on the side of the British were 11 wounded; the force engaged being 3 guns, 140 mounted men, 340 infantry, with 250 native troops.

Active operations in the Lydenburg district were after this brought to a close. Fort Burghers and other advanced posts were abandoned, and the troops withdrawn to various garrisons in the Transvaal and on the borders of Zululand†.

---

* The thermometer was 110° in the shade.

† In October, 1879, operations against Sekukuni were resumed, the forces employed being commanded by Lieutenant-General Sir Garnet Wolseley, K.C.B. These operations resulted in the defeat of the tribe and the capture of the stronghold on the 28th November, 1879, Sekukini himself, who had taken refuge in a cave, surrendering on the 2nd December. A detailed account is given in "The Chief of the Staff's Journal of the Military Operations in the Transvaal, 1879.'

II. The Events which preceded the Outbreak of Hostilities—August, 1878, to 10th January, 1879.

It is now necessary to consider the aspect of affairs in Natal in August, 1878, when General Thesiger arrived in that Colony.

The feeling of restlessness and hostility to the white inhabitants, which has been spoken of as pervading the South African races, was not wanting among those tribes whose territories lay near Natal, and it was not certain to what extent their kinsmen who dwelt within the boundaries of the Colony were influenced by the same sentiments.

As the coloured population of Natal amounted to more than 300,000 persons, in the midst of whom some 20,000 white settlers were scattered, the mere possibility of a native rising was sufficient to cause grave anxiety to those responsible for the direction of affairs. When, however, in addition to this, the prospect of a war with the Zulu nation presented itself, this anxiety was proportionately intensified.

The Zulus had been consolidated into a nation in the early part of the present century by Chaka, a bloodthirsty chief, whose military talents and aggressive disposition had raised his tribe to the position of the dominant native race in South Africa.

Under Chaka and his successors the Zulus had frequently been involved in hostilities with their neighbours, among whom were the Boers who had emigrated from the Cape Colony, and in these encounters gallantry and numerical superiority had enabled the savage warriors to claim some not inconsiderable successes, even against the firearms of the Europeans. With the British in Natal they had not come into collision, and the relations maintained were generally friendly. In recent times, indeed, the moral support of the Colonial Government had been exerted on the side of the Zulus when certain differences had occurred between them and the Boers of the Transvaal Republic.

The principal cause of these differences had been the disputed territory near the Blood river, to which reference has already been made. This question was still unsettled in April, 1877, when the Transvaal was annexed to the British Dominions. In August, 1878, no definite arrangement had been arrived at, and by this time the Zulus were quite ready to transfer to the English the ill feeling which the dispute had previously caused them to entertain towards the Boers.

The dispute was of long standing and had given rise to much trouble. It had brought on the war between the Boers and Sekukuni in 1876; it was the cause of the war with that chief now in progress; and it might at any time lead to a rupture between the British and the Zulus. This was a contingency of a very serious nature. Ketchwayo, who had been crowned King of the Zulus in 1873, was an ambitious chief, who was desirous of rivalling the exploits of his uncle Chaka. With this view the military system of his predecessors was maintained and improved, and at this time an army of some 40,000 men, bold, vainglorious, and eager for distinction, were ready to obey his orders. It was known, moreover, that this army was well supplied with fire-arms, many of them breech-loaders, and that a considerable amount of ammunition had found its way into Zululand.

Previous to the annexation of the Transvaal Ketchwayo's military preparations were regarded in Natal as a measure of defence against the Boers, but after the annexation had taken place this reason for the maintenance of the Zulu army no longer existed. It was ascertained, however, that the army was maintained, unimpaired in numbers and efficiency, and as Zululand was now encompassed by British possessions, it was plain that the Zulu warriors could gain distinction only by coming into collision with British subjects.

Under these circumstances the importance of setting at rest the border dispute had been fully recognised. In December, 1877, messengers had been sent by the Lieutenant-Governor of Natal to Ketchwayo, suggesting that the matter should be settled by arbitration, and to this course he had willingly agreed. It had been accordingly arranged that Sir Bartle Frere, Her Majesty's High Commissioner, should be the final arbitrator, and in February, 1878, three Commissioners* had been appointed by the Lieutenant-Governor of Natal to visit the ground, examine witnesses, and report on the conflicting claims. The Transvaal and Zululand had each sent three representatives,† and the Commission had held its first sitting at Rorke's Drift, on the Blood river, on the 12th March, 1878. As already mentioned, a decision had not been arrived at in the following August.

While the work of the Commissioners had been in progress the attitude of the Zulus had not been reassuring, as in the

April, 1878. month of April all the missionaries resident in Zululand were forced by the threats of Ketchwayo to abandon their mission stations and leave the country, while in July two sons of an influential chief named Sirayo, had, with a force of some 70 men, pursued and captured within the limits of Natal two refugees who had sought the protection of the British Colony.

It was therefore necessary for General Thesiger, when he arrived in Natal, to regard a war with the Zulus as a possible if not a probable contingency.

Besides the 1 | 13th and 80th Regiments, which were now required for the Transvaal, the only troops which were immediately available consisted of three companies of the 2 | 3rd at

---

* Hon. M. H. Gallwey, Attorney-General of Natal; Hon. J. W. Shepstone, Acting Secretary for Native Affairs; Col. Durnford, R.E., Commanding R.E.

† Mr. H. C. Shepstone, Mr. G. M. Rudolph, and Mr. P. L. Uys, for the Transvaal; Umudulu, Gebula, and Sirayo, for Zululand.

Pietermaritzburg, the 2 | 24th, which had lately arrived in the Colony, and three companies of the 90th, who were in garrison at Utrecht.

A column under Colonel Wood, V.C., composed of the remainder of the 90th, with 30 mounted men of the 2 | 24th, and Harness's Battery (N | 5 R.A.), moving from King William's Town to Natal, was halted at Kokstadt on account of disturbances in Pondoland, and the Frontier Light Horse were on the march to Lydenburg. **Kokstadt to Pietermaritzburg, 125.**

Colonel Wood's column was now ordered to resume its march, and arrived at Pietermaritzburg on the 2nd September. **2nd Sept., 1878.**

About a fortnight later, when difficulties as to transport had been overcome, Colonel Wood, with five companies of the 90th and four guns of Tremlett's Battery (11 | 7 R.A.), proceeded to Utrecht, there joining the three companies of the 90th which had been in garrison at that place since the previous month of May.

In the operations which were now impending, the point of primary importance was to secure Natal and the Transvaal from invasion by the Zulus.

The frontier to be defended was about 200 miles long, and was divided into two nearly equal faces, forming a re-entering angle in the neighbourhood of Rorke's Drift. While the country along the greater part of the Transvaal frontier, which forms the northern of these two faces, is open and can be watched with comparative ease, the district beyond the Buffalo and Tugela rivers, which constitutes the southern face, is broken and mountainous, and in many places clothed with thick forests. Considerable facilities were therefore offered to a Zulu force, unhampered by wheeled transport, to assemble unseen at any convenient point in this long line, and, unless prevented by floods in the boundary rivers, to make a raid into Natal and to return before the troops guarding the frontier could reach them.

It was accordingly recognised that, in the event of war, the British troops would have to take the offensive promptly, and invade Zululand as the surest mode of guarding Natal.

The invasion of Zululand, however, could only be attempted by such tracks as were passable by the long train of wagons necessarily accompanying European troops, and information as to these tracks was difficult to obtain. No maps of the country existed, and the statements of traders and others who had visited the interior of Zululand were conflicting, and in many cases proved to be misleading. Eventually, however, the principal wagon routes were ascertained, and in September, 1878, General Thesiger drew up a memorandum proposing that, on the declaration of war, five columns should march on Ulundi, Ketchwayo's principal kraal.

Their starting points were to be as follows:—No. 1 from the Lower Tugela Drift; No. 2 from Middle Drift; No. 3 from Rorke's Drift; No. 4 from Utrecht; and No. 5 from Luneburg. Each column was to consist of a complete battalion of eight companies, with one reserve battalion, and a depôt company at the principal base of operations, Pietermaritzburg. In addition to this, 12 companies were required for the protection of stores at various places, making in all a force of over eight battalions necessary.

At this time six battalions represented the British force available in Natal and the Transvaal, and on the 28th September General Thesiger made an urgent appeal for two more battalions of infantry and two companies of Engineers. This request was complied with, and the 2 | 4th and 99th Regiments with the 2nd and 5th Companies R.E. were despatched from England towards the close of the year.

28th Sept., 1878.

In the meantime the political prospect had not improved. During the month of September a surveyor employed by the Natal Government was captured by a party of Zulus when on the right bank of the Tugela river, near Fort Buckingham, and detained for a short time, and towards the end of the same month the German settlers in the Luneburg district were ordered by a Zulu Chief to leave their farms, as the land was required by Ketchwayo. In consequence of this Luneburg was occupied on the 19th October by two companies of the 90th from Utrecht.

19th October.

On hearing of the unsuccessful result of the expedition of Colonel Rowlands against Sekukuni, General Thesiger ordered one wing of the 1 | 13th to Middleburg, and the other to Derby, Pretoria being now garrisoned by two companies of the 80th, while the remaining companies of this regiment were left to observe the roads leading from Sekukuni's country to Middleburg and Lydenburg.

26th October.

29th October.

On the 29th October Her Majesty's ship "Tyne" arrived at Durban from the Mauritius with three companies of the 2 | 3rd Regiment, which were at once moved along the coast road to Stanger. The rest of this regiment was already on the frontier, four companies being at Thring's Post, and one at the Lower Tugela Drift, where a fort was commenced early in November.

In the month of October it had been arranged that the garrison duties at Cape Town should be performed by Volunteers, and in this way it became possible to relieve five companies of the 1 | 24th at King William's Town by four companies of the 88th, who had been at Cape Town. These five companies of the 1 | 24th were moved to Natal, there joining two companies of the regiment which had arrived at the end of September, while the 8th Company remained at the mouth of the St. John's river, Pondoland.

In order to supplement the small military force available, a Naval Brigade was landed from Her Majesty's ship "Active" on the 19th November. This, consisting of 170 sailors and marines, with two 12-pr. Armstrongs, one Gatling, and two rocket-tubes, and commanded by Captain Campbell, R.N., proceeded by the coast road to Fort Pearson, the work which was being constructed at the Lower Tugela Drift. The Naval Brigade arrived

19th Nov.

here on the 24th November, relieving two companies of the "Buffs," who next day rejoined the Head-quarters of their regiment at Thring's Post. **24th Nov., 1878.**

It was recognised that in the event of a war with the Zulus, the employment of both local troops and native levies would be absolutely necessary.

The local troops available consisted of 80 men of the Natal Mounted Police, and of about 300 Mounted Volunteers, both being similarly armed with carbines and revolvers.

All natives resident in the various "locations" within the Colony of Natal are legally liable to military service at the call of the Lieutenant-Governor, whom they recognise as their supreme Chief, and early in November General Thesiger obtained the necessary authority for raising and organising 7,000 of these natives in seven battalions of 1,000 men each.*

In order to reduce the risk of thus arming possible enemies, rifles were only issued to 10 per cent. of the rank and file, while a strong white element of 95 officers and non-commissioned officers per battalion was introduced, and no use was made of the tribal organisation under which the natives are accustomed to dwell.

His Excellency Sir Bartle Frere, High Commissioner for South Africa, had arrived at Pietermaritzburg on the 28th September, 1878, and after lengthy communications with the Lieutenant-Governor of Natal and with the Administrator of the Transvaal, gave his decision on the Transvaal-Zululand frontier question about the middle of November.

This decision was that the boundary line from the Buffalo to the Pongolo should be accepted as running "from the junction of the Buffalo and Blood rivers, along the latter river to its main source in the Magadela mountains, and thence direct to the round hill between the two main sources of the Pongolo river in the Drakenberg."

The boundary claimed by the Boers, and beaconed off in 1864, lay considerably to the east of this line. Starting from Rorke's Drift, it ran in a north-easterly direction by the Inseke to the Zungi mountain, and thence to a point on the Pongolo about 50 miles from its source. The disputed territory between these two lines was now acknowleged as forming part of Zululand, and thus the award, though it did not recognise Ketchwayo's claims to their full extent, was decidedly in his favour.

By this time, however, the aggressive bearing of the Zulus, and the known power of their army, had produced a condition of affairs which their European neighbours found to be intolerable, and it was finally decided that certain demands should be made on Ketchwayo when the award was communicated to him. These demands were embodied in an "ultimatum," of which the main stipulations were as follow:—

1st. That the sons of Sirayo, who had violated Natal terri-

---

* *Vide* Appendix D.

24th Nov., 1878. tory, should be surrendered for trial, and that a fine of 500 head of cattle should be paid for their outrage.

2nd. That a fine of 100 head of cattle should be paid for the outrage on the surveyor.

3rd. That a man named Umbelini, who had made a raid into British territory north of the Pongolo, should be surrendered, with his associates, whose names were to be notified at a later date.

4th. That the Zulu army should be disbanded and only brought together with the permission of the Great Council of the nation assembled, and with the consent also of the British Government.

5th. That every Zulu on arriving at man's estate should be free to marry, the King's permission being no longer required.

6th. That the administration generally should be reformed, and that accused persons should have a personal trial.

7th. That a British Resident should be received at the Zulu capital.

8th. That the missionaries and native converts should be allowed to return to the mission stations.

9th. That if a missionary or other European should be involved in a dispute, the matter should be heard by the King in presence of the Resident, and that any sentence of expulsion from Zululand should receive the approval of the Resident before being carried into effect.

11th Dec. On the 11th December, 1878, a number of Deputies sent by Ketchwayo arrived at the Lower Tugela Drift, and crossed to the Natal side, where they were met by Commissioners appointed by Sir Bartle Frere to announce the award on the land dispute and to communicate this ultimatum.

The award was first made public, and was received by the Zulus with satisfaction. The meeting was then adjourned for half an hour, and on its re-assembly the ultimatum was read to the Deputies, who were informed that a definite reply was required by the 31st December, and that the accused persons were to be delivered up and the fines of cattle paid on or before the 10th January, 1879.

The Zulu Deputies, who were regarded as representing the peace party, listened to the ultimatum with marked attention. With reference to its stipulations, they observed that they could not understand why the disbandment of the Zulu army was demanded, as they considered that their nation had as much right to maintain an army as the English. The sons of Sirayo, they said, had fled, and could not be found, and they requested that the limit of time might be extended. They were informed, however, that no change could be made in the terms, and the meeting being concluded, they recrossed the Tugela into Zululand.

The known temper of Ketchwayo rendered the acceptance of the terms of the ultimatum more than doubtful, and it was now necessary to make active preparation for the war which his rejection of them would bring on. For the contemplated offensive operations, the transport question was of primary importance, and efforts were made to overcome the very serious difficulties connected with it.* It was decided that the number of invading columns should be reduced to three, advancing simultaneously from the Lower Tugela Drift, Rorke's Drift, and Utrecht, and that a fourth column, consisting mainly of native troops, should move forward at a later date between the lines of advance of the centre and right columns.

The command of the right column was given to Colonel Pearson, 2 | 3rd Regiment; that of the centre to Colonel Glyn, 1 | 24th Regiment; and that of the left to Colonel Wood, V.C., 90th Regiment, while the column of natives was under Colonel Durnford, R.E.

The country in which active operations were now impending extends over some 15,000 square miles, and in its physical features resembles the adjoining British Colony of Natal. The greater portion consists of high open grassy downs, furrowed by deep watercourses, and broken by rocky eminences, the remainder being a strip of low-lying alluvial country, from 20 to 40 miles wide, running along the coast. The whole country is well watered, but the rivers are all fordable except when in flood. Wood for fuel is tolerably plentiful in the coast district and in the valleys of the principal rivers, but on the uplands it is very scarce and bad, consisting merely of the brushwood which grows on the mountain sides and in the ravines, or "kloofs." Being within a few degrees of the tropics, the climate of the coast region is warm, damp, and feverish, but the air of the uplands, some 3,000 feet above the sea level, is dry and bracing, and proved to be exceptionally healthy. It was through this latter region than the centre and left columns were to advance, while the right column was to traverse part of the coast district.

In front of the left or northern column there was no serious natural obstacle; but the Buffalo and Tugela rivers crossed the tracks to be taken by the centre and right columns respectively, and for passing these streams provision had to be made. The Buffalo at Rorke's Drift, though rapid, is seldom unfordable for any length of time, but the Tugela below its junction with the Buffalo, is, during the rainy season,† an obstacle of considerable importance. The preparations at Rorke's Drift, therefore, were on a comparatively small scale, and consisted in supplementing the existing pont by a barrel raft, but at the Lower Tugela Drift, where a rapid stream some 300 yards wide and liable to heavy floods had to be passed, more extensive works were necessary. A new pont was constructed here, and steel wire hawsers for working it sent from Durban.

On the 6th of January, 1879, one of these hawsers was taken 6th January, 1879.

* A description of the vehicles employed, &c., is given in Appendix E.

† October to March.

across the river by the Naval Brigade, and its end made fast to an anchor on the Zulu shore. On the 8th a flood carried it away

10th January, 1879. into the middle of the stream, but by the 10th it was again made secure.

During the period allowed for the receipt of Ketchwayo's reply, stores were being collected at points near the frontier as rapidly as the difficulties of transport would permit. These points were, Stanger and Fort Pearson for the right column, Greytown, Ladysmith, and Helpmakaar for the centre, and Newcastle and Utrecht for the left; the main depôts being Durban and Pietermaritzburg. From the sea base at Durban the lines of communication were as follows:—Durban to Fort Pearson, 66 miles; Durban, Pietermaritzburg, Greytown, Helpmakaar, 155 miles; and Durban, Pietermaritzburg, Ladysmith, Newcastle, Utrecht, 260 miles.

The road from Greytown to Helpmakaar was not in general use, and, to make it practicable, ponts had to be placed on the Mooi and Tugela rivers. The portion of the road, however, between these streams required constant repair, and was a frequent source of delay, while after heavy rain it became temporarily impassable.

The arming and organization of the Natal Native Contingent had been actively carried on, and by the end of December, 1878, this force had begun to assume a definite shape. The seven battalions of which it was composed were formed into three regiments, commanded by Colonel Durnford, R.E., Major Graves (2 | 3rd Regiment), and Commandant* Lonsdale respectively. The 1st Regiment, which formed the bulk of Colonel Durnford's column, had three battalions under Commandant Montgomery, Major Bengough (77th Regiment), and Captain Cherry (32nd Regiment). The 2nd Regiment, which was attached to Colonel Pearson's column, had two battalions under Major Graves and Commandant Nettleton, and the 3rd Regiment, which belonged to Colonel Glyn's column, had also two battalions under Commandant Browne and Captain Cooper.

At this time there was no regular cavalry in South Africa, but two squadrons of Mounted Infantry,† which had been formed for duty in the late Kaffir war, were available, while the Mounted Volunteer Corps of Natal, which had been called out early in December, were encamped at various points along the frontier.

4th January. On the 4th of January the reinforcements from England began to arrive, the first troops to land being a portion of the 99th Regiment. One company of this regiment was left in garrison at Durban, and another at Stanger, the remainder, with

Right column. the 2nd Company R.E., moving on to join Colonel Pearson at

* This title was given to commanders of local corps, who had no army rank.

† Men taken from the various infantry regiments in the command, and mounted on horses purchased in South Africa. The men at first carried the regulation infantry rifle and bayonet, but were afterwards armed with Swinburn-Martini carbines and a bowie knife, which fixed on to the carbine muzzle. The 2nd squadron ultimately had swords. The saddlery was of the regulation cavalry pattern.

the Lower Tugela Drift, while the 5th Company R.E. was ordered up country to join the centre column.

The Naval Brigade, which was attached to the right column, was on the 6th of January reinforced by a party of about fifty seamen and marines from Her Majesty's ship "Tenedos," under Lieutenant Kingscote, R.N.

By the 11th of January, Colonel Pearson's force was nearly complete and on that date was composed of eight companies the Buffs, six companies 99th Regiment, two guns, 11 | 7 R.A., 2nd Company R.E., Naval Brigade ("Active," "Tenedos"), No. 2 Squadron Mounted Infantry and Mounted Volunteers, with two battalions Native Contingent, and No. 2 Company Native Pioneers, or a total of about 300 mounted men, 1,500 European infantry, and 2,000 natives, with 4 guns, 1 Gatling, 2 rocket tubes, and 1 trough.*

Telegraphic communication between Durban and Stanger had been opened on the 29th of December, and early in January the line was extended to Fort Pearson.

Centre column.

The arrangements for the advance of the centre column were in a less forward condition, as the distances over which supplies had to be conveyed were longer, and the roads in worse condition.

Early in January Lord Chelmsford's† Head-quarters were established at Helpmakaar, where a part of Colonel Glyn's column was encamped. The other part of this column, consisting of a wing of the 2 | 24th, two companies of the 1 | 24th, and some native troops, had been moved forward into the valley of the Buffalo, and was on the Natal side of the river, near Rorke's Drift. By the 9th of January the whole of the centre column was concentrated in this neighbourhood, and consisted of seven companies 1 | 24th Regiment, eight companies 2 | 24th Regiment, N | 5 R.A., No. 1 Squadron Mounted Infantry, the mounted police, and mounted Volunteers, with two battalions Native Contingent, and No. 1 Company Native Pioneers, or a total of about 300 mounted men, 1,300 European infantry, and 2,500 natives, with six 7-pr. guns and two rocket troughs.

Helpmakaar to Rorke's Drift, 10.

Five companies of the 2 | 4th Regiment and the 5th Company R.E. were advancing in rear of this column, and Colonel Durnford's force of some 3,000 natives, with three rocket tubes, was at no great distance.‡

Left column.

At the beginning of January the left column, under Colonel Wood, V.C., was assembled near Balte Spruit, and consisted of eight companies 1 | 13th Regiment, and eight companies 90th, four guns 11 | 7 R.A., with the Frontier Light Horse, mounted Boers, and Wood's Irregulars, or a total of about 200 mounted men, 1,500 European infantry and 300 natives, with four guns and two rocket troughs.

---

* For operations of Col. Pearson's column, *vide* section III.

† General Thesiger assumed the title in November, on hearing of the death of his father, which had taken place on the 5th October, 1878.

‡ For operations of Col. Glyn's column, *vide* section IV.

Batte Spruit to Blood river, 5.

This column advanced on the 4th of January to the Blood river, leaving a detachment with two guns at the old camp. The river was in flood when the column reached it, but on the morning of the 6th the passage was effected, and the column en-

Blood river to Bemba's Kop, 1.

10th January, 1879.

camped at Bemba's Kop. On the 10th the detachment from Balte Spruit joined the column, and on the same day Bemba, the chief of this district, submitted, and with his followers was sent to Utrecht. Colonel Wood's column was now about 35 miles from Rorke's Drift, where the centre column was to cross the next morning, and, as some opposition to this crossing was anticipated, orders had been issued for the left column to move southwards in support of Colonel Glyn.*

Of the other two columns which had been originally constituted, neither was to take part in the advance. No. 5, under Colonel Rowlands, was to remain near Luneberg, and No. 2, under Colonel Durnford, which was to have crossed the Tugela at Fort Pearson, if the middle drift were impassable, was now ordered to remain in Natal and guard the frontier against Zulu raids.

On the 10th of January the three invading columns were concentrated at Fort Pearson, Rorke's Drift, and Bemba's Kop respectively, and the general plan was that they should follow the routes converging on Ulundi from these points, the right column forming an advanced depôt at Etshowe,† while the centre established one near the Isipezi hill, and the left another at the Inyayeni hill.

This concentration of British troops on the frontier was consequent on Sir Bartle Frere's memorandum of the 4th of January, 1879,‡ which placed the further prosecution of the demands on

---

* For a continuation of the operations of Col. Wood's column, *vide* section V.

† Or Ekowe.

‡ The text of this document was as follows:—

NOTIFICATION BY HIS EXCELLENCY THE HIGH COMMISSIONER.

Pietermaritzburg, Natal, January 4th, 1879.

Towards the latter end of July last, two large armed bodies of Zulus, retainers of the chief Sirayo, and led by three of that chief's sons, and by one of his brothers, entered Natal and took away by force and violence out of Natal territory two refugee women from two different kraals, one of them belonging to a Border Police Guard of the magistrate of the Umsinga division. The women were dragged across the border into Zululand, and there, it is reported, murdered.

2. These two separate acts of outrage were promptly brought to the notice of Cetywayo, on the 1st and the 16th of August, by separate messengers from His Excellency the Lieutenant-Governor of Natal, and explanations and redress by the surrender of the offenders for trial by the colonial courts of law, were then and afterwards demanded from Cetywayo.

3. In the place of complying with this just demand, Cetywayo replied excusing the outrage as a boyish excess, and offering a sum of money as a solatium for the violation of British territory.

4. This offer of money was declined, with a repetition of the demand for the surrender of the offenders, but they were not surrendered; and on the 11th of December a final demand was made on the Zulu King, in the name of the High Commissioner, that the three sons and brother of Sirayo should be given up for trial, and that a fine of cattle for non-compliance with the demands already made should be paid within twenty days from the date of demand.

Ketchwayo in the hands of Lord Chelmsford. By this document the General was authorized to take such measures as the force at his command might permit for compelling the submission of the Zulu king, unless an intimation of an unqualified and complete acceptance of the terms previously proposed should be received before the close of the 11th of January.

---

5. Those twenty days expired on the 31st of December, 1878, and the demand not having been complied with, the High Commissioner entertains no hope that it is the intention of the Zulu King to afford the redress Her Majesty's Government has a right to demand.

6. It appears clear to the High Commissioner, from Cetywayo's omission to comply with his demands, that the Zulu King's intentions are not friendly to the British Government, nor calculated to ensure the preservation of peace between the Zulus and the subjects of Her Britannic Majesty in South Africa.

7. I, therefore, hereby make known, for the information of Cetywayo and all the Zulu people, that I have placed the further prosecution of this and all other demands for redress and reparation in the hands of His Excellency Lieutenant-General Lord Chelmsford, commanding Her Majesty's forces in South Africa, with a request that His Excellency will take such steps as he finds necessary to protect the British territory from further aggression, and to compel the Zulu King to comply with all the demands made on him, whether for satisfaction due to the British Government, or for the greater security of British territory, or for the better and more peaceable government of the Zulu people.

8. Lieutenant-General Lord Chelmsford will carefully notify to all Zulu chiefs and people who may come within his reach for making such communication, that the demands of the British Government are made on Cetywayo as much in the interest of the Zulu people as of the English nation, and that till the 11th of January the Lieutenant-General will be willing to receive and to transmit to me any intimation of the unqualified and complete acceptance by Cetywayo of all the terms offered him on the 11th of December.

9. If such intimation of unqualified and complete acceptance be received by the Lieutenant-General before the 11th of January, no further hostile movements will be made, unless they should be rendered necessary by the action of the Zulu forces. Lord Chelmsford will place his own forces in such positions as shall best ensure compliance with all his demands, and up to the 11th of January he will be ready to consider any steps the Zulu King may propose to take for the purpose of giving real and permanent effect to the demands of the British Government.

10. But unless such unqualified and complete acceptance of the terms imposed be intimated to the Lieutenant-General on or before the expiration of the time specified, namely, the close of the 11th of January, the Lieutenant-General will no longer be bound by any of the terms offered on the 11th of December for Cetywayo's acceptance, but will take such measures as the forces at his command will permit for compelling the submission of the Zulu King, always bearing in mind that the British Government has no quarrel with the Zulu nation, and that the future good government and well-being of the Zulus is as much an object of the steps now taken as the safety and protection of the British territories of Natal and the Transvaal.

11. And I do hereby warn all residents and inhabitants of Her Majesty's possessions and colonies in South Africa, of whatever race, to be guided by this my notification, and I do strictly charge and command all Her Majesty's officers, ministers, and subjects, and all others whom it may concern, to govern themselves, and to act accordingly, and to take due notice of, and to pay due regard to, the tenor hereof.

(Signed) H. B. E. Frere,
High Commissioner.

III. Operations of the Right Column, 11th to 23rd January.

The 11th of January, 1879, passed away without any communication being received from Ketchwayo, and the invasion of Zululand by Colonel Pearson's column began at daybreak on Sunday the 12th.

12th January, 1879. A party of the Naval Brigade were first taken across the Tugela in the pont, and established themselves on the left bank without opposition. These were followed by some of the Natal Mounted Volunteers, after whom the infantry were ferried across.

The working of the pont, a flat-bottomed vessel some 30 feet long by 11 broad, was found satisfactory. It was hauled across by oxen, and two to three trips per hour were made.

By the evening of the 12th, the Buffs, part of the 99th, the artillery with two guns (11 | 7 R.A.), the Naval Brigade, and some of the mounted infantry were encamped on the further bank, where an entrenchment had been commenced by the first arrivals.

13th January. On Monday the 13th, the remainder of the troops, including the 2nd Company R.E., which had reached Fort Pearson the evening before, were taken across, a battalion of the Native Contingent being left at Fort Pearson.

A fort on the left bank, called Fort Tenedos, was commenced this day, and in it a large store house was erected.

The next few days were employed in conveying the stores, wagons, and oxen to the left bank, and in working at the new fort.

15th January. On Wednesday, the 15th of January, a reconnaissance was made by the mounted infantry under Major Barrow, to a distance of some 9 miles in advance, without discovering the presence of any force of the enemy; and on the afternoon of the same day the Head-quarters and two companies of the 99th Regiment joined the column.

17th January. By the evening of the 17th, Fort Tenedos was completed, and as the necessary stores and means of transport had by this time been collected on the left bank, it was now possible to commence the advance. The right column was to move forward in two sections, marching at such an interval as would admit of mutual support in case of attack, and a convoy of supplies was to follow with a small escort as soon as the safety of the road was assured.

18th January. Starting at 6 A.M. on Saturday, the 18th January, the leading section*, under Colonel Pearson, proceeded as far as the

---

* Detachment R.A. (11 | 7), No. 2 Company R.E., 2 | 3rd Regiment (5 companies) Naval Brigade (Her Majesty's ship "Active"), 1 battalion Natal Native Contingent, half company Natal Pioneers, No. 2 Squadron Mounted Infantry, the Natal Hussars, and the Stanger and Victoria Mounted Rifles.

Inyoni river, encamping there about 2 P.M. This section was accompanied by 50 wagons, and its march across an undulating grassy country, nearly free from bush, was uninterrupted by the enemy. Tugela to Inyoni, 10.

The second section of the column,* under Colonel Welman, 99th Regiment, with eighty wagons, started from the Tugela at 6 A.M. on the 19th, and reached the camp on the Inyoni before the first section had marched off. This now moved on to the farther side of the Umsundusi, and there encamped. A portion of the second section followed the first to the Umsundusi the same evening, but a large number of the wagons remained at the Inyoni. To allow these wagons to come up, and to make preparations for crossing the Amatikulu, an important water-course some 4 miles in front, the column remained halted at the Umsundusi on the 20th. From here a working party was sent forward to improve the approaches to the ford of the Amatikulu, and this party returned to camp the same evening. 19th January 1879. Inyoni to Umsundusi, 5. 20th January.

On the morning of the 21st the column again moved on, and traversed, unmolested, a somewhat bushy district. The Amatikulu, though rather deep, was fordable, and was passed without much difficulty, but the track on the northern bank led through heavy sand, and the progress of the wagons was slow, so that it was very late before the tail of the column arrived at the new camping ground. This was at a spot named Kwasamabela, and from here the first section of the column moved off at 5 A.M. on the 22nd of January, the second section following later. 21st January. Umsundusi to Kwasamabela, 8. 22nd January.

The mounted men in advance reported that there was some tolerably open ground on the banks of the Inyezane, and Colonel Pearson, on arriving there with the head of the column about 8 A.M., determined to halt on the farther side of the stream for two hours to rest the oxen and allow the men to breakfast. Kwasamabela to Inyezane, 4.

The track, which from the Tugela to this point skirts the base of the hills, and is comparatively level, here bears to the left and commences the ascent of the ranges. This ascent is made on a low ridge running up the middle of a valley between two hills of considerably greater height, which rise steeply on either side. At 8 A.M., when the column halted, a few Zulu scouts were seen on the eastern of these hills, known as Majia's, which lay about three-quarters of a mile in front. Though on the previous day Zulu scouts had been observed on the distant hill tops, none had appeared so close to the British troops, and Colonel Pearson now ordered this party to be dispersed by the company of the Natal Native Contingent which had led the column. This was done, and the scouts all disappeared from the top as the base of Majia's hill was approached, but as another party now showed themselves on a spur of the same hill, the company turned in their direction and proceeded to dislodge them. In order to reach this spur it was necessary to cross a 22nd Januar

* 3 companies 2 | 3rd Regiment, 4 companies 99th Regiment, 1 battalion Natal Native Contingent, half company Natal Pioneers, and the Durban Mounted Rifles.

22nd January, 1879.

wooded ravine or kloof with a marshy bottom, and when the company emerged on to the open ground beyond, they were met by a heavy fire from a large body of Zulus who now appeared on Majia's hill, distant some 400 yards on their left flank.

To this fire the native troops could make no effective reply, as only ten in the company, besides the European non-commissioned officers, carried rifles; and, to avoid being cut off by the Zulus who now descended the hill, a hasty retreat became necessary. This was carried out with the loss of one lieutenant and four European non-commissioned officers, besides three natives.

The foremost wagons of the column were being parked for the halt when the heavy firing of the Zulus was heard in front. On learning that the enemy was present in force, Colonel Pearson advanced with the leading troops of the column, consisting of two guns R.A., two companies of the Buffs, and two of the Naval Brigade, and occupied a knoll rising from the ridge already mentioned, along which the road ascends towards Etshowe. From this knoll dense masses of the enemy were seen about a mile off, working round the right flank towards the rear of the column, where the long string of wagons was slowly moving up, and against these masses shells and rockets were directed with good effect.

Two companies of the Buffs and the 2nd Company R.E. now advanced on the right of the road in skirmishing order, and, supported by a detachment of the 99th sent forward from the second section, forced the advancing Zulus back out of some bushy ground into the open, where they again came under a flanking fire from the knoll.

Meanwhile, however, following their usual tactics, the Zulu right wing had pushed forward, and had occupied the high hill on the west of the road, as well as a kraal on the central ridge. From this kraal and from the hills above a galling fire was opened on the troops who occupied the knoll. To this the artillery and the rockets of the Naval Brigade replied, and a party of officers and non-commissioned officers of the Native Contingent,* supported by a portion of the Naval Brigade, pushed forward, and took the kraal which was then set on fire. This force being joined by a company of the Buffs, a further advance up the road was made, and in spite of a heavy fire from the Zulus who occupied the adjacent heights, the dominating crest of Majia's hill was cleared of its defenders. This point won, the Zulus retreated rapidly, and by about 9.30 A.M. the last shot had been fired. In this action the casualties were as follows:—10 killed (of whom 2 were officers of the Natal Native Contingent), and 16 wounded. The Zulu losses were estimated at about 300.

---

* The men of the contingent seem on this occasion to have shown little inclination to advance.

To face page 24.

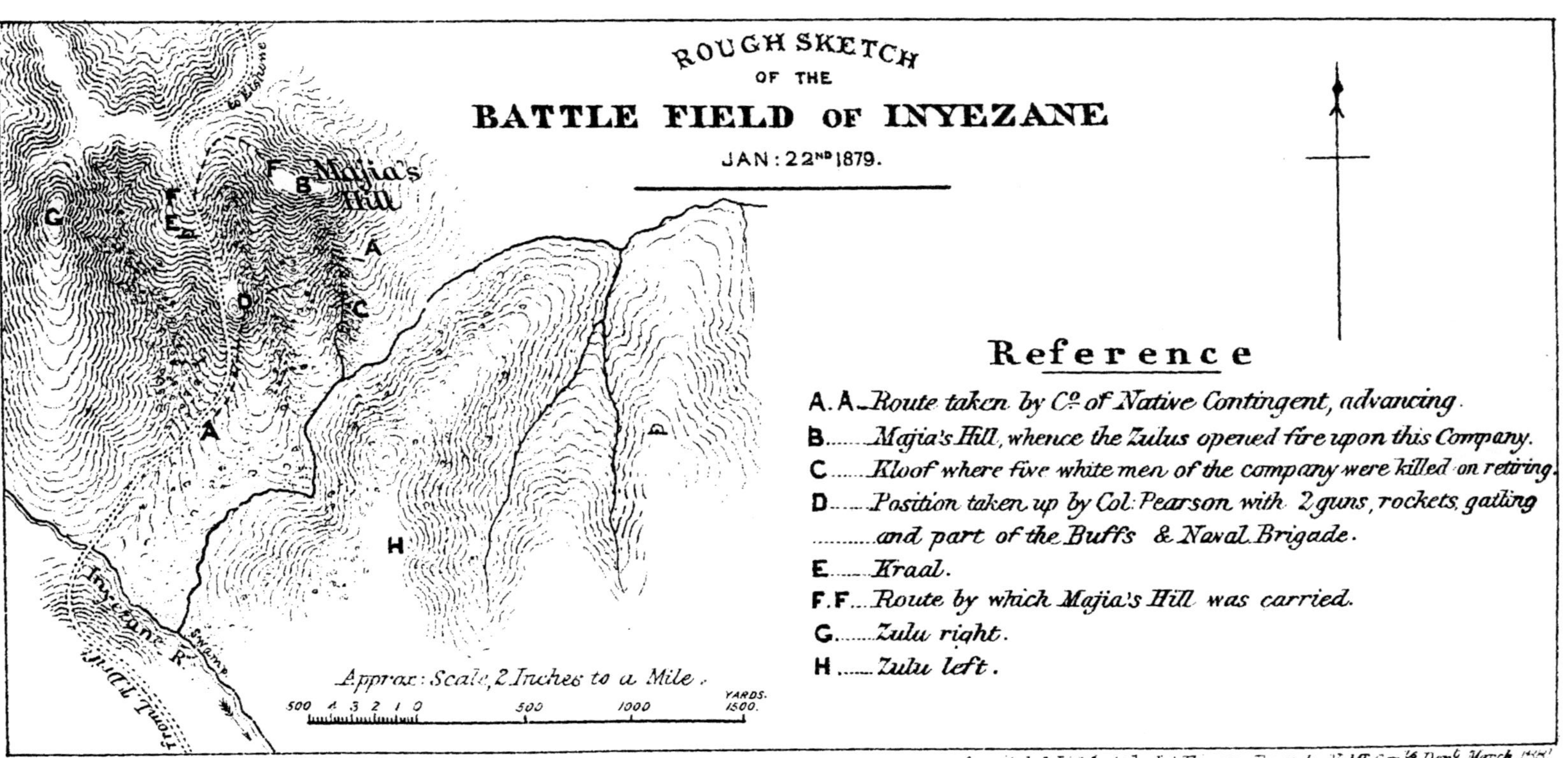

Compiled & Lith. at the Intelligence Branch, Qr. Mr. Genl's. Dept. March. 1881.

After a halt, the march was continued for about 4 miles beyond the Inyezane to a ridge on which the troops bivouacked. **Inyezane to Ridge, 4.**

Early next morning the column again advanced, and occupied the Mission Station of Etshowe without opposition. The mission buildings, though deserted for many months, were not in bad repair, and, as they were well suited for storehouses, steps were now taken to surround them by an entrenchment, Etshowe having been designated as a depôt for this line of invasion. Beyond this point it was contemplated that the advance on Ulundi should be made by a flying column acting in concert with the forces under Lord Chelmsford and Colonel Wood.* **23rd January, 1879. Ridge to Etshowe, 6.**

---

* For a continuation of the operations of the right column, *vide* section VI.

IV. Operations of the Centre Column—11th to 23rd January, 1879.

As already mentioned, the centre column, under Colonel Glyn, was encamped on Friday, the 10th January, on the right bank of the Buffalo river at Rorke's Drift. On the evening of that day orders were issued that the troops should cross the following morning, the invasion here commencing one day earlier than at the Lower Tugela.

11th January, 1879. At daybreak on the 11th January the mounted men and natives began to cross by the ford, while the British infantry were taken over in the ponts which had been prepared. The operation was covered by Harness's battery, which occupied a knoll overlooking the points of passage, but no opposition was attempted, and by 6.30 A.M. the whole of the troops were on the left bank. The mounted men were sent out in front, and during the day wagons, stores, and camp equipage were ferried across, and a camp was formed on the Zulu side of the Buffalo, the two battalions of the 24th in the centre, with a battalion of the Native Contingent on either flank.

Having seen the crossing satisfactorily carried out, Lord Chelmsford started with an escort of mounted infantry and Volunteers to communicate with Colonel Wood, whom he knew to have crossed the Blood river, and to be approaching the left flank of the centre column.

Riding in a northerly direction for a distance of about 12 miles, Colonel Wood with his advanced force was met, and after a consultation with him, Lord Chelmsford returned to his own camp at Rorke's Drift, where, later in the day, he had an interview with Colonel Durnford, commanding No. 2 Column.

12th January. At 3.30 A.M. on the 12th January a force under Colonel Glyn, consisting of four companies of the 1 | 24th Regiment, the 1 | 3rd Natal Native Contingent, and most of the mounted men, left camp to reconnoitre the country to the eastward, where the kraal of the chief Sirayo was known to be situated.

Lord Chelmsford and his Staff accompanied this force, which, after a march of about five miles arrived at a ravine in the valley of the Bashee river, in which a considerable number of cattle had evidently been collected. A small body of Zulus was seen on the hills above, and against these the mounted men advanced, while the 1 | 3rd Native Natal Contingent with three companies of the 1 | 24th pushed up the valley towards where the cattle had been observed. These were in some broken rocky ground about the base of the cliffs, and, from the cover there afforded by boulders and shrubs, the Zulus who were guarding them opened fire on the advancing force. They were speedily dislodged, however, and the cattle taken.

Meanwhile the mounted men had met with some resistance

from the Zulus on the high ground, but these also were dispersed without much difficulty. The whole affair was over soon after 9 A.M., having lasted about half an hour. Sirayo's kraal, which lay further up the Bashee valley, was burnt later in the day, and the troops returned to their camp at Rorke's Drift the same evening. 12th January, 1879.

The losses on each side were as follow:—Zulus, 30 killed, 4 wounded, 10 prisoners; British forces, 2 natives killed, 1 officer and 1 non-commissioned officer wounded, and 12 natives wounded.

The stock captured consisted of 13 horses, 413 cattle, 332 goats, and 235 sheep.

On the 14th January a force consisting of four companies of the 2 | 24th, the 1 | 3rd Natal Native Contingent, and some Native Pioneers moved to the Bashee Valley, some 4 miles from Rorke's Drift. 14th January.

From the 14th to the 19th January the two portions of the column remained in the same positions, and during this time wagons and stores continued to be brought up from Helpmakaar and ferried across the Buffalo, and bad places in the road were rendered passable by strong working parties.

It must here be observed that though footpaths and cattle tracks led through Zululand, roads did not exist. The only wheeled transport which had previously traversed this region was the wagon of an occasional trader or sportsman, and the old grass-covered ruts which these had left were the sole guides in selecting the route for the line of advance.

On the 15th January a reconnaissance was made to the Isipezi hill, and on the 17th Lord Chelmsford rode out to the Isandhlwana hill, which, as fuel was there obtainable, he had selected as the next halting place of the column. 15th January.

The country, which was generally open and treeless, appeared quite deserted. No Zulus had been seen near Rorke's Drift, and no earthworks covering the crossing place had been constructed there. At the camp on the Bashee river, however, a low wall was formed on the exposed faces.

Two companies of the 1 | 24th being left at Helpmakaar, and one of the 2 | 24th at Rorke's Drift, the centre column advanced on Monday the 20th January. The troops marching from the Buffalo were preceded by those who had been encamped on the Bashee, and the whole column moved on the Isandhlwana hill* accompanied by about a hundred wagons for regimental transport. These were in charge of the officers commanding corps, subject to the general control of the transport officer of the column. 20th January.

The track was boggy and bad in places, and though these had been improved by working parties, the advance of the column was slow. By about mid-day, however, the camp had

* Also, erroneously, called Isandula. The name Isandhlwana signifies "the little hand."

20th January, 1879.

been laid out on the eastern side of the precipitous crag known as the Isandhlwana hill. This hill, which forms a conspicuous landmark, is elongated, its greatest length being from north to south, and its shape has been compared to that of a sphinx or lion couchant. The highest part of the hill, or head of the animal, is to the south, and still further to the south is a small stony hill or koppie, beyond which the ground is extremely rugged and broken. The country to the north of the Isandhlwana hill is similar in character, so that a barrier is thus formed across the route taken by the column, and in this barrier the only track passable by wheeled vehicles is that which leads over the neck of land uniting the koppie to the Isandhlwana hill.

The ground on the eastern side of the hill falls gently like a glacis towards a watercourse in front, and on the upper part of this slope the camp was formed. So much delay, however, occurred in passing various obstacles on the way from Rorke's Drift, that the whole force did not reach the camp on the evening of the 20th, about one-third of the total number of wagons failing to get beyond a watercourse 1 mile west of Isandhlwana. At this point they halted for the night, guarded by a wing of the 2 | 24th Regiment, whose regimental transport formed part of the number of wagons thus delayed. The wagons of the column on arriving at the camp were formed up in rear of the ground occupied by the corps to which they were attached. The distribution of the corps is shown on the Survey of the Battle Field, and it will be perceived that the left was assigned to the two battalions of the Native Contingent. Under ordinary circumstances these would, for sanitary reasons, have been put "down stream," *i.e.*, on the right flank, but the koppie commanding the pass over the neck above mentioned was considered of such importance that the camp of the 1 | 24th was pitched close by it, and the natives were put on the other flank, which was moreover regarded as less liable to any hostile attack.

In front of the camp thus formed, with its back to the Isandhlwana hill, an open plain extended to a distance of some 8 miles. This plain, which is much intersected by watercourses, is about 4 miles wide, and is bounded on the south by the 'Ndlazagazi range, and on the north by rolling hills of no great height connected with the 'Ngutu range, which lies a few miles behind. Thus, while the view from the camp towards the front was extensive, it was limited on either side by the crests of these two nearly parallel ranges of hills between which the plain lies. Nothing of the nature of an entrenchment was formed for the defence of the camp, which was guarded by a chain of vedettes from 2 to 3 miles distant, and by an infantry outpost line closer in.

This line was composed of men belonging to the four battalions present, each of which had one company on piquet, the 24th being on the right and the Native Contingent on the left. By night this outpost line was brought to within about 500 yards of the tents, and, being made continuous, encircled the camp and the Isandhlwana hill, while a detached piquet of the Native Contingent was stationed some 1,200 yards to the northward to watch a pathway leading down from the high ground. 20th January, 1879.

Lord Chelmsford and his Staff arrived at the site of the camp about noon, and at 1 P.M. started again on a reconnaissance with an escort of the mounted infantry. The object was to examine a fastness known as Matyana's stronghold, some 8 or 10 miles to the south-east of the camp, and believed to be occupied by that chief and his retainers. The stronghold consisted of a deep ravine or glen with precipitous sides, the Amangene stream, which forms a waterfall at its head, running through it, and eventually joining the Buffalo. From the high ground overlooking this chasm no signs of a Zulu force could be perceived, and the General returned to the camp at Isandhlwana, where he arrived about 6.30 P.M.

It was, however, reported that many Zulus were in the valleys near this stronghold, and on the night of the 20th orders were issued for a reconnaissance to be made in this direction on the following day by the mounted Volunteers, police, and native troops. The mounted Volunteers and police, under Major Dartnell, were directed to proceed by the track on the high ground taken that day by the General, while the two battalions of the Native Contingent, under Commandant Lonsdale, were to work round the southern side of the Malakata mountain, and search out the valleys below.

The latter force started at 4.30 A.M. on the 21st, the mounted men, about 150 strong, leaving an hour later, both parties carrying rations for one day. Major Gosset, A.D.C., accompanied Major Dartnell's force, while Captain Buller, A.D.C., and the Hon. W. Drummond went with Commandant Lonsdale and the infantry. This consisted of 16 companies, eight from each of the two native battalions, two companies of each being left in camp. 21st January

It had been arranged that 50 of the wagons which had accompanied the troops should be sent back to Rorke's Drift to bring up more supplies, and the men who remained in camp this day were employed in unloading these wagons, and in preparing the track in front for the next advance.

During the forenoon Lord Chelmsford went to see a brother of Sirayo, named Gamdana, who had previously submitted, and had been allowed to remain in his kraal near the Malakata mountain. This man was away when the General arrived, but was sent for, and later in the day came into the camp and had an interview with Lord Chelmsford outside his tent, after which he returned to his home.

On the morning of the 21st a small party of mounted infantry under Lieutenant Browne had been sent out to make an independent reconnaissance towards the Isipezi hill. They returned about mid-day, reporting that they had seen some Zulu scouts

21st January. 1879. and a small party of the enemy, with whom they had had a skirmish.

About 4 P.M. Lord Chelmsford and Colonel Glyn, when riding out to a hill* where one of the most advanced vedettes was posted, met Major Gosset and Captain Buller returning from the force sent out that morning to reconnoitre, and these officers reported that a considerable Zulu force had been seen, and that Major Dartnell requested reinforcements to be sent to him. Lord Chelmsford, however, declined to accede to this request.

The proceedings of this reconnoitring force had been as follows:—The two battalions of the Native Contingent, under Commandant Lonsdale, proceeding nearly due south from Isandhlwana, had, after a march of about 5 miles, reached the deep thorny valley of a stream which flows beneath the northern side of the Malakata mountain. The contingent was sent up this valley with a battalion on each bank of the stream, but no Zulus being found here, Commandant Lonsdale ordered his men to ascend the 'Ndhlazagazi range, which rises above this glen. The slopes of this range were also unoccupied by the enemy, but some cattle were discovered and captured. At about 2 P.M., when the contingent reached the level top of the range, the mounted men were seen near its eastern end, and Lonsdale's force moved on to join them.

The Volunteers and police, who formed the mounted section of the reconnoitring force, had left camp about 5.30 A.M., and had proceeded south-eastwards by the Qudeni forest track to within about a mile of the Amangene stream. Here the two parties had separated, the Volunteers, under Captain Shepstone, ascending the 'Ndlazagazi heights to co-operate with the Native Contingent, while Major Dartnell, with the police, about 40 or 50 strong, advanced still further along the track. This latter party had crossed the Amangene stream when a considerable force of the enemy was seen about a mile off, moving towards the north-east, and this force presently took up a position on the left of the road along which Dartnell's party was moving. Finding the enemy in considerable strength, Major Dartnell pushed his reconnaissance no further, but recrossing the Amangene, ascended the 'Ndlazagazi range, where he joined the Contingent and the Volunteers. Major Gosset, Captain Buller, and Mr. Drummond then rode back to camp to report to Lord Chelmsford, while the reconnoitring force remained on the eastern end of the 'Ndhlazgazi, where it was proposed that it should bivouack that night.

Blankets and provisions were sent out from camp on pack horses, in charge of a small party of mounted infantry, and these arrived at the bivouack just before dark.

From the bivouack there was a clear view over the hills to the eastward, and the number of Zulus seen here at sunset was so large that Major Dartnell sent in a note to the camp, stating

---

* B on Plate IV.

that he and Commandant Lonsdale did not consider the force at their disposal sufficient to attack, and requesting that a reinforcement of two or three companies of the 24th might be sent out to them next morning.

This note was received by Major Clery, Staff Officer to Colonel Glyn, at 1.30 A.M. on the morning of the 22nd January, and Lord Chelmsford, on hearing its contents, gave orders that the mounted infantry, with four guns of Harness's Battery, six companies of the 2 | 24th Regiment, and the Native Pioneers, should march out at once in support of the troops who were on the 'Ndhlazagazi range. 22nd January 1879.

The wagons which had been unloaded on the 21st were to have returned to Rorke's Drift this day, but the orders on this head were now countermanded, as the force remaining was too small to furnish the necessary escort.

The troops above mentioned paraded under Colonel Glyn before daybreak. The men were in light marching order, without great coats or blankets, and each carried one day's cooked rations and 70 rounds of ammunition. The force moved off about 4 A.M., and was accompanied by Lord Chelmsford and his Staff.

The troops left in camp consisted of 30 mounted infantry for vedettes, about 80 mounted Volunteers and Police, two guns, and 70 men Royal Artillery, five companies 1 | 24th Regiment, one company 2 | 24th, two companies 1 | 3rd Natal Native Contingent, two companies 2 | 3rd Natal Native Contingent, and 10 Native Pioneers.

Before leaving, Lord Chelmsford sent orders to Colonel Durnford, R.E., who was at Rorke's Drift, to advance at once to Isandhlwana with all his mounted men and the rocket battery, and as senior officer to take command of the camp. This, till his arrival, was left in charge of Lieutenant-Colonel Pulleine, 2 | 24th Regiment, who received orders in writing to the effect that, in the absence of the force then starting, the cavalry vedettes were to be kept far advanced, but the line of infantry outposts to be drawn in closer, and that if attacked he was to act on the defensive. A wagon loaded with ammunition was to be kept ready to follow the force marching out, in case they should be seriously engaged.

After the departure of the column nothing unusual occurred in camp till about 8 A.M., when a report was sent in by a few mounted men posted some 2,000 yards to the north,* that a body of the enemy was in sight approaching from the north-east. 22nd January, 8.0 A.M.

On this the troops were got under arms, and drawn up in front of the camp, facing in the direction from which the enemy

---

* A on Plate IV.

22nd January, 1879. was reported to be coming, a mounted man being sent off with a brief despatch to acquaint Lord Chelmsford of the circumstance.

9.0 A.M. From the camp no Zulus were visible till about 9 A.M., when a small number were seen on the crest of the hills,* apparently coming from the direction reported. These withdrew almost immediately, and about the same time the party on the heights sent in word that the enemy were in three columns, of which two were retiring, and that the third had passed out of sight, moving in a north-westerly direction.

Colonel Durnford, R.E., who commanded No. 2 Column, had on the 11th January received directions from Lord Chelmsford that on the advance of Colonel Glyn's column he was to move his mounted force and rocket battery,† with one battalion of the Native Contingent, to the neighbourhood of Rorke's Drift, and that he was to be prepared to follow the centre column with the rocket battery and mounted men.

On the night of the 21st, therefore, Colonel Durnford, with five troops mounted Basutos, the rocket battery, and two companies 1 | 1st Natal Native Contingent were encamped on the left bank of the Buffalo at Rorke's Drift, having crossed the river on the 20th.

At about 6 A.M. on the morning of the 22nd January, Lieutenant Smith-Dorrien conveyed to Colonel Durnford Lord Chelmsford's order to advance immediately to Isandhlwana, and at 7.30 A.M. the force moved off, accompanied by 10 wagons.

10.0 A.M. About 10 A.M. Colonel Durnford arrived at Isandhlwana, where he found the troops still drawn up under arms. He then took over command of the camp from Colonel Pulleine, who gave him a verbal statement of the number of the troops, and of the orders he had received.

On learning that a force of Zulus had been seen on the left front of the camp an hour previously, Colonel Durnford sent back one troop of his mounted natives to protect his wagons, which were following in rear, and despatched two troops‡ to the heights on the left flank to reconnoitre, while he himself advanced into the plain in front with the remaining two troops of mounted natives, the rocket battery, and one company of the 1 | 1st Natal Native Contingent. This party he appears to have wished to be increased by two companies of the 24th, but

10.0 to 11.0 A.M. Colonel Pulleine strongly represented that the instructions, as conceived by him, did not warrant such a step. Colonel Durnford, therefore, only took with him that portion of his own force which is mentioned above.

---

* B on Plate IV. It would appear that the vedettes who had been posted here had withdrawn.

† Three rocket tubes, &c., carried on pack mules. The personnel consisting of an officer and a bombardier R.A., with eight men of the 1 | 24 Regiment.

‡ No. 1 under Lieutenant Raw, who was accompanied by Captain G. Shepstone (Political Agent to Colonel Durnford), and No. 2 under Captain Barton and Lieutenant Roberts.

With this he left the camp about 11 A.M., and advanced along the plain in front, with the object of preventing the columns of the enemy, reported as in retreat, from joining the force with which Lord Chelmsford was at that time believed to be engaged 22nd January, 1879. 11.0 A.M.

Before starting Colonel Durnford ordered a company of the 1 | 24th (Lieutenant Cavaye's) to move to the heights some 1,500 yards north of the camp, and about the same time the rest of the troops who had been drawn up returned to their private parades, and were broken off.

At 12 o'clock, when Colonel Durnford and his party were still absent in front, and the troops in camp were engaged in preparing for dinner, firing was heard from the hill where Lieutenant Cavaye's company had been posted. 12.0 noon.

It appears that Lieutenant Raw's troop of Basutos, which had been sent out to reconnoitre on the high ground north of the camp, had, after going some 3 or 4 miles, come on a herd of cattle which they had followed over a small rising ground. From the top of this they had seen the Zulu army about a mile off advancing in line, and extending towards its left. Captain George Shepstone and a Mr. Hamer, who had gone out with Lieutenant Raw, had ridden back to the camp to report the presence of this large force, while the troop of Basutos fell back before the enemy.

An open valley lies to the north of the range, along which this troop was retiring, and while the bulk of the Zulu army was advancing direct on Isandhlwana, its right horn was pushing up towards the head of this valley. Crossing the neck by which the hills immediately north of Isandhlwana are united to the main 'Ngutu range, this right horn began to descend into the valley to the westward, and soon came under the fire of Cavaye's company, which was on the ridge overlooking this valley. The Zulus, however, did not turn aside to attack the company; but passing its front at a distance of about 800 yards streamed onwards in loose order to carry out their usual encircling movement.

When the information reached the camp the troops again fell in, and Captain Mostyn's company of the 1 | 24th was sent out to support Lieutenant Cavaye. On reaching the heights Captain Mostyn extended his men along the crest between the main portion of Lieutenant Cavaye's company, and a section* which that officer had detached some 500 yards to his left. On Cavaye's right a company of the Native Contingent which had arrived on the heights about the same time as Captain Mostyn's, prolonged the line, while still further in this direction the mounted Basutos were descending from the range.

About five minutes after Captain Mostyn's company had joined Lieutenant Cavaye's, orders were received that the troops on the heights were to retire slowly as the enemy appeared to 12.20 P.M.

* This section was commanded by Lieutenant Dyson.

22nd January, 1879 be threatening the front of the camp. This retreat was carried out in good order, and a fresh line was formed facing the

12.45 P.M. heights, and about 400 yards from them, the two companies of the 1 | 24th being supported by a third (Captain Younghusband's), which was drawn up in échelon on their left, and like them in extended order.

The company of the Native Contingent which had been on Cavaye's right appears to have been that detailed by the 2nd Battalion Natal Native Contingent for piquet duty, and it would seem that when the troops left the heights this company joined the piquet furnished by the 1st Battalion Natal Native Contingent, which at this time was on the low ground to the left front of the camp.

In the meantime Colonel Durnford, with Captain Davies' and Captain Henderson's troops of Basutos, had pushed on across the plain in front of the camp, outstripping the rocket battery and its escort of the Native Contingent, which followed him as fast as the difficulties of the ground would permit.

After passing a small pointed hill on the left front of the camp Colonel Durnford's party, bearing to their left, ascended the ridge, and advanced more than a mile beyond it. Here a message, brought by two Carabineers, was received to the effect that a large Zulu force was close by, and was trying to surround the party. Shortly afterwards the enemy came in sight, and a retreat on the camp was ordered. This was carried out steadily, fire being maintained by alternate troops, and after a distance of about 2 miles had been traversed they came on all that remained of the rocket battery.

When this, following Colonel Durnford, had got about 3 miles from the camp a Carabineer had been met, who had reported that the Basutos* were heavily engaged on the further side of the ridge, and had offered to point out a short cut, by which the battery might join them. Almost at the same time a large number of Zulus had appeared on this ridge, and a rocket had been fired at them, but a party of the enemy, issuing suddenly from a ravine 100 yards off, had replied with a volley which had frightened the mules, and had led to the retreat of the native escort.

The Zulus now rushing in, a hand-to-hand fight ensued, in which Major Russell, R.A., who commanded the battery, 5 of the 8 men and the mule drivers were killed. This struggle was still going on when Colonel Durnford's party approached, and on this the Zulus withdrew.

This party continued its retreat on the camp, halting and opening fire where the ground was favourable, and making a determined stand at the watercourse in front of the camp, where

1.0 P.M. they were supported by those of the mounted infantry and Volunteers who had remained behind when the column had marched out that morning.

---

* Raw's troop probably.

The two guns of N | 5 R.A., with their detachments turned out along with the other troops at 12 o'clock, and came into action on the left of the camp, and about 400 yards from it. From this point a large body of Zulus was seen advancing, and fire was immediately opened on them at a range of about 3,400 yards. A force was also reported on the right flank, and one of the guns was presently moved a few hundred yards in this direction, but was afterwards brought back to its original position.

22nd January 1879.

12.10 P.M.

12.25 P.M.

When the troops turned out at 12 o'clock two companies of the 1 | 24th were sent, as already mentioned, to the support of Lieutenant Cavaye. The remaining two companies of the 1 | 24th were also sent to the left of the camp, and formed up in skirmishing order near the guns which were already in action.

Lieutenant Pope's company of the 2 | 24th, which, having come off piquet that morning, had not marched out with the rest of the battalion, paraded along with the companies of the 1 | 24th at noon. This company appears to have been sent direct to the front, and to have been drawn up in extended order near the wagon track.

It would seem that the same report of Zulus threatening the right, which caused the gun to be moved towards that flank, led also to the right company of the 1 | 24th being extended in this direction, till it approached the left of Lieutenant's Pope's company.

12.30 P.M.

On this portion of the field, owing to the Zulu advance being retarded by the mounted men, the pressure was as yet less severely felt than on the left, where the enemy, descending from the heights which they had occupied on the withdrawal of Mostyn's and Cavaye's companies, soon forced the defenders to fall back still further, and to take up a fresh position within about 300 yards of the camp. This movement, while tending to unite the two portions of the force, had the effect of leaving the Native Contingent in a somewhat advanced position at the salient of the defensive line, which now formed two nearly continuous faces, one towards the north, and the other towards the east. The troops thus engaged were exclusively occupied with the enemy's forces in their immediate front, and, so far as can be ascertained, occupied the following positions about 1 P.M.

1.0 P.M.

On the left, facing the north, Younghusband's, Mostyn's, and Cavaye's companies were extended in the order named. The two companies of the Native Contingent were on Cavaye's right front, and near them were the guns, firing towards the east. To the right of the guns, one company of the 1 | 24th in extended order faced the east, and the remaining company of the 1 | 24th was stretched over the space between this and Lieutenant Pope's, which formed the right of the infantry line at the wagon track. Beyond this, and some distance in advance, was a force of mounted men, composed of those left behind in camp, and of

22nd January, 1879. those who had been out in front with Colonel Durnford. The remainder of the Native Contingent was drawn up somewhat in rear of the defensive line, and was to have been employed to pursue the enemy when recoiling from the attack, which (following the experience of previous Kaffir warfare) he was to be encouraged to make.

The camp itself was in no respect prepared for defence. The tents were still standing as they had been left when the troops had marched out that morning, and were occupied by officers' servants, bandsmen, clerks, and non-combatants, who were entirely unconscious of danger. The 50 wagons which were to have gone back to Rorke's Drift, had been drawn up the evening before in three lines on the neck, between the track and the Isandhlwana hill, and were still in the same position. The rest of the wagons were in rear of the camps of the corps to which they were attached. The oxen, having been collected for safety when the Zulus were first seen near the camp, were with the wagons, and, owing to a mistake on the part of the native drivers, many were regularly yoked in, instead of being merely tied up to the wagons as ordered.

Meanwhile the advance of the Zulus was continued steadily, and without check or halt. Moving from the north-east in a loose but deep formation of horseshoe shape, their left horn was directed towards the right of the British line, while their right was descending the valley at the back of the Isandhlwana hill, and their central mass was aimed directly at the camp.

The enormous force of their adversaries could now be realised by the defenders of the camp. These extended in a long thin line,* saw themselves outnumbered about six to one† by an enemy who pressed forward from all sides, regardless of the heaviest losses. Soon after 1 P.M. the foremost ranks of the Zulus had got within some 200 yards of the men of the
1.10 P.M. Native Contingent, who then turned and fled.

A gap in the line was thus left, into which a mass of Zulus poured, and in an instant all was confusion. Before Mostyn's and Cavaye's companies of the 24th, which were extended on the left, had time to rally, or even to fix bayonets, the Zulus were among them, and slaughtered them to a man. Captain Younghusband's company, which was on the extreme left, succeeded, however, in retreating, and eventually gained a sort of ledge or terrace on the southern side of the Isandhlwana hill.

The two guns, after discharging a few rounds of case into the dense advancing mass of the enemy, limbered up and retired towards the camp. This was already in the hands of the Zulus, who had come up from the west, and before it was traversed nearly every gunner had fallen stabbed by assegais.

On reaching the neck the track to Rorke's Drift was found

---

* Over 2,000 yards in length.

† The Zulu army was about 14,000, strong of whom 10,000 attacked the camp.

22nd January, 1879.

to be completely blocked by the enemy, and an attempt was made to take the guns over the rough and rocky ground to the southward, where a space, as yet unoccupied by the Zulus, seemed to offer a hope of escape to the numerous fugitives now hastening in this direction. Most of these fugitives were entirely ignorant of the country through which they were seeking to make their way, and numbers were overtaken and massacred by the pursuing Zulus, who, exceptionally fleet of foot, were able on such rough ground to outstrip even horsemen.

The guns did not get far. About 800 yards from the neck, a deep watercourse was reached, which proved impassable for vehicles, and here drivers and horses were assegaied, two officers and a sergeant alone escaping.*

The route taken by the majority of the fugitives was along this watercourse, and hence to a point on the Buffalo, distant something over 4 miles from the camp. The Zulus, however, pursued so hotly that no dismounted European succeeded in traversing more than half this distance, and of those horsemen who reached the river many were drowned in trying to cross, and many were slain on its banks. The few who survived struggled on to Helpmakaar.

Of the conflict in and around the camp, but little trustworthy information exists. For a short time after the defensive line was broken, men fought hand-to-hand among the tents. The only companies which appear to have made any organised resistance were Captain Younghusband's and the two on the right, which rallied, and were joined by men of other companies and corps. The former, on the terrace below the Isandhlwana hill, and the two latter near the camp of the 1 | 24th, held their ground in compact bodies, till, their ammunition being expended, they were overpowered, and died where they stood.

Colonel Durnford on his return to the neighbourhood of the camp appears to have remained near the mounted men, who, by holding the watercourse on the extreme right, were keeping the Zulus at bay. These, however, finding a direct advance impossible, extended to their left, and crossing the watercourse still lower down outflanked the mounted men, and threatened to cut off their retreat. On this it would seem that Colonel Durnford determined that the forces under his command should adopt a more compact formation, and that with this object he ordered the "Retire" to be sounded. This was done, and the time of its occurrence appears to have been just previous to the rush of the Zulus, which penetrated the defensive line.

The troopers, whose horses had been under cover in the watercourse, rode back some 1,500 yards, and took up a fresh position on the eastern slope of the neck of land before mentioned, over which a stream of fugitives must now have been hastening. But the stony koppie to the south was already in

* One of these officers (Major Stuart Smith) was afterwards killed at the Buffalo river. Of the Artillery left in camp, 8 men also escaped.

22nd January, 1879. the hands of the enemy, and from the west, their right horn was rapidly closing in, so that on this spot the final stand was made. Here Colonel Durnford, with a party of mounted Volunteers, 24th men, and others, who had rallied round their commanding officer, held their ground gallantly like the companies of the 24th near at hand, but attacked from all sides by overwhelming numbers, when the last cartridge had been fired, the end could not long be delayed.*

By 2 P.M. the only survivors of the force which had occupied the camp were those who were endeavouring to make good their escape to the Buffalo.†

As already mentioned, the column for the support of Dartnell and Lonsdale left the Isandhlwana camp at 4 A.M. on the 22nd January. Lord Chelmsford and his Staff pushed on ahead, and about 6 A.M. arrived at the place where the Native Contin-

4.0 A.M.

6.0 A.M.

---

* Extract from a statement made by Methlagazulu, son of Sirayo, when confined in *Pietermaritzburg Jail.* September, 1879:—

"We were fired on first by the mounted men, who checked our advance for some little time. About the same time the other regiments became engaged with the soldiers who were in skirmishing order. When we pressed on the mounted men retired to the donga, where they stopped us twice. We lost heavily from their fire. My regiment (Ngobamakosi)‡ suffered most. When we saw that we could not drive them out of the donga we extended our horn to the bottom of the donga, the lower part crossing and advancing on to the camp in a semi-circle. When the mounted men saw this they came out of the donga, and galloped to the camp. Our horn suffered a great deal, both from the mounted men, and a cross fire from the soldiers, as we were advancing on to the camp, the Nonkenke and Nodwengu regiments forming the left§ horn, circled round the mountain to stop the road, the main body closing in on to the camp. I then heard a bugle call, and saw the soldiers massing together. All this time the mounted men kept up a steady fire, and kept going further into the camp. The soldiers when they got together fired at a fearful rate, but all of a sudden stopped, and then they divided and some commenced to run. We didn't take any notice of those running away, thinking that the end of our horn would catch them, but pressed on to those who remained. They got into and under wagons and fired, but we killed them all in that part of the camp (those that ran away took the direction of the Buffalo river, some throwing their guns away, and others firing as they ran). When we closed in we came on to a mixed party of mounted and infantry men, who had evidently been stopped by the end of our horn; they numbered about a hundred. They made a desperate resistance, some firing with pistols and others using swords. I repeatedly heard the word "*fire*" given by some one, but we proved too many for them, and killed them all where they stood. When all was over I had a look at these men, and saw an officer with his arm in a sling, and with a big moustache, surrounded by Carabineers, soldiers and other men that I didn't know. We ransacked the camp, and took away everything that we could take; we broke up the ammunition boxes, and took out all the cartridges. We practised a great deal at our kraals with the rifles and ammunition. Lots of us had got the same sort of rifle that the soldiers used, having bought them in our country, but some did not know how to use them, and had to be shown by those who did."

† Captain Essex who was one of the last to escape before the Zulu circle was completed, left Isandhlwana about 1.30 p.m.; and when Commandant Lonsdale rode into the camp about 2.0 P.M., resistance had ceased. See also note on p. 48.

---

‡ Methlagazulu states that he commanded one wing of this regiment.

§ Evidently a mistake for "right."

gent and the Carabineers had bivouacked. These had passed the night undisturbed except by a panic which had occurred among the natives, and which had resulted in some of them being injured by their comrades. **22nd January, 1879.**

The mounted portion of this outlying force was now sent off under Major Dartnell towards the left of the enemy's position; while the Native Contingent was ordered to descend into the valley and move against the hills to the north-east, on which the Zulus had been seen in force the evening before.

An order was at the same time issued for the mounted infantry of Colonel Glyn's column under Lieutenant-Colonel* J. C. Russell, 12th Lancers, to move round a hill on their left front, while the artillery and 2 | 24th were to continue their advance by the track. This order was received by Colonel Glyn about
6.30 A.M. and was acted on. **6.30 A.M.**

The two battalions of the Native Contingent, having been **7.30 A.M.**
formed in line on the plain, were sent up the hills in front, while Colonel Glyn, moving his column eastwards in support of this force, was now on its left rear, and to the north of the track which he had been following. The ground here, however, was found to be much intersected by watercourses, and the delays occasioned by making these passable for artillery rendered the progress of the column so slow that Colonel Glyn eventually moved on without the guns, which were left to follow with two companies of the 2 24th detached as an escort.

The hills ascended by the Native Contingent were found to
be unoccupied, but Major Dartnell's force which had moved **8.0 A.M.**
round behind these heights came on a number of Matyana's tribe, and killed some 30 of them; while many more who had taken refuge in caves and among the rocks were afterwards despatched by the Native Contingent, who, on reaching the spot, worked through these hiding-places.

All efforts to reach the main body of the Zulus, however, proved fruitless, as they constantly fell back from range to range in a north-easterly direction, abandoning very strong positions
without firing a shot, and showing that they had no intention of **8.0 to 9.0 A.M.**
waiting to be attacked.

At 9.30 A.M., soon after Lord Chelmsford and his staff had **9.30 A.M.**
halted for breakfast, a messenger arrived from the camp with Colonel Pulleine's report referred to on page 32. This note ran as follows:—"Staff Officer—Report just come in that the Zulus are advancing in force from left front of the camp.

(Signed) H. B. PULLEINE,
8.5 A.M. Lieutenant-Colonel.
"Received 9.30—22/1/79. (Signed) H. P†."

Lord Chelmsford received this note from Major Clery, and in

---

* Local rank.

† The initials are those of Captain Hallam Parr, the Staff Officer who received the note.

22nd January, 1879. consequence of the intelligence it contained, sent Lieutenant Milne, R.N., to a hill from which the camp was visible, with orders to examine it with his telescope and to report.

10.0 A.M. Soon afterwards the 1 | 3rd Natal Native Contingent arrived at the place where the Head-quarters Staff had halted, and this battalion was ordered to march back to the Isandhlwana camp, examining on the way the dongas which intersected the open country in front of that camp.

Lieutenant Milne, on reaching the top of the hill, was unable to detect any sign of the Zulus reported by Colonel Pulleine as advancing on the camp, and announced to Lord Chelmsford by flag signal that the cattle had been driven in close to the tents, this being the only point which appeared to require notice. After remaining on the hill for an hour and a half, Lieutenant Milne rejoined Lord Chelmsford, without having ascertained anything further.

Almost simultaneously with the departure of the Native Contingent, orders were sent to Lieutenant-Colonel Harness, R.A., who was some distance in rear, that he was to abandon his attempts to advance, and was to make his way with his guns and their escort to the Amangene valley, where it was intended that a new camp should be formed.

As this new camp was to be occupied at once by the greater portion of the force which had accompanied Lord Chelmsford, Captain Alan Gardner, who, with Major Stuart Smith and some 10.30 A.M. other officers, left the column about 10.30 A.M., was the bearer of an order for the requisite tents, &c., to be sent out from Isandhlwana.*

11.45 A.M. At about 11.45 A.M. Lord Chelmsford remounted and proceeded over the high ground to the place where the action with 12.30 P.M. Matyana's people had taken place. On arriving here at about 12.30 P.M., the engagement was over, but the Native Contingent were still searching the caves and broken ground. Lord Chelmsford then moved on to the Amangene valley, and pointed out the position where the new camp was to be formed.

Harness's proceedings. Lieutenant-Colonel Harness, R.A., on receiving the order mentioned above, turned round, and having regained the Qudeni forest track, proceeded along it towards the new camping ground.

12.0 noon. About noon he halted his force on a ridge where this track begins to descend into the Amangene valley, and half an hour 12.30 P.M. later while thus halted, it was noticed by some of the party that

---

* Captain Gardner on reaching the camp sent back the following note addressed to Major Clery : " Heavy firing near left of camp. Shepstone has come in for reinforcements, and reports the Basutos falling back. The whole force at camp turned out and fighting about 1 mile to left flank. (Signed) Alan Gardner, Captain, S.O." (This note did not reach Major Clery, but appears to have been received by Major Gosset about 3 P.M.).

Lieutenant-Colonel Pulleine also replied to the order, his note being addressed to " the Staff Officer." " Heavy firing to left of our camp ; cannot move camp at present. (Signed) H. B. Pulleine, Lieutenant-Colonel." (This note appears to have been delivered to Lord Chelmsford, probably about the same hour as the former.)

the two guns left behind at Isandhlwana were firing, but this 22nd January, 1879.
does not seem to have caused uneasiness or alarm. From the
spot where Harness's party was halted, the camp itself could not
be seen, but the ground to the northward where the guns had
come into action lay fairly visible with field glasses, the distance
being about 9 miles.*

Soon after noticing the guns firing, a large body of natives, 12.45 P.M.
recognised as belonging to the Native Contingent, was observed
in the low ground, directly between Lieutenant-Colonel Harness's
party and the camp. From this body a mounted man was seen
hastening, and Captain Church, commanding one of the companies of the 2 | 24th, rode towards him on an artillery horse,
accompanied by a sergeant of the battery. Captain Church, on
his return about half an hour later, reported that this mounted 1.15 P.M.
man was an officer† of the 1 | 3rd Natal Native Contingent, who
was bearing the following message from Commandant Browne:
—"For God's sake come with all your men; the camp is surrounded and will be taken unless helped."

Major Gosset, A.D.C., was present when Captain Church brought this information, and when Lieutenant-Colonel Harness decided, in consequence of it, to move towards Isandhlwana, Major Gosset rode back again to acquaint Lord Chelmsford, accompanied by an officer of the battery.‡

Lord Chelmsford had reached the site of the new camp in
the Amangene valley about 1 P.M., and very soon after his 1.0 P.M.
arrival here had received a report from a native that Zulus were
near the Isandhlwana camp, and that heavy firing was going
on. On this Lord Chelmsford and his Staff had gallopped up to
a hill from which the Isandhlwana camp was visible, and on 1.15 P.M.
seeing with their field glasses that the tents were standing and
that all was apparently quiet, had concluded that this report
and a similar one which had previously been received from
another native source were alike unfounded.

The height from which Lord Chelmsford was examining the camp was within half a mile of the spot where the guns had been halted, and the report of Harness's movement, which Major Gosset carried, reached the General at this place.

On receiving this report Lord Chelmsford gave orders for
Lieutenant-Colonel Harness to retrace his steps, and move as 1.25 P.M.
previously arranged to the new camping ground by the Amangene river. This order was carried by Major Gosset, who overtook Harness's party after they had gone about a mile and a half, 1.45 P.M.
and in accordance with it they turned back.

At about 2.0 P.M. Lord Chelmsford started to return to 2.0 P.M.
Isandhlwana, accompanied by the mounted Volunteers, and had
not gone far when he met Lieutenant-Colonel Russell. This

---

* By the track it is about 10½ miles from this ridge to Isandhlwana.

† Captain Develin.

‡ Lieutenant Parsons, R.A. This officer was sent for the purpose of conveying any order which the General might issue on learning the step taken by Lieutenant-Colonel Harness.

22nd January, 1879.

Russell's Proceedings.

officer, having been detached early on the day with the mounted infantry to explore the valleys near the Isipezi hill, had found this hill occupied in force by the enemy.

No collision, however, had occurred, and the party, after traversing these valleys during the forenoon, halted and off-

1.15 P.M. saddled between 12 and 1 o'clock. About 1.15 P.M. a mounted European of the Native Contingent arrived at their halting-place, and stated that he had been sent to tell the General that the camp was attacked.

At this time it was not known where Lord Chelmsford was, as he had not been with this party since the early part of the day, and efforts were made to find him, but without success. As some of the mounted infantry stated that they had seen the guns in camp firing, and as a second mounted European bearing a message similar to the first was met about this time, Lieutenant-Colonel Russell moved his party to a point near the track to Isandhlwana, with the view of joining the remainder of the force which he presumed would now move in that direction. Leaving the mounted infantry here, he pushed on to find the General, and on the way met Harness's party marching towards

1.45 P.M. Isandhlwana, in consequence of the message conveyed by Captain Develin.

After a conversation with Lieutenant-Colonel Harness, Russell moved on, and about a mile further met Lord Chelmsford with the mounted Volunteers, proceeding leisurely towards

2.10 P.M. Isandhlwana. On a report being now made of the purport of the messages received from the Native Contingent, no uneasiness was caused, as the camp had been seen within the last half-hour to all appearance undisturbed (*vide* p. 41). It was considered that if any small bodies of Zulus should be encountered on the way to Isandhlwana, the mounted troops accompanying Lord Chelmsford would be quite sufficient to drive them off. Russell turned again towards Isandhlwana with the General and his Staff, and very soon afterwards Harness and his party were met, retracing their steps as mentioned above, and moving in the direction of the new camp. When the General arrived at the spot where the mounted infantry were drawn up, these joined the Volunteers, and the force moved slowly towards Isandhlwana.

2.30 P.M. At about 2.30 P.M. Lord Chelmsford came up with Commandant Browne's battalion of the Native Contingent, halted in front.

Browne's proceedings.

The proceedings of this battalion, which had been ordered back at 10 A.M., had been as follows:—Shortly after leaving the General, a Zulu scout had been captured, from whom it was ascertained that an attack on the Isandhlwana camp was contemplated. On this, Commandant Browne, sending back an officer* to inform Lord Chelmsford, moved his battalion forward with the design of reinforcing the defenders of the camp. After

* Lieutenant Pohl.

advancing about 3 miles, it could be seen that the attack had 22nd January,
commenced, and that the guns had opened fire. A sergeant* 1879.
was now sent to report the state of affairs, and as a large number 12.0 noon.
of Zulus were seen in front, Commandant Browne decided to
withdraw his battalion, and retired towards his left rear. The
battalion thus reached the position where it was seen by Lieu- 12.45 P.M.
tenant-Colonel Harness's party, and it was from here that Captain Develin was despatched to give any Staff Officer he could meet the message:—"For God's sake, come back; the camp is surrounded, and things, I fear, are going badly."†

Somewhat later the mounted infantry came in sight, and Commandant Browne sent away another messenger, bearing a written memorandum to the effect that "there was a large force of the enemy between him and the camp."

This note‡ was received by Lieutenant-Colonel Russell as he was escorting Lord Chelmsford back to Isandhlwana, and was communicated to the General, who, being entirely unconscious of the disaster which had happened, regarded the report merely as an explanation of the halt of the Native Contingent. This was now ordered to advance immediately, and its march towards the camp was resumed, Lord Chelmsford with the mounted men leading the way.

At about 3.30 P.M.,§ when the united force had reached a 3.30 P.M.
point some 5 miles from Isandhlwana, a solitary horseman was met.

This proved to be Commandant Lonsdale, who, in order to make some arrangements about his men's rations, had returned earlier than the General, and had reached the camp at Isandhlwana soon after 2 P.M.‖ Riding on unsuspectingly, he had got within 10 yards of the tents when he was fired at, and had then recognised that all the men in red tunics whom he saw about him were Zulus, and that the camp was entirely in the enemy's hands. Turning his pony away with some difficulty, he fortunately escaped untouched by the bullets which were aimed at him, and was thus able to bring this news to Lord Chelmsford.

Orders were now sent back for Colonel Glyn's troops at the bivouack to march for Isandhlwana forthwith, and the General

---

* Sergeant Turner. Lieutenant Pohl and Sergeant Turner are believed to be the two messengers who reached Lieutenant-Colonel Russell's party as mentioned above.

† Captain Develin was met by Captain Church as mentioned on p. 41.

‡ It was afterwards lost.

§ This hour is arrived at by the fact that Major Gosset, who carried the order, issued in consequence of the news given by Commandant Lonsdale, reached the site of the new camp, about 6 miles back, at 4.5 P.M., accurately observed by Captain Symons, 24th Regiment.

‖ The statement as to the hour of this occurrence is supported by the facts that Commandant Lonsdale parted from Major Clery to return to camp (about 12 miles distant) soon after 12.0 noon; and also that he met Lord Chelmsford about 5 miles from camp, not later than 3.30 P.M. As after leaving the camp his pony was so tired that he had to lead it most of the way, it must have taken him about an hour and a quarter to get over these 5 miles.

22nd January, 1879. having formed the native battalion in line, with the mounted men on each flank, continued the advance towards Isandhlwana for about 2 miles.

Here the force halted behind a ridge, which concealed it from the camp, and the mounted infantry were sent forward to reconnoitre. The report which they brought in about an hour later, was that Zulus to the number of many thousands were in occupation of the camp.

Colonel Glyn had received the order to move to Isandhlwana
4.5 P.M. at 4.5 P.M., and the march had been commenced with as little delay as possible.

6.10 P.M. At 6.10 P.M. his force came up with Lord Chelmsford, who then, sending out the mounted men in front, formed the column with the guns in the centre, three companies of the 2 | 24th on either side of them, and the natives on the flanks, and gave the order to advance.

6.30 P.M. It was about 6.30 P.M. when the advance was resumed, and
7.0 P.M. at 7.0 P.M., when the sun set, the camp was still some 2 miles distant. Daylight rapidly faded, and about 7.45 P.M., when the column was within half a mile of Isandhlwana, darkness completely covered the camp. Merely the black outline of the hills was visible, and on the crests of those to the northward parties of Zulus could be seen against the sky.

The column was now halted, and a fire of shrapnel was opened by the artillery against the neck south of the Isandhlwana hill, over which the road to Rorke's Drift passes. To this no reply was made, and the troops then advanced to within 300 yards of the neck, on which fire was again opened, while three companies of the 2 | 24th under Major Black were sent forward with orders to seize the koppie to the south of it. This was done without opposition, and then the remainder of the column moved forward through the camp, which was silent and deserted.

8.30 P.M. It was now 8.30 P.M. and quite dark, so the troops halted and bivouacked on the neck, Major Black and his three companies remaining on the koppie.

At about 4 A.M. on the following morning the column started for Rorke's Drift.

When the centre column advanced on the 20th January, one company of the 2 | 24th Regiment, under Lieutenant Bromhead, had been left at Rorke's Drift to guard the ponts, some sick, and a certain amount of stores. On a rocky terrace, on the Natal side of the Buffalo about a mile from the crossing-place, stood two stone buildings, with thatched roofs, belonging to a Swedish mission station. The company of the 24th was encamped close to these buildings, of which the eastern, formerly the church, was now converted into a storehouse, while

To face page 45

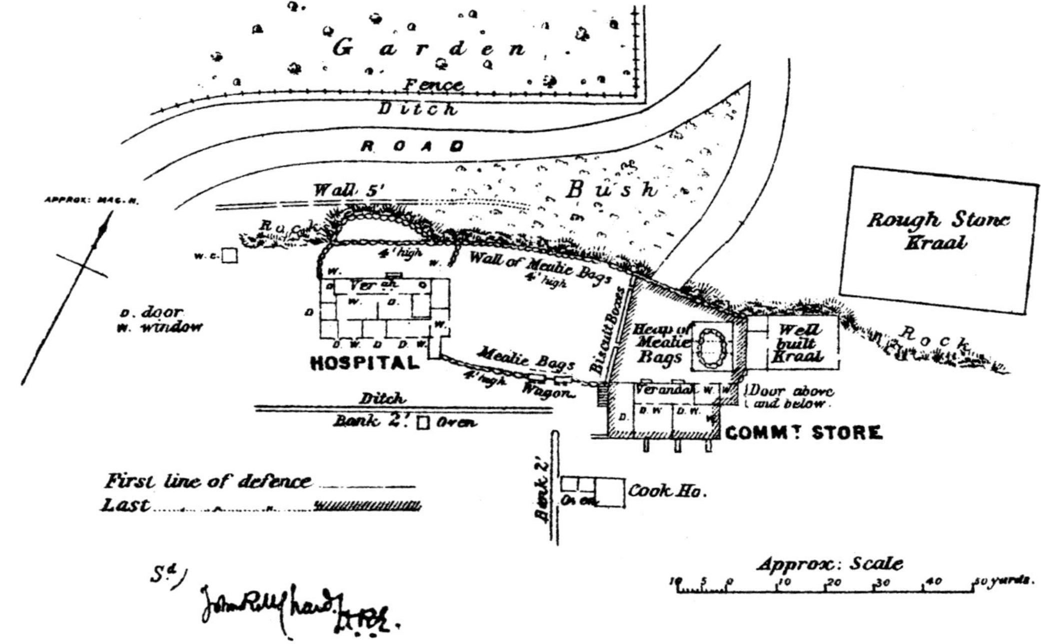

the other, which had been the missionary's dwelling, formed the hospital. 22nd January, 1879.

A force of native troops, under Colonel Durnford, had arrived at Rorke's Drift on the 20th; but on the removal of the greater part of them to Isandhlwana on the morning of the 22nd, the defence of the post at Rorke's Drift was left to this one company of the 2 | 24th and a detachment of the Natal Native Contingent.

The nearest troops were two companies of the 1 | 24th at Helpmakaar, 10 miles distant; and at 2 P.M. on the 22nd Major Spalding, D.A.Q.M.G., who was in charge of this part of the line of communications, rode over to that place to bring up one of these companies to reinforce the small garrison at Rorke's Drift.*

When Major Spalding left, the command at Rorke's Drift devolved on Lieutenant Chard, R.E. This officer at 3.15 P.M. was watching the ponts at the river, when Lieutenant Adendorff and a Carabineer galloped up from the direction of Isandhlwana, and informed him of the disaster which had happened there. The Carabineer was sent on with the news to Helpmakaar, and the two officers hastened to the military post, where preparations for defence had already been commenced by Lieutenant Bromhead, in consequence of a report brought in by a man of the mounted infantry. These preparations consisted in striking the tents, barricading and loopholing the storehouse and hospital, and in connecting these two buildings, which at their nearest points were about 30 yards apart, by a parapet. Materials for this were fortunately at hand in the bags full of Indian corn which formed part of the commissariat stores, and with these and a few wagons a defensible line was formed. The pont guard was called in, all the men available were told off to their respective posts, and the work of building the parapet was proceeded with as rapidly as possible. Soon after 4 P.M. firing was heard to the south, and the enemy were reported to be close at hand, upon which the detachment of the Native Contingent, who were within the post, quitted it with their officer. The garrison was now reduced to the company of the 2 | 24th, about 80 strong, and some men of other corps, the total number within the post being 139, of whom 35 were sick in hospital. The length of parapet to be defended was too great for this diminished garrison, and Lieutenant Chard at once commenced an inner retrenchment, forming a parapet of biscuit boxes across the larger enclosure. This was only two boxes high when the enemy, who had crossed the river below Rorke's Drift, advanced on the post. The following is Lieutenant Chard's description of the struggle which ensued:—

"About 4.30 P.M. 500 or 600 of the enemy came in sight round the hill to our south, and advanced at a run against the

---

* This company had been ordered to Rorke's Drift previously, and ought to have arrived there on the 20th January.

22nd January, 1879. south wall. They were met by a well-sustained fire, but notwithstanding their heavy loss, continued to advance to within 50 yards of the wall, where they met with such a heavy fire from the wall and cross-fire from the store, that they were checked, but taking advantage of the cover afforded by the cookhouse, ovens, &c., kept up a heavy fire. The greater number, however, without stopping, moved to the left, around the hospital, and made a rush at our north-west wall of mealie bags, but after a short but desperate struggle, were driven back with heavy loss into the bush around the work.

"The main body of the enemy were close behind, and had lined the ledge of rock and caves overlooking us, about 400 yards to our south, from where they kept up a constant fire, and, advancing somewhat more to their left than the first attack, occupied the garden, hollow road, and bush in great force.

"Taking advantage of the bush, which we had not time to cut down, the enemy were able to advance under cover close to our wall, and in this part soon held one side of the wall, while we held the other. A series of desperate assaults were made, extending from the hospital, along the wall, as far as the bush reached; but each was most splendidly met and repulsed by our men with the bayonet, Corporal Schiess, Natal Native Contingent, greatly distinguishing himself by his conspicuous gallantry.

"The fire from the rocks behind us, though badly directed, took us completely in reverse, and was so heavy that we suffered very severely, and about 6 P.M. were forced to retire behind the retrenchment of biscuit boxes.

"All this time the enemy had been attempting to force the hospital, and shortly after set fire to its roof.

"The garrison of the hospital defended it, room by room, bringing out all the sick who could be moved before they retired. Privates Williams, Hook, R. Jones, and W. Jones, 24th Regiment, being the last men to leave, holding the doorway with the bayonet, their own ammunition being expended. From the want of interior communication and the burning of the house, it was impossible to save all. With most heartfelt sorrow I regret we could not save these poor fellows from their terrible fate.

"Seeing the hospital burning, and the desperate attempts of the enemy to fire the roof of the stores, we converted two mealie bag heaps into a sort of redoubt, which gave a second line of fire all round, Assistant Commissary Dunne working hard at this, though much exposed, and rendering valuable assistance.

"As darkness came on we were completely surrounded, and, after several attempts had been gallantly repulsed, were forced eventually to retire to the middle, and then inner, wall of the kraal on our east. The position we then had we retained throughout.

"A desultory fire was kept up all night, and several assaults were attempted and repulsed, the vigour of the attack continuing until after midnight. Our men firing with the greatest coolness, did not waste a single shot, the light afforded by the burning hospital being of great help to us. 22nd January, 1879.

"About 4 A.M., the 23rd instant, the firing ceased, and at daybreak the enemy were out of sight, over the hill to the south-west. We patrolled the grounds, collecting the arms of the dead Zulus, and strengthened our defences as much as possible.

"We were removing the thatch from the roof of the stores, when about 7 A.M. a large body of the enemy appeared on the hills to the south-west.

"I sent a friendly Kaffir, who had come in shortly before, with a note to the officer commanding at Helpmakaar, asking for help.

"About 8 A.M. the 3rd Column* appeared in sight, the enemy, who had been gradually advancing falling back as they approached."

Major Spalding, who had started for Helpmakaar, at 2 P.M., on the 22nd, reached that place at 3.45 P.M., and afterwards returned towards Rorke's Drift, with two companies of the 1 | 24th Regiment, under Major Upcher. Pushing on in advance of the infantry, Major Spalding arrived at sunset, within about 3 miles of the post, and there met a body of Zulus, who opposed his progress. From this point the Mission House was seen to be on fire, and the assertion of the fugitives that the post had fallen appeared to be correct. On rejoining the infantry, therefore, Major Spalding ordered them to march back to Helpmakaar. This place was the principal advanced depôt for the centre column, and contained large stores of ammunition and provisions, and for the protection of these stores, the defences which had been commenced by the fugitives from Isandhlwana were strengthened on the return of the troops, at 9 P.M.

The night, however, passed without any attack being made. 23rd January.

The march of the force with Lord Chelmsford, from Isandhlwana to the Buffalo, on the morning of the 23rd January, was made without opposition, though a large body of Zulus was seen at some distance on the left flank of the column. When the force arrived at Rorke's Drift, the men were supplied with food, and measures were taken to improve the defences of the post.

52 officers and 806 white non-commissioned officers and men were killed at Isandhlwana, on the 22nd January. Of the native troops in camp it seems probable that from 200 to 300 fell, but the number who perished has not been ascertained with accuracy. This disaster also deprived the centre column of the whole of its transport, and rendered the troops who composed it incapable of making any offensive movement. Officers

---

* Lord Chelmsford's force.

22nd January, 1879. and men found themselves on the 23rd January with nothing but what they stood in, for those who had marched out on the morning of the 22nd had gone in light marching order, and those who escaped from the camp had saved nothing. All the documents of the Head-quarter Office were lost, as well as those of both battalions of the 24th. The colours of the 2nd Battalion had been left in the guard tent, when the regiment marched out of camp, and they were never seen again. The regimental colour of the 1 | 24th had been left at Helpmakaar, but the Queen's colour was in the camp, and when the success of the Zulu attack was evident, this colour was taken by Lieutenant Melvill, the adjutant, who, accompanied by Lieutenant Coghill, endeavoured to bear it to a place of safety. These officers followed the same ravine as the other fugitives, and reached the Buffalo, but were both killed at that river,* from the bottom of which the colour was recovered on the 4th February.

By the capture of the camp the Zulus became possessed of two 7-pr. guns with their ammunition, and of about 800 Martini-Henry rifles, with some 400,000 cartridges.

From statements made by Zulus who were present at Isandhlwana, it appears that Ketchwayo's army, 13,700 strong, and commanded by Tshingwayo, left the military kraal of Nodwengu, near Ulundi, on the afternoon of the 17th January, and marched to the White Umvolosi. On the 20th the army had reached the Isipezi hill, and on the 21st halted under the 'Ngutu hill, about 7 miles to the north-east of the camp at Isandhlwana.

The Zulu army was organized in three bodies, the Nodwengu Regiment (1220), the Nokenke (830), and the Umcityu (2880), forming the right; the 'Mbonambi (1240), and the 'Nkobamakosi (3260), the centre; and the Tulwana (2450), and Qikazi (1220), the left. It is asserted that there was no intention of attacking the British on the 22nd, as the state of the moon was considered unpropitious, and that the ceremonies which usually precede an action had not been performed.

On the morning of the 22nd, however, on the sound of firing being heard, the Nokenke regiment advanced, thinking that one of the regiments on its left (the 'Nkobamakosi) was engaged.
8.0 A.M. This firing was the action near Matyana's, and when the Nokenke found all quiet in the neighbourhood of the 'Nkobamakosi, they retired to their original position.

Soon afterwards some mounted men came upon, and fired at, the Umcityu regiment, which thereupon sprang up and advanced against them. The other two regiments of the right wing, the Nodwengu and Nokenke, followed the Umcityu, as did the 'Mbonambi and 'Nkobamakosi, which formed the centre.

---

* Lieutenant Melvill's watch was found to have stopped at 10 minutes past 2.

Tshingwayo ordered the Tulwana and Qikazi, which were on the left, to form circle, and remain in reserve, but afterwards sent these two regiments forward, directing them to move to the extreme right by the west of the Isandhlwana hill. These regiments, who were commanded by Dabulamanzi, a brother of Ketchwayo's, seized the road to Rorke's Drift, and, when the camp had been captured, moved off to that place and formed the force which attacked the post.

In the attack on the camp, the Zulu regiments were in the following order:—On the right was the Nokenke, with the Nodwengu, 'Mbonambi, and Umcityu next to it, in the order named; the left being formed by the 'Nkobamakosi, which was the strongest of the regiments engaged.

There is some difficulty in fixing the amount of the Zulu losses on this day, but it appears probable that at Isandhlwana not less than 1,000 fell, while at Rorke's Drift about 400 bodies were found round the post.

On the evening of the 22nd January the Zulu army, after pillaging the camp, returned to its halting place under the 'Ngutu hill, and shortly afterwards dispersed.

V. Operations of the Left Column—11th to 23rd January.

The left column (No. 4), under Colonel Evelyn Wood, was encamped at Bemba's Kop, on the Blood river, on the 10th

10th January, 1879. January. At 2 P.M. on that day, Colonel Wood started with 2 guns (11 | 7 R.A.), 6 companies 90th Regiment, 6 companies 1 | 13th Regiment, the greater part of the Frontier Light Horse, and Wood's Irregulars, and marched down the left bank of the Blood river.

The difficulties of this march were considerable, as, in addition to the delays caused by passing marshy ground, it was necessary to cross numerous tributary streams which run down from the Incanda and Halatu mountains. To render the deep beds of these streams passable by vehicles, their banks had to be cut down, but by 6 P.M. a distance of 9 miles had been

11th January. covered. Halting till 2 A.M. on the 11th, Colonel Wood again moved forward with merely a flying column, composed of the Frontier Light Horse, the 2 guns, 24 marksmen from the two infantry regiments, carried in mule wagons, and 600 of Wood's Irregulars. The remainder of the force, under Lieutenant-Colonel Gilbert, was ordered to follow in support, for a distance of 9 miles.

Colonel Wood, with his flying column, pushed on through darkness and fog, and guided by Mr. P. L. Uys reached a spot about 12 miles from Rorke's Drift, at 8 A.M. Here he had the interview with Lord Chelmsford which has been already mentioned, and thus learned that the centre column had crossed the Buffalo without opposition.

After a short halt Colonel Wood started on his return, and having rejoined the main body of his column, the whole force marched back towards the camp at Bemba's Kop. It did not

13th January. arrive there, however, till the morning of the 13th, as on the 12th the country became almost impassable by reason of heavy rain.

During these movements, though large numbers of cattle were captured, no hostile encounter took place, as the Zulus, though well armed and present in large numbers, were at this time without definite orders as to the attitude they were to assume towards the British.

From the 13th to the 17th January, the column remained halted at Bemba's Kop; reconnaissances being made on the 15th and 17th by the mounted troops.

18th January. On the 18th the column advanced eastwards to the Insegene, or Sand river, a distance of about 10 miles, and during this march Wood's Irregulars had a slight skirmish on the farther side of the White Umvolosi river.

A halt was made on the 19th, and on the 20th the column moved on to the White Umvolosi, and encamped near Tinta's kraal. This chief submitted, and was sent with his people to Utrecht, a company of the 90th escorting them as far as the Blood river. On this day, the 20th, a reconnaissance was made by the Frontier Light Horse, and part of the Dutch Contingent to the top of the Zungi range, a large, table-topped mountain, where they met with so much opposition that they were obliged to withdraw. **20th January, 1879.**

On the 21st a stone laager fort was completed on the White Umvolosi, and in it most of the stores of the column were deposited in charge of a company of the 1 | 13th, and of the company of the 90th which had now returned from its escort duty with Tinta's tribe. **21st January.**

At midnight, on the 21st January, the remainder of the column started on a patrol towards the Zungi range. This name is given to the western portion of a more or less continuous line of hills which extends from west to east, for a distance of over 20 miles. The central eminence in this line is known as the Inhloblana mountain, and the eastern as the Ityenteka. Colonel Wood's force was divided into three sections. One of these, consisting of the Frontier Light Horse and the Dutch Contingent, with 2 guns, was sent under the command of Lieutenant-Colonel Buller to ascend the valley of the White Umvolosi, and gain the western end of the Zungi range; while another, consisting of the 90th and Wood's Irregulars, under the command of Colonel Wood himself, marched direct to a point in the range, about 3 miles to the eastward of that on which the mounted men were moving. The third section, consisting of the 1 | 13th Regiment, under the command of Colonel Gilbert, left camp later than the others, and, marching about 12 miles, encamped beneath the south-eastern extremity of the Zungi mountain. **22nd January.**

Both the parties which ascended the mountain arrived on the summit unopposed, about 6 A.M., and after a halt, proceeded together along it towards the east, driving away some Zulus, and capturing the cattle which they had been guarding.

When the force reached the eastern extremity of the Zungi range a number of Zulus, estimated at about 4,000, were seen drilling on the north-western slopes of the Inhlobana mountain. Their evolutions, which were plainly visible with the aid of a glass, were executed with ease and precision, a circle, a triangle, and a hollow square with a partition across it, being formed rapidly by movements of companies. Colonel Wood's force now descended the mountain, and at 7 P.M. arrived at the camp, which had been formed by the 1 | 13th Regiment.

Here the left column remained halted on the 23rd, and advanced again on the morning of the 24th January. At 7.30 A.M., when a distance of about 8 miles had been traversed, a force of Zulus was encountered to the north of the Inhlobana mountain, and dispersed without difficulty. During this skirmish news of the Isandhlwana disaster reached Colonel Wood, who **24th January.**

decided to withdraw to his former position on the White Umvolosi.

After a halt of two hours and a half, the return march was commenced, and at 7 A.M., on the 25th, the column reached Fort Tinta.*

25th January 1879.

---

* For a continuation of the operations of the left column *vide* section VIII.

To face page 53.

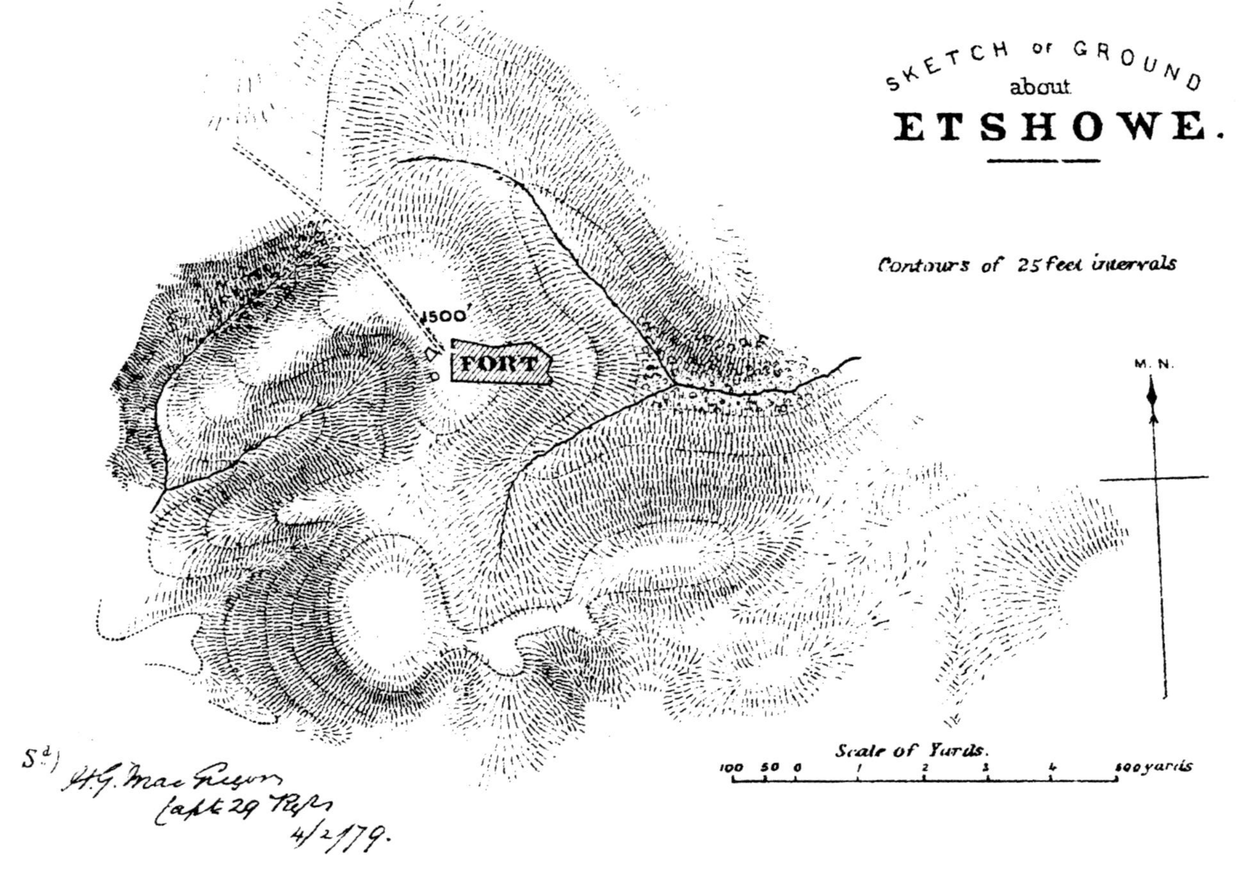

Lithd at the Intelligence Dept War Office. March, 1881.

VI. The Blockade of Etshowe—24th January to 3rd April.

The force under Colonel Pearson, on its arrival at Etshowe on the 23rd January, 1879, lost no time in forming the Mission Station into a defensible post, as this was a necessary preliminary to the advance on Ulundi.

On the 25th January 48 empty wagons left Etshowe for the Lower Tugela, escorted by two companies of the Buffs and two of the 99th. This convoy arrived without interference at Fort Tenedos on the 27th. **25th January, 1879.**

The troops at Etshowe, busily employed in the construction of the fort and in preparations for their next advance were entirely ignorant of the movements of the other invading columns and of the events which had occurred at Isandhlwana until the 27th January, when a brief message from Sir Bartle Frere announced that Colonel Durnford had been defeated.

About 9 A.M., on the 28th January, Colonel Pearson received the following telegram from Lord Chelmsford:—"Pietermaritzburg, 27th January, 1879. Consider all my instructions as cancelled, and act in whatever manner you think most desirable in the interests of the column under your command. Should you consider the garrison of Etshowe as too far advanced to be fed with safety you can withdraw it. Hold, however, if possible, the post on the Zulu side of Lower Tugela. You must be prepared to have the whole Zulu force down upon you. Do away with tents, and let the men take shelter under the wagons which will then be in position for defence and hold so many more supplies." **28th January**

Though the extent of the disaster which had befallen the centre column could not be realised from this message, it was evident that the situation was materially changed, and the course to be adopted was discussed at a council of war, composed of Staff and Commanding Officers, held the same day. At this council it was decided by a small majority not to retreat to the Tugela.

Etshowe, which had been selected as a depôt by reason of the buildings which existed there, had many disadvantages as a permanent post. On three sides the fort was commanded at short range, and some dangerous wooded ravines lay close below it. Plenty of good water was near at hand, but there was no large stock of provisions in the fort. Even though the convoy of supplies, now on its way, should arrive safely, the provisions available would still be inadequate for the entire force during a protracted blockade, and the difficulties of the road by which the position was reached gave little hope of a further supply being soon received. While, therefore, it was determined that Etshowe should be held, and fortified as strongly as the site permitted, it was decided at once to reduce the garrison by sending back all the mounted men and nearly the whole of the two battalions of the Native Contingent.

These troops left Etshowe at 2 P.M., and the mounted men under Major Barrow reached Fort Tenedos at 11·30 P.M. the
29th January, 1879. same night. At daybreak the following morning the men of the Native Contingent began to arrive, but their march had been conducted in such an irregular manner that it was late in the afternoon before all had got to the Tugela.

The convoy of supplies* for the right column was still on
28th January. the road to Etshowe on the 28th, and on the afternoon of that day a message was despatched to Colonel Ely, who commanded it, urging him to hasten his march as much as possible. The convoy had by this time got within a few miles of the post, and spans of oxen were sent out to aid in bringing up the wagons. Seventy-two of these wagons arrived late in the evening, but at a distance of about 7 miles from Etshowe it had been found necessary to abandon six wagons containing food and one containing forage.

30th January. On the 30th January, in accordance with Lord Chelmsford's instructions, the whole of the garrison moved within the work and took shelter beneath wagons ranged along the inside of the parapet instead of occupying tents outside. The strength of the garrison at this date was as follows:—Combatants, 1,292 whites and 65 blacks; non-combatants, 47 whites and 290 blacks, or a total of 1,339 whites and 355 blacks.

The large number of animals which had accompanied the column could not find pasture for any length of time within reach of the fort, and it was therefore decided that a considerable portion of them should be sent away in charge of their drivers, to reach the Tugela if possible. Accordingly on the 30th about a thousand animals were despatched, but of these some 900 were promptly captured by the Zulus and the remainder were driven back to the fort.

2nd February. On the 2nd February runners arrived at Etshowe with letters and telegrams giving some particulars of the Isandhlwana disaster, but the garrison did not become fully aware of its extent till some days afterwards. On this day Colonel Pearson wrote to Lord Chelmsford suggesting that the troops in Etshowe should be reinforced by seven companies, proposing, under these circumstances, to form an entrenched camp outside the existing work.

6th February. On the 6th February another despatch from Lord Chelmsford, dated the 2nd, was received, as well as a telegram dated the 4th. In the latter Colonel Pearson was reminded of the inadvisability of reinforcements being sent to Etshowe, and a withdrawal to the Lower Tugela with a portion of the garrison was suggested.

---

* The escort consisted of three companies 99th Regiment, which were reinforced by two companies of the Buffs, and two of the Native Contingent, sent back from Etshowe on the 24th.

Colonel Pearson replied the same day, admitting that it would be unwise to send him reinforcements, and reporting on the existing state of the entrenchments. In this letter Colonel Pearson suggested that a convoy of 20 wagons of food should be sent up under escort, and that two companies of the Buffs from the Lower Tugela should relieve the three companies of the 99th at Etshowe, these latter being accompanied on their return to the frontier by half the company of the Royal Engineers, the Volunteers, and the native troops. 6th February, 1879.

This despatch reached Fort Pearson safely on the 8th, and its substance was telegraphed to Lord Chelmsford, who was then at Durban.

On the 7th February another despatch, dated the 6th, reached Etshowe, and in this Colonel Pearson was recommended to retire to the Lower Tugela with half his force, the sick and the wounded, and to reduce the size of the entrenchments to suit the diminished garrison. 7th Feb.

By the same messenger who brought this despatch, tolerably full particulars of the Isandhlwana disaster were received, and the garrison of the fort now for the first time realised the position in which they stood.

The recommendations contained in Lord Chelmsford's despatch were to a certain extent contingent on an unsuccessful attack on the post having been made, and it was decided that these recommendations should not be followed, and that no reduction should be made in the garrison.

On the 11th February messengers arrived at Etshowe bearing a despatch from Lord Chelmsford dated the 8th. This was in reply to Colonel Pearson's despatch of the 6th, and repeated the recommendations of the previous despatches. A rapid withdrawal to the Lower Tugela, without wheeled transport, was counselled, and warning was given that no convoy would be able to start for Etshowe for six weeks. 11th Feb.

On receipt of this despatch Colonel Pearson sent off a reply to it and to that of the 6th, and informed Lord Chelmsford that on hearing again, he would be prepared to march out at midnight on the 16th with three companies of the 99th, the Naval Brigade, and half the company of Engineers.

By this time, however, the road had become very unsafe for messengers, and this despatch never reached its destination. The Zulus showed themselves in large numbers round the fort, and after this date they prevented the arrival of messengers from the Tugela.

The course of events for the garrison thus shut up without means of communication with the outer world was very monotonous. Work on the fort was continued and its defences improved, but the Zulus who hovered round did not venture to attack it. They did not even avail themselves of the commanding positions on the hills overlooking the fort, from which they might easily have opened a harassing fire on the garrison.

As, on the 16th, no further communication had been received 16th Feb.

from Lord Chelmsford, the movement which Colonel Pearson had been prepared to make did not take place.

18th Feb., 1879. On the 18th February a messenger from Etshowe succeeded in passing to the Tugela, and bore a despatch reporting that no attack had been made on the fort and that the health of the garrison was good.

20th Feb. On the 20th February the property of those who had marched out on the 29th January was examined, and the stores of food which were thus brought to light were put up to auction and realised large prices. Of the necessaries of life there was no scarcity, but by this time the want of tea and tobacco began to be felt. The garrison had plenty of employment, for additions were constantly made to the defences and a road inside the fort was constructed. The bands, both of the Buffs and of the 99th, were with the besieged force, and these played daily.

When Major Barrow's force marched out, a certain number of sick horses had been left behind, and with these and some officers' horses a small mounted party was organised. This little force did excellent service in furnishing vedettes and in scouting, and on the 21st and 22nd February, as well as on other occasions, made successful attacks on small parties of Zulus who had fired on the cattle guard.

1st March. On the 1st March a force of 400* infantry with one gun and about 30 mounted men marched out to a distance of some 7 miles from Etshowe, and burnt a kraal belonging to the Chief Dabulamanzi. On their return the troops were fired on by Zulus who occupied the bush through which the track passed, but no casualties occurred.

At this time the latest news which the garrison had received was dated the 8th February, and therefore intense excitement

2nd March. was caused on the 2nd March by the discovery that a bright light seen in the direction of the Tugela, and which was at first taken for a burning kraal, was in reality a flashing signal.

3rd March. At first nothing could be read, but on the 3rd the following portion of a message was made out :—" Look out for 1,000 men on the 13th, sally out when you see me to ——"

5th March. Nothing could be read on the 4th, but on the 5th March the signalling was fairly distinct, and a message was received in these terms :—" From Colonel Law to Colonel Pearson. About 13th instant, by General's orders I advance to your support with 1,000 men, besides natives, as far as Inyezane. Be prepared to sally out to meet me with your surplus garrison there, by signal. I may come by Dunn's road. Make answer by flag on church."

9th March. The next few days were cloudy, and communication by flashing was impossible, but on the 9th a runner succeeded in reaching the Tugela with letters which informed the signallers that their messages had been understood. Efforts were made by the garrison to reply by signal, but appliances were wanting,

---

* 4 companies Buffs, 1 company 99th, 1 company R.E., and 20 marines.

and the first attempts were without success.* Eventually, how ever, all difficulties were overcome, and by the 14th March intercommunication was satisfactorily established, and thenceforward was only interrupted by cloudy weather.

At the beginning of March a running survey of a route leading from the fort to a point on the track to the Lower Tugela had been made by the Engineer officers. By the use of this route, which ran through a fairly open country, a long détour might be avoided; and as it was considered practicable, work was commenced on it on the 7th March. The length of the new road was about 3 miles, and the principal operations necessary to open it consisted in cutting down the steep banks of watercourses and in carrying the track along the sides of hills. On this working parties were now daily employed, and though they were fired at occasionally by the enemy, no serious interference was attempted.

On the 13th March a message was received that the relief was postponed till the 1st April, when the whole garrison would be removed, and accordingly the contemplated march of a portion of the force this day towards the Inyezane did not take place. **13th March, 1879.**

By this time sickness had appeared within the fort to a serious extent. Up to the end of February the general health of the garrison had been tolerably good, but about that date the number of sick showed a marked increase.

Early in March the whole of the slaughter oxen were consumed, and the meat rations were now supplied from the lean carcases of the draught or "trek" oxen. The meat ration was $1\frac{1}{2}$ lb. at this time, but it was tough and innutritious, and the want of fatty matter was very severely felt.

On the 15th March large numbers of the enemy were seen moving past Etshowe from the direction of the Inyezane, but they took no notice of the fort or its defenders. **15th March.**

On the 20th March, for the first time since the 11th February, a runner arrived from the Tugela with letters and a despatch. By this Colonel Pearson was definitely informed that the relief column would start on the 29th. **20th March.**

During the previous fortnight the work on the road had been going forward, and by the 21st March it was nearly complete.

Towards the end of the month, in anticipation of the termination of the blockade, preparations were made for the removal

---

* A fire balloon made of tracing paper had been tried, and also a screen 12′ × 15′, set up on the sky line, but both these failed. Efforts were then made to direct the sun s rays by means of a small mirror on the point near the Tugela whence the flashing proceeded. Captain MacGregor accomplished this by "laying" a long straight piece of iron tubing (found in the church) on the point in question, and then arranging the mirror so as to illuminate two bits of paper fixed at each end of this tube When it was found that only one bit of paper was illuminated, the mirror was readjusted. Flashes were made by covering and uncovering the mirror.

of the wagons, which had been used as traverses within the fort, and beneath which officers and men had been sleeping.

29th March, 1879. On the 29th March Lord Chelmsford sent orders by signal that a force of 500 men was to sally out from Etshowe and act in concert with the relief column when this should become engaged.

31st March. 1st April. Two days afterwards the mounted men of the column were seen in the distance, and on the afternoon of the 1st April the laager formed by Lord Chelmsford's main body was plainly visible in the valley of the Inyezane.

A force was detailed to move out as directed, but before **2nd April.** this had started on the morning of the 2nd, the relief column was seen to be hotly engaged. Gingihlovo, the scene of this action, was in a direct line, only a few miles distant from Etshowe, but the country which lay between was so impracticable that it could only be reached by a wide détour. To traverse this three or four hours would have been required, and, as it was seen that useful co-operation was impossible, the force detailed did not leave the fort.

The progress of the battle of Gingihlovo and its successful result were easily seen and anxiously watched, and on its conclusion Colonel Pearson sent congratulations to Lord Chelmsford by signal.

3rd April. On the evening of the 3rd April Lord Chelmsford, with a portion of the relief column, arrived at the fort, and the blockade of Etshowe was terminated.

During the ten weeks that it had lasted 4 officers and 27 men had died, and at this date the number of sick amounted to [illegible] 120

VII. Proceedings in Natal from 23rd January to 3rd April, and Relief of Etshowe.

Lord Chelmsford, with what remained of the central column arrived, as has been already mentioned, at Rorke's Drift on the morning of the 23rd January. During the day the improvised fortifications at this place were strengthened, and as they were now held by a garrison of some 700 men, the post was perfectly secure from assault. **22nd January, 1879.**

The confidence of the Native Contingent, however, had been rudely shaken, and on the night of the 23rd January many of those whose comrades had fallen at Isandhlwana, deserted from the two battalions at Rorke's Drift.

Lord Chelmsford determined to proceed at once to Pietermaritzburg, and at 9 A.M. on the 24th January started from Rorke's Drift. On arriving at Helpmakaar, he found that the battalion of the Native Contingent at that place had refused to march to Umsinga as ordered, and it was only by making it clearly understood that deserters would be shot that obedience was secured. **24th January.**

At 2 P.M. Lord Chelmsford left Helpmakaar, and, proceeding by way of Ladysmith,* arrived at Pietermaritzburg on the evening of the 26th.

After the General's departure from Rorke's Drift, the whole of the Native Contingent who had remained at that place deserted, those who had rifles, however, being previously disarmed.

On this day the artillery and mounted men were moved to Helpmakaar, so that at Rorke's Drift there were only seven companies of the 2 | 24th, viz., the one which had defended the post, and the six which had been out with Lord Chelmsford on the 22nd.

At Helpmakaar were two companies of the 1 | 24th, and these were joined by half the 5th Company R.E., the other half of this company moving on to Rorke's Drift.

Of the 2 | 4th Regiment which had left England a few days after the 99th, three companies had been sent to Cape Town, and the remainder had disembarked at Durban on the 13th and 16th January. These companies were moving up country to occupy posts on the line of communications when the news of the Isandhlwana disaster was received, and four of them were sent to Helpmakaar, one being left in garrison at Greytown.

In the period immediately following the withdrawal from

---

* After the Isandhlwana disaster, the working parties and wagon drivers who were employed on the Greytown-Helpmakaar road, deserted *en masse* and refused to return. This road accordingly ceased to be used.

Zululand of the centre column, a purely defensive attitude was assumed by the troops in this part of Natal. Helpmakaar and Rorke's Drift were strongly fortified, and no offensive movement was attempted.

4th February, 1879. On the 4th February a small party under Major Black 2 | 24th Regiment, went from Rorke's Drift down the course of the Buffalo river to the spot known as the Fugitive's Drift, where the greater number of those who had escaped from Isandhlwana had endeavoured to cross over into Natal. Near this spot the bodies of Lieutenants Melvill and Coghill were found and buried, and the Queen's colour of the 1 | 24th was recovered from the bed of the river, and on the following day was restored to the custody of the regiment.

While about this time a few marauding parties crossed from Zululand into Natal and caused serious alarm, Ketchwayo's intentions remained unknown, and no reliable information was forthcoming as to the position of his army which had fought at Isandhlwana.

Under these circumstances very grave fears of invasion were felt, not only in the more exposed portions of Natal, but also in regions remote from the frontier. At Pietermaritzburg and Durban, as well as at Utrecht, Greytown, Stanger and other towns and villages near the border, central posts or laagers were prepared in which in case of need the white inhabitants might assemble, and where they might stand a siege.

Lord Chelmsford on his arrival at Pietermaritzburg took measures for informing the Secretary of State for War, both by
27th January. telegraph and by despatch, of the Isandhlwana disaster, and at the same time asked for reinforcements. South Africa not being in telegraphic communication with Europe, the General's message had to be conveyed by steamer from Cape Town to St. Vincent, the vessel being dispatched on the 27th instead of on the 28th, in order that the news might be delivered as speedily as possible.

When the information reached Cape Town, arrangements were promptly made for having the duties carried on by the colonial troops, and for sending to Natal the three companies of the 2 | 4th Regiment which had formed the garrison. These companies leaving Cape Town on the 26th January arrived at Durban on the 30th, and marched into Pietermaritzburg on the 2nd February.

2nd February. Four companies of the 88th which had been on the eastern frontier of the Cape colony, on being relieved by Volunteers from Cape Town, proceeded by sea to Natal, and arrived at Durban on the 8th February. The Head-quarters of the regiment and
8th February. one company went to Pietermaritzburg, two companies to Stanger, and one remained at Durban. Those which went to Stanger relieved two companies of the 99th, which moved on to Fort Pearson.

Lord Chelmsford who had arrived at Durban on the 6th February, and had sent messages thence to Colonel Pearson,

proceeded on the 11th to Fort Pearson. At this time Colonel 11th Feb., 1879.
Pearson's return from Etshowe with a portion of his force was contemplated, and it was proposed to aid him, if attacked on the march, by a force from the Lower Tugela. The two companies
of the 99th from Stanger arrived on the 14th, and the force 14th Feb.
available was thus raised to five companies of the 99th, two of the Buffs, and the "Tenedos" Naval Brigade, with Barrow's mounted infantry, the Volunteers, and the Native Contingent, the whole being under the command of Lord Chelmsford himself.

As has been already mentioned, no portion of Colonel Pearson's force left Etshowe at this time, and Lord Chelmsford, after remaining at the Lower Tugela for about a week, returned to Pietermaritzburg, where he arrived on the 21st February.

In consequence of a request from Colonel Wood, the mounted infantry and Natal Carabineers which had remained at
Helpmakaar since the 24th January, marched on the 14th Feb- 14th Feb.
ruary to join the left column, and on the same day two companies of the 2 | 4th Regiment also left Helpmakaar for Utrecht.

By the middle of February, the fears of an invasion of Natal were considerably allayed, and Lord Chelmsford's efforts, on his return to Pietermaritzburg, were principally directed to the collection of transport to replace that lost at Isandhlwana, and to the reorganization of the Native Contingent, now formed into five battalions. Additional native levies were also enrolled, and the mode in which they should be employed led to a long correspondence between Lord Chelmsford, Sir Bartle Frere, and Sir Henry Bulwer.

It was finally decided that the bulk of these levies, which were enrolled for the defence of Natal, should not cross the Zulu frontier.

In the meantime, however, reinforcements were on their way to Natal.

On the 6th February the news of the Isandhlwana disaster 6th February.
reached St. Helena, and it was determined that the garrison of the island, consisting of a battery R.A. (8 | 7) and a company of the 88th Regiment, should be at once embarked on board Her Majesty's ship "Shah," which was in port at the time, and be conveyed to Durban. The "Shah" was on her way home from the Pacific station, but under these circumstances her commander, Captain Bradshaw, considered himself justified in changing her destination. In addition to the troops, a naval contingent of about 400 men could be furnished from this vessel, so that a reinforcement of some 650 men would in this manner become available. Coal was purchased at St. Helena, and the voyage was performed under steam. On the 23rd February the "Shah" arrived at Simon's Bay, and, after coaling, proceeded to Durban,
which was reached on the 6th March. 6th March.

Lord Chelmsford's telegram of the 27th January reached the Secretary of State for War early on the 11th February, and before the day was over the reinforcements to be sent out had been detailed, and the preliminary measures for their transport and supply had been taken. It was decided that these rein forcements should consist of two regiments of cavalry, two batteries of artillery, and an ammunition column, one company of engineers, six battalions of infantry, three companies Army Service Corps, and one company Army Hospital Corps. Two of the troop ships sailed on the 19th February, and the remainder followed as shown in the table forming Appendix B.

Prince Louis Napoleon, son of the late Emperor of the French, accompanied the expedition, and went out in the steamship "Danube."

At the time when the news of Isandhlwana was received in London, the 57th Regiment, which had been in garrison in Ceylon, was about to be relieved by the 102nd Fusiliers, who had proceeded from Gibraltar in Her Majesty's ship "Tamar."
11th March, 1879. Orders were sent by telegraph for the "Tamar" to convey the 57th to Natal, and this regiment having embarked on the 22nd February, landed at Durban on the 11th March.

The next reinforcements were furnished from Her Majesty's ship "Boadicea," from which a naval brigade 200 strong was
15th March. landed on the 15th March, and on the 17th March the 91st
17th March. Regiment disembarked from the "Pretoria" which had made the voyage from Southampton in 26 days.

Lord Chelmsford had returned to Durban early in March, and on the arrival of the "Shah" had proposed to send forward a column from the Lower Tugela towards Etshowe to co-operate with Colonel Pearson, who was to sally out with a portion of the garrison. This relief column under Lieutenant-Colonel Law, R.A., was to have been composed of detachments of the Buffs, 88th, and 99th, with seamen and marines from the "Tenedos," and Barrow's mounted men, and, as mentioned in the account of the blockade of Etshowe, was to have started on the 12th March.

This scheme was, however, abandoned, and the relief of Etshowe was postponed till the arrival of further reinforcements should allow of its being carried out by a column of a strength sufficient to bear down all probable opposition.

During the months of February and March heavy floods came down the Buffalo and Tugela, and this fact to a great extent accounts for the inaction of the Zulus in the period following their success at Isandhlwana. The scene of this disaster to the British arms remained unvisited by any Europeans till the
14th March. 14th March, when about 25 mounted men,* under Lieutenant-Colonel Black, 2 | 24th Regiment, proceeded from Rorke's Drift by the track followed on the 20th January, and reached Isandhlwana unopposed. On passing over the neck of land which has been previously mentioned, the wrecked camp was before them. A few natives were seen running away from a kraal

---

* 3 officers, 1 sergeant 2 | 24th Regiment, 13 officers Natal Native Contingent, and 10 troopers Natal Mounted Police.

near at hand, but the ground on which the struggle had taken place was deserted. The Zulus had removed the bodies of many of their comrades, but here the remains of the British soldiers lay unburied and decaying. The tents had been taken away or destroyed, and the site of the camp was strewn with books, papers, and other articles of no value in the eyes of the Zulus, but neither arms nor ammunition remained. Of the missing colours not a trace could be found, and the two 7-pr. guns had likewise disappeared.

Having ascertained that the whole of the transport appliances, baggage and effects of what had been the centre column was now represented by a certain number of uninjured wagons, the little party returned to Rorke's Drift unmolested.

The arrival at Durban of six companies of the 3 | 60th Rifles on the 20th March, completed the reinforcements which Lord **20th March,** Chelmsford considered necessary for undertaking the relief of **1879.** Etshowe.

These troops were at once sent forward to join the column on the Lower Tugela; of which Lord Chelmsford took personal command on the 23rd March. **23rd March.**

The force assembled near Fort Pearson consisted of the 57th and 91st Regiments, six companies of the 3 | 60th, five companies of the 99th, and two companies of the Buffs, with a naval brigade formed of men from the "Shah," "Tenedos,' and "Boadicea." In addition to these, there were the mounted infantry and Volunteers with the 4th and 5th Battalions of the Native Contingent, so that the strength of the column amounted to 3,390 whites, and 2,280 natives, with two 9-pr. guns, four 24-pr. rocket-tubes, and two Gatlings.

Two brigades were formed, of which one was commanded by Lieutenant-Colonel Law, R.A., and the other by Lieutenant-Colonel Pemberton, 60th Rifles.

On the 28th March this force, together with 122 carts and **28th March.** wagons containing provisions, was assembled on the left bank of the Tugela, and the advance commenced at 6 A.M. on the 29th March. **29th March.**

The route adopted was not the same as that by which Colonel Pearson had marched in January, but was nearer the coast, and passed through a more open country. Heavy rain **Fort Tenedos** had fallen on the 27th and 28th, and progress was slow, but by **to Inyoni, 10.** midday the Inyoni river had been reached. Here an entrenched camp was formed, the wagons being drawn up in a square with a shelter trench at about 20 yards distance outside. No tents had been taken, and the troops bivouacked in the space between the wagons and the shelter trench. The oxen which had been sent out to feed as soon as the column had halted, were collected at dusk and driven within the wagon enclosure for the night.

On the following morning the column again moved forward, **30th March,** and in the afternoon formed a similar entrenched camp on the **Inyoni to** right bank of the Amatikulu. This river was crossed on the **Amatikulu, 9.**

31st March, and a fresh camp established about a mile and a half beyond it.

1st April, 1879. About noon on the 1st April the column having marched some 6 miles, occupied a slight eminence about a mile from the Inyezane river, where an entrenched camp, like those on the Inyoni and Amatikulu, was formed.* The Gingihlovo stream ran close to the site of this camp which was surrounded by country generally free from bush, though clothed with long grass, affording a considerable amount of cover.

On the 1st April, some large parties of Zulus were seen in the distance, and during the following night the numerous fires on the hills to the northward made it evident that a considerable force of the enemy was in the neighbourhood.

2nd April. The night, however, passed without any alarm, and at dawn on the 2nd April the mounted men were sent out to reconnoitre, while the infantry stood to their arms within the entrenchments. It was not intended that the column should advance this day, and the cattle were about to be turned out to graze, when, shortly before 6 A.M., information was sent in by the mounted men and by the advanced piquets, that the Zulu army was approaching, and exactly at 6 o'clock the enemy came in sight of the camp.

Two columns appeared on the farther bank of the Inyezane, and, after passing this stream at different points, rapidly deployed outwards and assumed a loose formation which allowed all advantage to be taken of the cover which the ground afforded.

The right of these two columns advancing from near the ruined mission station soon became engaged with the front or north face of the laager, while the left, whose point of crossing had been lower down the stream, was hastening forward to attack the north-eastern angle.

These two columns formed the left wing of the Zulu army, and the right wing was but little behindhand in coming into action. This wing advanced in column from the westward, and on emerging from the bush to the north of the Umisi hill deployed and embraced the southern and western faces of the laager in its attack. In the assault on the latter the co-operation of the right column of the left wing was received, as this, checked in its first attempt, had circled round to its right, and was now endeavouring to make an impression on the western face.

Thus, within a short time after the commencement of the action, the defenders of the camp were on three sides hotly engaged with an enemy, who, pushing on in spite of the deadly fire of breech-loaders and Gatlings, at some points got to within 20 yards of the shelter trench. Closer than this it was impossible to approach, and when the Zulus had realised that this struggle was one in which the assegai would be useless, they

* Wagon enclosure a square of about 130 yards side.

ROUGH SKETCH OF THE ZULU ATTACK ON THE GINGIHLOVO LAAGER

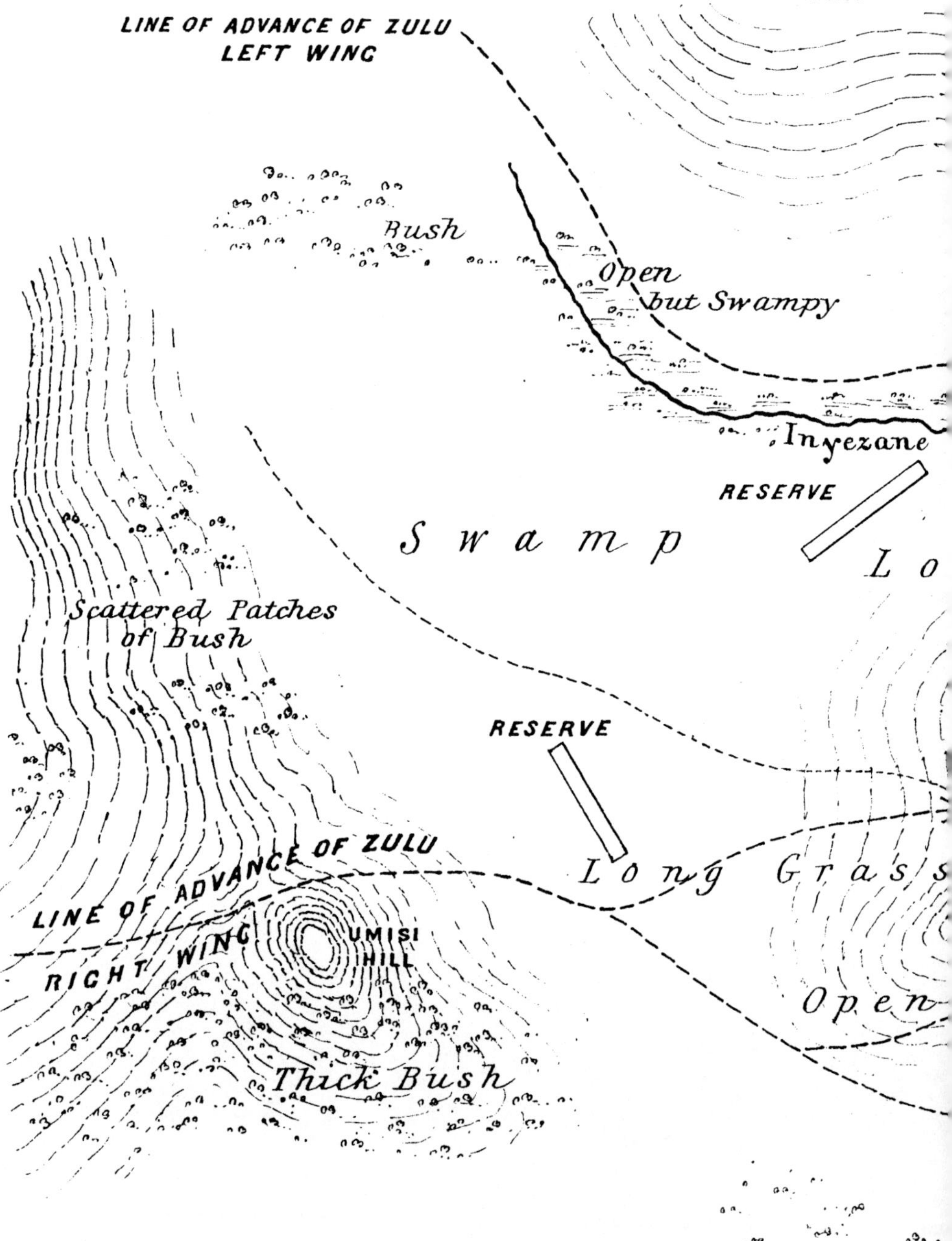

W.C.F. Molyneux Capt. ADC.

on the 2nd April 1879.

To face page 64.

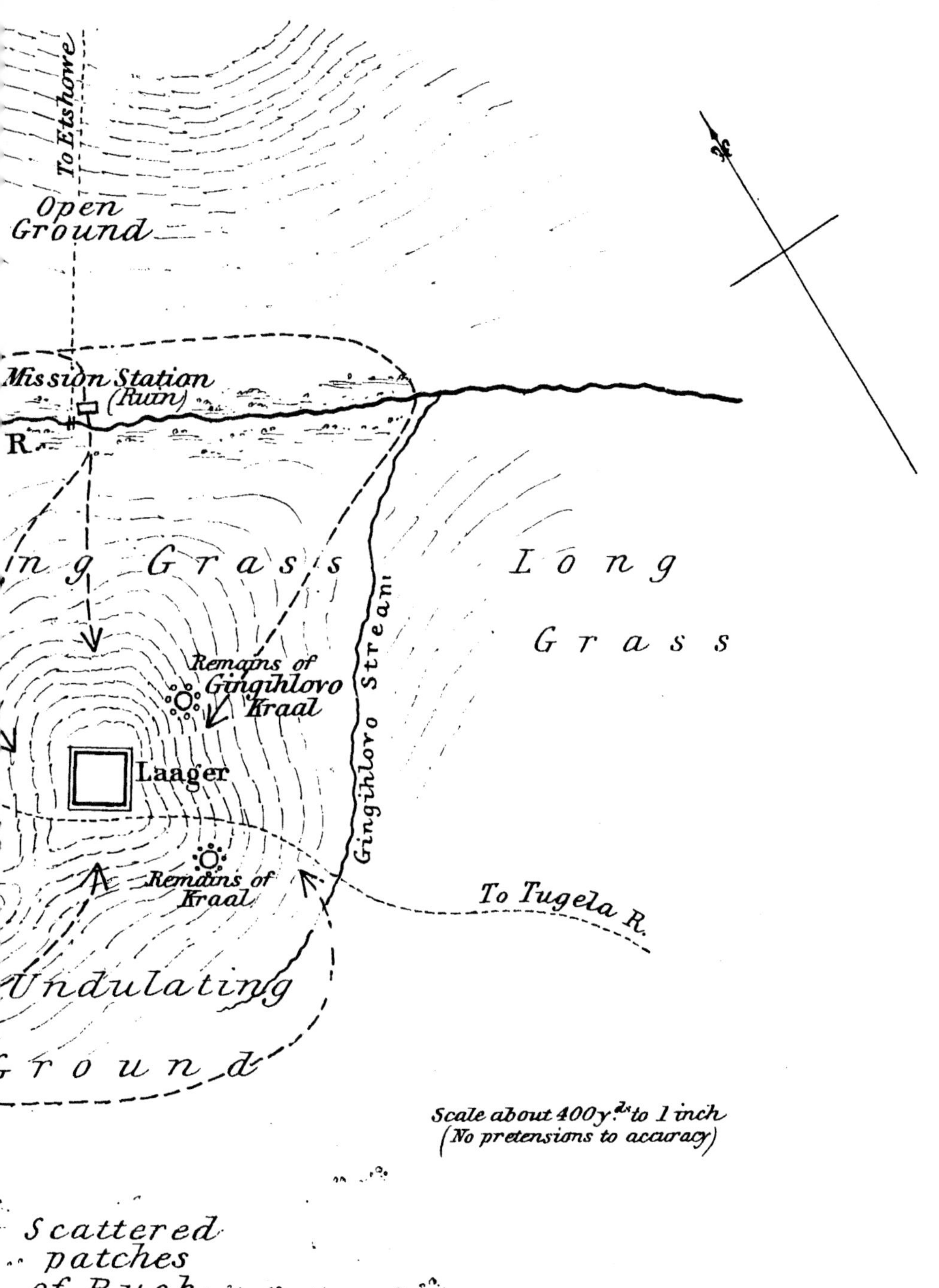

Scale about 400 yds. to 1 inch
(No pretensions to accuracy)

Lith.d at the Intelligence Dep.t War Office March 1881.

recoiled from the hopeless attack. On the first signs of wavering in their ranks, the mounted men under Major Barrow were directed to move outside, and assailed the right flank of the enemy. A few shots were fired at the advancing horsemen, and then the Zulus turned and fled.

In the pursuit which now took place, the fugitives suffered severely from the mounted infantry, who, following for about 2 miles, used with good effect the sabres with which they had been armed a short time previously. The Native Contingent were also sent out after the flying Zulus, and killed considerable numbers.

2nd April, 1879.

In this action, which lasted about an hour and a half, and which resulted in such a complete victory for the British, their loss was 9 killed and 52 wounded.

The Zulu army was about 10,000 strong, and had only arrived in the neighbourhood of Gingihlovo on the previous evening. It was commanded by Dabulamanzi, who was ignorant of the real strength of the relief column. The Zulu losses in this engagement amounted to nearly 1,200.

Congratulations from Etshowe having been received and acknowledged by signal, the troops of the relieving column passed the remainder of the 2nd April at Gingihlovo, engaged in reducing the size of the laager and in strengthening its defences, as Lord Chelmsford had determined that a part of his force should remain here, while he advanced to Etshowe with merely a flying column. Lord Chelmsford also decided that Etshowe, on account of its inaccessibility, should be abandoned, and orders were flashed to Colonel Pearson to prepare for its evacuation as soon as he was relieved.

3rd April.

At 8 A.M. on the 3rd April, Lord Chelmsford's flying column, consisting of the 57th, 60th, and 91st, with part of the Naval Brigade, left Gingihlovo for Etshowe. These troops escorted a convoy of 58 carts of stores for the garrison, and on the march were preceded by the mounted infantry and Volunteers, under Barrow, and by a number of native scouts organised by Mr. John Dunn.*

By road the distance to Etshowe was about 15 miles, and the route led up the right bank of the Inyezane as far as the crossing-place near which Colonel Pearson's action of the 22nd January had been fought. From hence the ranges near Majia's hill were ascended by the track followed after that action, and by this track, though it was in two places partially destroyed, Lord Chelmsford's column eventually arrived at the commencement of the new road to Etshowe, which had been formed by the garrison.

During this march the country was found quite free from any hostile force, but the progress of the column was much delayed

* Mr. John Dunn had been a resident in Zululand for many years previous to the outbreak of the war. His knowledge of the country was accurate, and proved of great value during the campaign. At its close he was appointed chief of one of the districts into which the country was divided.

by the difficulties of the road. But little saving of time was effected by the use of the short cut, as the ground was in bad condition from the heavy rain which had fallen, and it was 6 P.M. before the mounted men reached the fort, and nearly midnight before the main body arrived, and thus accomplished the relief of Etshowe.

VIII. Operations of the Left Column—24th January to 3rd April.

The left column, which had fallen back to Fort Tinta when the news of the Isandhlwana disaster was received, halted at that post during the 25th January, taking up the loads of 73 wagons there deposited, and on the 26th marched 9 miles towards the 'Ngabaka Hawane mountain. Next day the movement was continued to the White Umvolosi, where the column halted till the 31st January. On this day Colonel Wood marched to Kambula hill, an eminence on the south-eastern side of the 'Ngabaka Hawane, where water was plentiful and wood obtainable, and here a strong entrenched camp was formed. 25th January, 1879. 26th Jan. 27th Jan.

At 4 A.M. on the 1st February, a force of the Frontier Light Horse and Dutch Burghers, about 140 strong, under the command of Lieutenant-Colonel Buller, left Kambula and proceeded to the Makulusini kraal. This kraal was known to be a centre of resistance and a rallying point for the most hostile natives in this region, and its destruction was considered advisable. It lay some 30 miles east of Kambula, in the centre of a basin surrounded by precipitous hills. Leaving a force of 30 men to guard the pass by which these hills were traversed, Lieutenant-Colonel Buller's party descended into the basin, and at 12·30 P.M. galloped up to the kraal from which the Zulus fled in all directions. The kraal which contained about 250 huts, was burnt, some cattle were captured, and the party returned to Kambula the same evening without any casualty. 1st February.

On the 3rd February, Fort Kambula was finished and armed with two guns, and on the 5th Lieutenant-Colonel Buller with a party of the Frontier Light Horse, the Dutch Contingent, and some of Wood's Irregulars proceeded to the Eloya mountains, while another party was sent to seek some Zulu raiders reported as being in the southern part of the Utrecht district. Neither of these parties met with any force of the enemy, and both returned to camp on the 7th. 3rd Feb. 5th Feb. 7th Feb.

On the 10th February, Lieutenant-Colonel Buller headed an expedition to the Inhlobana mountain, which resulted in the capture of 500 head of cattle without any serious resistance. 10th Feb.

Fuel for the Kambula camp was obtained from wood growing on the top of the 'Ngabaka Hawane, and as the transport of this fuel was an important consideration, it was now determined to build a new fort nearer the mountain. A site was accordingly selected some 2 miles higher up the same spur on which the original Fort Kambula was situated, and the work was commenced on the 11th February. 11th Feb.

On the 13th February, the new fort was occupied, and on the same day Lieutenant-Colonel Buller started for Luneberg with 70 of the Frontier Light Horse and the Burghers, in order 13th Feb.

13th Feb., 1879. to restrain a chief named Manyanyoba who was reported as killing and plundering in the Intombi valley. Manyanyoba had, however, been joined by Umbelini, the turbulent chief who, in September, 1878, had ordered the Germans to quit their farms near Luneberg, and on the night of the 10th February, their combined forces had committed many barbarous murders in the Intombi valley.

To avenge this raid, a small party under Lieutenant Schwartzkopf had on the 11th made a successful attack on some of the enemy, and on Lieutenant-Colonel Buller's arrival at Luneberg, he determined to punish them further. Accordingly, at day-
15th Feb. light on the 15th February, he advanced against Manyanyoba's stronghold, which consisted of a series of caves on the Intombi river.* Mr. Piet Uys with a portion of the force moved along the high ground over these hiding places, while Lieutenant-Colonel Buller attacked them from below. The Zulus made little resistance; 34 of their number were killed, and a quantity of cattle captured. The attacking force, which had two natives killed, one missing, and three wounded, returned to Luneberg the same night, and on the following day Lieutenant-Colonel Buller marched back to Kambula.

On the 15th a force† under Colonel Rowlands, V.C., was also engaged. This officer, while marching on the road from Luneberg to Derby, found the Tolaka mountain occupied by the enemy, who held the caverns and rocks on its southern side. An attack made on this position was partially successful, a loss of 7 killed being inflicted on the defenders, and 197 head of cattle captured.

20th Feb. On the 20th February some of Colonel Rowlands' troops had an action with the Zulus at the Eloya mountain, and on the 25th February another attack was made on Manyanyoba, but neither of these affairs had decisive results, and the road between Derby and Luneberg remained unsafe except for strong parties.

About this time the attitude of the Boers of the Transvaal
6th Feb. had become extremely unsatisfactory, and on the 26th February, in accordance with orders from Head-quarters, Colonel Rowlands and his staff started for Pretoria, and the troops in the Derby and Luneberg district were attached to Colonel Wood's command.

17th Feb. On the 17th February two messengers had arrived at the Kambula camp reporting that Uhamu,‡ a half brother of Ketchwayo, who had been kept a prisoner at the king's kraal, had escaped, and was anxious to give himself up to the English.
24th Feb. On the 24th February a white man named Calverley visited Kambula, under a flag of truce, with another message from Uhamu, and in consequence of these negotiations, the 21st and

---

* The force employed consisted of 13 Frontier Light Horse, 33 Dutch Burghers, 417 Wood's Irregulars, 8 Kaffrarian Rifles, and 100 Luneberg natives.

† 103 Transvaal Rangers, 15 Boers, 240 Fairlie's Swazies, and 75 Vos' natives.

‡ Also known as Oham.

26th February were spent by Lieutenant-Colonel Buller in expeditions with parties of mounted men for the purpose of meeting this chief and of escorting him to Kambula. These expeditions, which were made in the direction of the Inhlobana mountain, were however unsuccessful, as no sign of Uhamu or of any of his tribe was seen on either occasion.

It was now reported that, being hindered from attending by a Zulu force, he was in hiding among the Swazies, and the investigations made by Captain Norman Macleod, Political Agent in Swaziland, led to his discovering Uhamu on the evening of the 2nd March in a Swazie kraal. On the 4th March Captain Macleod brought him to Derby, and from this place he was forwarded to Luneberg, accompanied by his family and about 700 followers. On the way to Luneberg, he was met near the Intombi river by a party of the Frontier Light Horse, sent out as escort from Kambula on the 6th. **2nd March, 1879.** **4th March.**

Uhamu and those who accompanied him arrived at Luneberg on the 7th March, and remained there during the 8th and 9th. On the morning of the 10th March, the journey was resumed, and Kambula was reached at 11 o'clock the same night. His followers were now disarmed, and three of the rifles given up were found to be Martini-Henry's, which had belonged to the 24th. Uhamu was afterwards sent to Utrecht. **7th March.** **10th March.**

Luneberg at this time was occupied by five companies of the 80th Regiment, under Major Tucker, Schembrucker's corps of Kaffrarian Rifles*, which had been in garrison there for about three months previously, having gone to Kambula to join Wood's column.

Supplies for the garrison of Luneberg were forwarded from Derby, and about the date of Uhamu's journey a convoy of wagons was on the road between these two places. On the 7th March a company of the 80th Regiment under Captain Moriarty, marched out from Luneberg to meet this convoy and bring it in. **7th March.** **Luneberg to Intombi, 4½.**

The company halted at the Intombi river, on the further side of which seven wagons of the convoy were met, and with these wagons a commencement was made of a V-shaped enclosure resting on the river bank. The last of the convoy did not arrive till the 9th March, when this wagon laager was completed, the flooded state of the river rendering its passage impossible. More rain falling, the river remained swollen, and on the 11th March, when Major Tucker visited Captain Moriarty's company, he found it still encamped on the banks of the Intombi waiting for the flood to subside. **9th March.** **11th March.**

Major Tucker, on inspecting the arrangements for defence, considered the wagons too far apart, and objected to the space left between the last wagon of the laager and the river bank, but did not order any change to be made.

On the night following Major Tucker's visit, the general

*** Raised from descendants of the men of the German Legion settled in British Kaffaria after the Crimean War.**

11th March, 1879. disposition of the force at this camp was as follows:—On the north or left bank of the river there were 71 men of all ranks sleeping in tents, and under wagons, and on the right bank 35 men, in tents, guarding the supply-wagons which had been taken across a few days earlier when the river was still passable. There was a guard on each bank, each guard furnishing two sentries, but there were no piquets. Captain Moriarty was on the left bank, and the whole of the reserve ammunition was on the same side of the river. Lieutenant Harward was with the men on the right bank, who had the usual 70 rounds in their pouches.

12th March. At about 4·30 A.M. on the morning of the 12th, when officers and men on both sides of the river were lying asleep, and undressed, a shot was fired by one of the sentries on the left bank. On this the men on the right bank were roused, dressed themselves, and stood to their arms. On the left bank, however, though it appears that similar orders were issued, this was not done, and all were still lying down, when at about 5·15 A.M. a large Zulu force, which had got unobserved in the mist to within 70 yards of the wagons, rushed in and assegaid a large number of the detachment as they came out of the tents. Captain Moriarty was killed soon after leaving his tent, and his detachment on the left bank, completely surprised, could offer no resistance to this sudden attack.

The party on the right bank, taking advantage of the cover afforded by the wagons and by some large ant hills close to the stream, promptly opened fire on the Zulus, but were unable to prevent about 200 of them from crossing the river. Lieutenant Harward who commanded the party on the right bank, after giving his men directions to fire, ordered a retreat on a farmhouse in rear, and having saddled his horse, galloped away to Luneberg.*

---

* Lieutenant Harward was tried by a General Court-Martial at Fort Napier, Pietermaritzburg, on the 20th February, 1880. The following General Order, was issued by H.R.H. the Field-Marshal Commanding-in-Chief:—

G.O. 70.—Court-Martial.

(*Specially issued*, 13*th May*, 1880).

At a General Court-Martial lately held, an officer was arraigned upon the following charges:—

1st. Having misbehaved before the enemy, in shamefully abandoning a party of the regiment under his command when attacked by the enemy, and in riding off at speed from his men.

2nd. Conduct to the prejudice of good order and military discipline in having, at the place and time mentioned in the first charge, neglected to take proper precautions for the safety of a party of a regiment under his command when attacked.

The Court recorded a finding of "Not Guilty" on both charges.

The main facts of the case were not in dispute. The officer rode away from his men to a station, distant 4½ miles, at a moment of extreme danger, when to all appearance the small party under his command were being surrounded and overwhelmed by the enemy.

The charge alleged "misbehaviour," that is cowardice in so doing: the defence averred that it was to procure reinforcements, and either by their actual arrival, or by the imminence of their arrival, to ward off destruction.

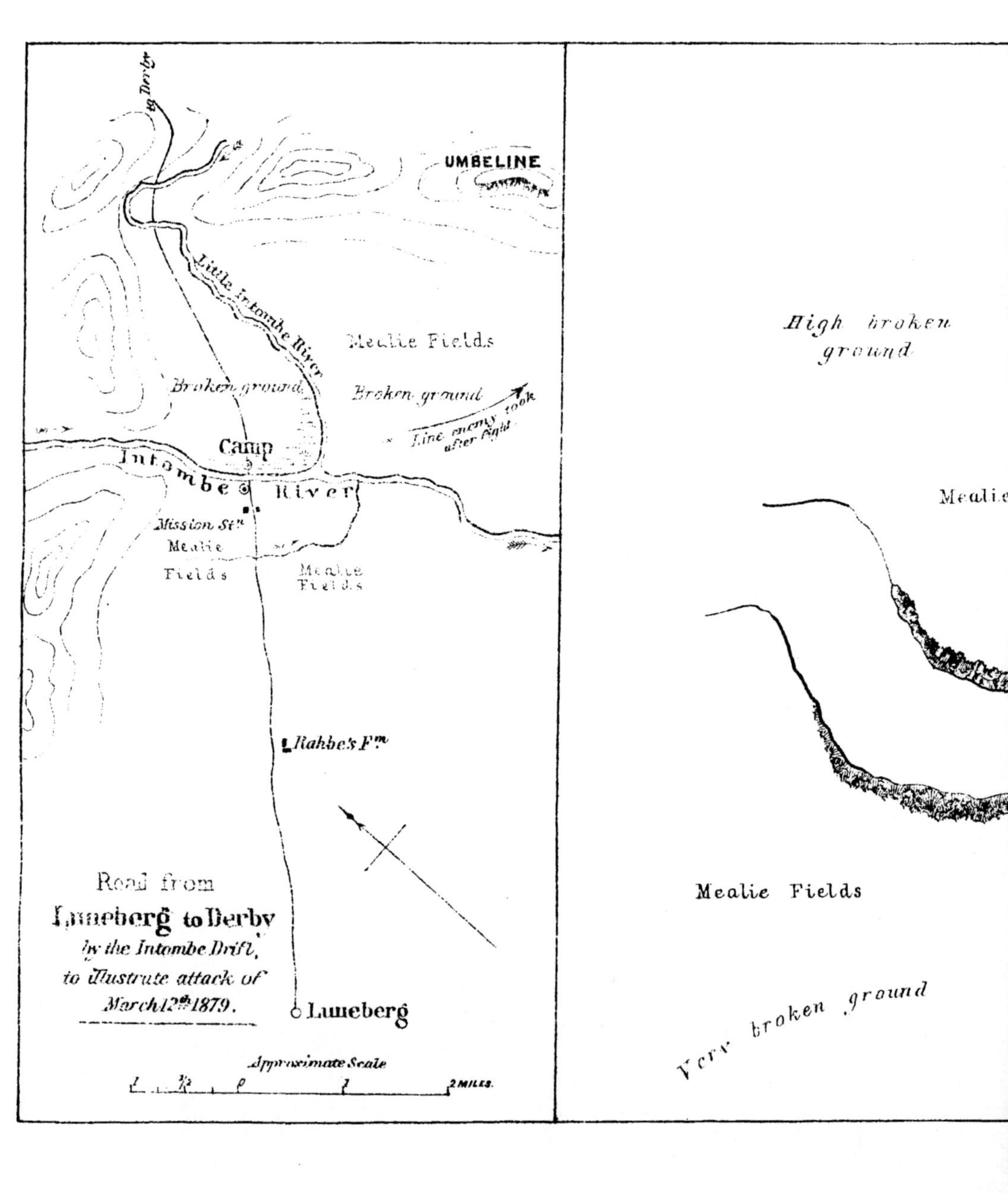

to Derby
UMBELINE
Little Intombe River
Mealie Fields
Broken ground
Broken ground
Line enemy took after fight
Camp
Intombe River
Mission Stn
Mealie Fields
Mealie Fields
Rahbe's Fm
Road from
Luneberg to Derby
by the Intombe Drift,
to illustrate attack of
March 12th 1879.
Luneberg
Approximate Scale
1 ½ 0 1 2 MILES.
High broken ground
Mealie
Mealie Fields
Very broken ground

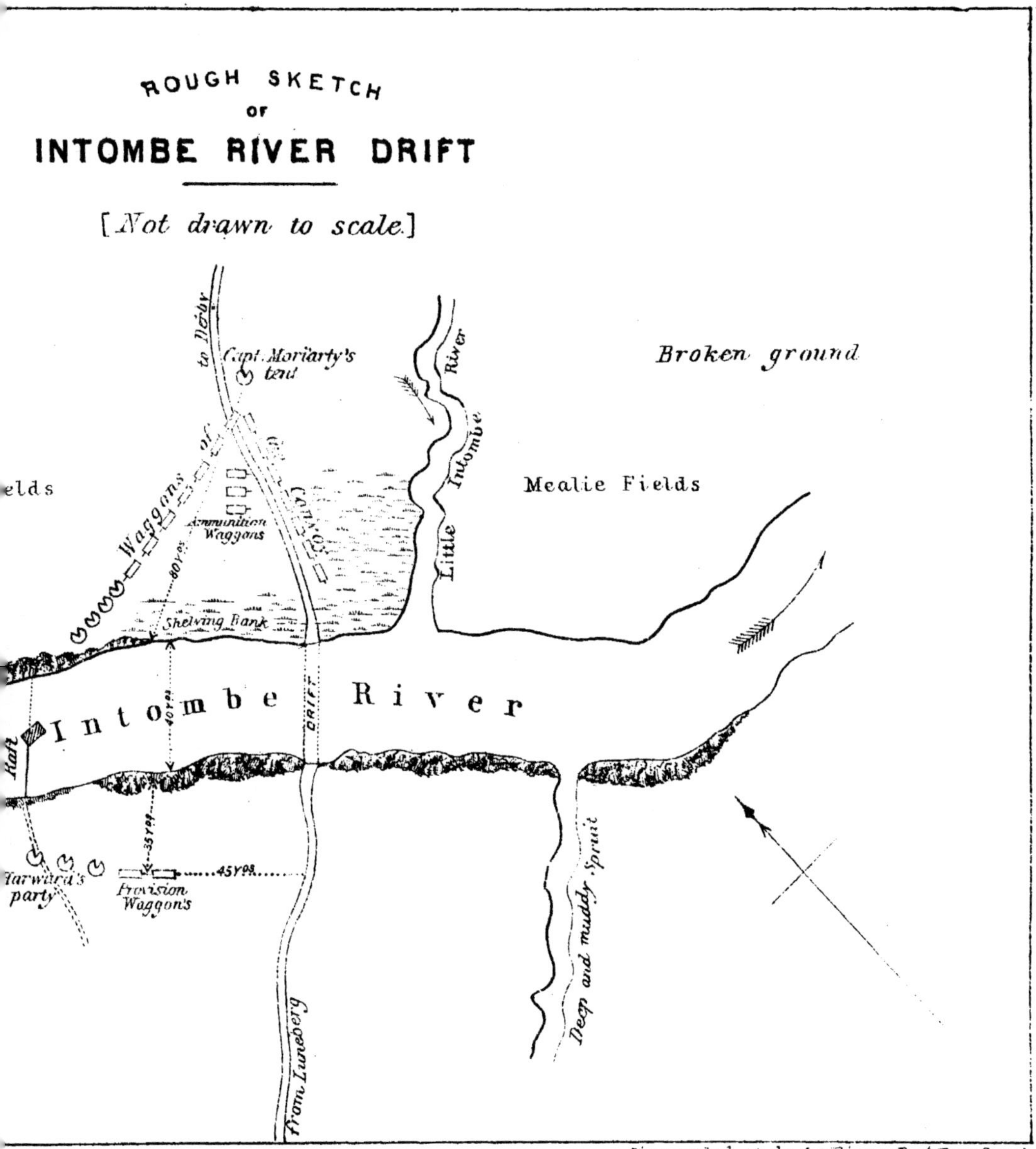

To face page 70.

ROUGH SKETCH OF INTOMBE RIVER DRIFT

[*Not drawn to scale.*]

to Derby
Capt. Moriarty's tent
Little Intombe River
Broken ground
elds
Mealie Fields
Waggons of Convoy
Ammunition Waggons
80 Yds
Shelving Bank
Intombe River
DRIFT
40 Yds
Raft
35 Yds
arward's party
Provision Waggons
45 Yds
Deep and muddy Spruit
From Luneberg

Zincographed at the Intelligence Dept, Horse Guards
March 1881

Sergeant Booth, the senior non-commissioned officer present, now rallied a small group of men and endeavoured to cover the retreat of those who were trying to escape from the farther bank; but to avoid being surrounded, this little band was soon obliged to fall back. The Zulus followed them for about 3 miles, but Sergeant Booth and his men, showing a bold front, and firing occasional volleys at their pursuers, held them in check and retired without loss. Their determination also secured the escape of several fugitives from the left bank, who, all without arms, and some without clothes, were now in full flight for Luneberg. 12th March, 1879.

As soon as the news of the disaster was reported by Lieutenant Harward to Major Tucker, the latter advanced to the Intombi river with the greater part of the Luneberg garrison. On their arrival at the site of the camp, however, they found that the Zulus had withdrawn, taking with them the whole of the oxen, small arm ammunition, rifles, blankets, and all other articles of value, except some rockets and artillery ammuniinot.

The Zulu force which was seen in the distance hastily retiring, was computed by Major Tucker at not less than 4,000 strong,* and, as ascertained from prisoners, was commanded by Umbelini.

Of the 71† men of the 80th who were on the left bank of the

In acquitting the prisoner, they have found that he was not guilty of cowardice.

The proceedings of the Court were submitted to the General Commanding, who recorded the following minute "Disapproved and not confirmed: Lieutenant . . . . . to be released from arrest, and to return to his duty."

The confirming officer has further recorded his reasons for withholding his approval and confirmation in the following terms:—

"Had I released this officer without making any remarks upon the verdict in question, it would have been a tacit acknowledgment that I concurred in what appears to me a monstrous theory, viz., that a regimental officer who is the only officer present with a party of soldiers actually and seriously engaged with the enemy, can, under any pretext whatever, be justified in deserting them, and by so doing, abandoning them to their fate. The more helpless the position in which an officer finds his men, the more it is his bounden duty to stay and share their fortune, whether for good or ill. It is because the British officer has always done so that he occupies the position in which he is held in the estimation of the world, and that he possesses the influence he does in the ranks of our army. The soldier has learned to feel that, come what may, he can in the direst moment of danger look with implicit faith to his officer, knowing that he will never desert him under any possible circumstances.

"It is to this faith of the British soldier in his officers that we owe most of the gallant deeds recorded in our military annals; and it is because the verdict of this Court-Martial strikes at the root of this faith, that I feel it necessary to mark officially my emphatic dissent from the theory upon which the verdict has been founded."

In communicating to the army the result of this Court-Martial, the Field-Marshal Commanding-in-Chief desires to signify his entire approval of the views expressed by the confirming officer in respect of the principles of duty which have always actuated British officers in the field, and by which, His Royal Highness feels assured, they will continue to be guided.

This General Order will, by His Royal Highness's command, be read at the head of every regiment in Her Majesty's service.

* Another estimate puts its strength at 800. This latter is supported by statements of Colonel Wood's spies.

† Including a civil surgeon attached.

river, only 12 escaped, and 3 of those on the right bank likewise fell, making the total number of casualties 62 out of 106. Two conductors and 15 drivers and leaders belonging to the Transport Department also perished.

At the end of February Colonel Wood's force at Kambula had been strengthened by the arrival of Raaf's corps,* followed on the 2nd March by Schermbrucker's† and Weatherley's,‡ and on the 14th March Lieutenant-Colonel Russell with the 1st squadron of mounted infantry marched in. This squadron had originally belonged to the centre column, and had remained at Helpmakaar from the 24th January till the 15th February, when it left for Dundee along with the Natal Carabineers.

14th March, 1879.

After a halt here of about 10 days, the mounted infantry had moved on, and on the 27th February had arrived at Balte Spruit, where they remained till the 13th March, when they set out for Kambula.

On arriving at Kambula on the 14th March, Lieutenant-Colonel Russell received an order directing him to follow in support of an expedition under Lieutenant-Colonel Buller, which Colonel Wood had himself accompanied. The object of this expedition, which had started at daybreak on the 14th, was to bring in a number of Uhamu's tribe who were hiding in caves near the Umkusi river, waiting for an opportunity to join their chief.

Buller's party of mounted men reached these caves, which where some 45 miles east of Kambula, about 10 P.M., and the remainder of the night was spent in collecting the tribe. At 9 A.M. the following morning, all were assembled, and the return journey was commenced. This was unopposed, except by some long shots fired from the Inhlobana mountain, near which place the returning party was met by Lieutenant-Colonel Russell and the mounted infantry, who, in accordance with Colonel Wood's orders, had left Kambula at 1 A.M. that morning.

15th March.

The whole party halted at the Zungi mountain on the evening of the 15th, and reached Kambula at 1 P.M. on the 16th. The number of Uhamu's people thus escorted to a place of safety was 958.

16th March.

Colonel Wood on this occasion had an opportunity of inspecting the southern side of the Inhlobana mountain, which appeared to be occupied by about 800 or 1,000 men.

This mountain, like many other eminences in Zululand, is table topped, and from its precipitous sides irregular masses of rock have fallen, which lie piled in confusion about the base of the cliffs. The holes which exist among these masses of rock are the so-called "caves," used by the Zulus as hiding places. On the southern side of the mountain there is an almost inaccessible ledge or terrace on which the native kraals were built, but the

* 100 whites and 50 coloured men.
† 106 of all ranks.
‡ 61 of all ranks.

top of the Inhlobana, which can only be reached by a few difficult paths, was uninhabited, and was used as a place of safety for the cattle belonging to the people who dwelt below.

In the latter part of March Colonel Wood received a despatch from Lord Chelmsford informing him of the steps he was about to take for the relief of Etshowe, and giving instructions that a diversion was to be made on the 28th March.

Colonel Wood therefore determined to send out a reconnaissance to the Inhlobana mountain, and his orders, published on the 26th March, directed that the summit was, if possible, to be gained on the 28th. **26th March, 1879.**

The force to be employed was to be furnished by the mounted men and native troops, and was divided into two portions to operate against the two ends of the mountain.* That sent against the eastern end was intended to form the main attacking force, while the other portion was to create a diversion and act in support, but was not to assault the position in the face of serious resistance.

The eastern reconnaissance was to be under Lieutenant-Colonel Buller, the western under Lieutenant-Colonel Russell, and both these officers were specially enjoined to send out scouts to watch for a large Zulu army reported to be advancing on Kambula.

On the 27th March, in accordance with these orders, Lieutenant-Colonel Buller left Kambula with a force of 400 mounted men and 300 natives, and marching about 30 miles, bivouacked some 5 miles to the south-east of the mountain. **27th March.**

About noon on the same day Lieutenant-Colonel Russell with 250 mounted men, a rocket detachment, a battalion of Wood's Irregulars and about 150 of Uhamu's people, also left Kambula, and marching about 15 miles bivouacked some 4 miles from the western extremity of the Inhlobana, on the ground occupied on the night of the 15th by the force returning with Uhamu's tribe.

Colonel Wood with his Staff,† an escort of eight mounted infantry and seven‡ natives, arrived at Lieutenant-Colonel Russell's bivouack at dusk on the 27th, and proceeding eastwards at 3.30 A.M. on the 28th, soon came on Commandant Weatherley with his force of the Border Horse, 54 strong. This party ought to have been with Lieutenant-Colonel Buller's force, but had become separated on the march out. **28th March.**

Buller, who had left his bivouack at 3.30 A.M., was at this time at the north-eastern end of the Inhlobana, and under cover of the morning mist succeeded in reaching the summit. The steep path was hardly passable for mounted men, and as it led up a re-entering angle in the centre of a concavity in the moun- **4.0 A.M.**

---

* The top of the Inhlobana is about 3 miles long.

† Captain the Honorable Ronald Campbell, Chief Staff Officer; Mr. Lloyd, Political Assistant; Lieutenant Lysons, Orderly Officer.

‡ One of these was Umtonga, Ketchwayo's youngest brother.

28th March, 1879.

tain side, it could not have been traversed in the face of any serious resistance. As it was, the few Zulus who were on the top, though surprised, were able to inflict on the Frontier Light Horse a loss of two officers killed and one man mortally wounded, in addition to numerous casualties among their horses.

Colonel Wood, who was moving forward, preceded by the Border Horse, on hearing this firing ordered Colonel Weatherley to push on after Buller's force up the eastern end of the mountain, and proceeded himself in the same direction. Buller was already on the summit, but the track he had taken was marked by the bodies of the dead and wounded horses which had fallen during his ascent. Most of the party with Colonel Wood now dismounted, and leaving their horses below a ledge of rock, advanced on foot. Colonel Wood himself was leading his horse up the steep slope, and, with his Staff and a small escort, was slightly ahead of Weatherley's men, when, at a short distance from the top, a severe and well-directed fire was opened on the party from some holes in the rocks above. By this fire Mr. Lloyd was mortally wounded, and Colonel Wood's horse was killed, and as these and other casualties appeared to be caused by shots from one cavern in particular, Colonel Wood ordered Colonel Weatherley to send some of his men to the front to dislodge the Zulus from this hiding place. As there was some little delay in obeying this order, Captain Ronald Campbell dashed forward, followed by Lieutenant Lysons and three men of the 90th, but just as they reached the dark entrance of the cavern Captain Campbell fell dead, shot through the head by a Zulu lying hidden within. His death was speedily avenged by his companions, and the cavern was cleared.

Colonel Weatherley and his men now moved on with the object of joining Buller's force on the summit, while Colonel Wood and his escort descended to a ledge to which Mr. Lloyd had been carried. He was now dead, so his body, along with that of Captain Campbell, was taken to a spot lower down the hill side, and there both were buried.

Buller's proceedings.

Lieutenant-Colonel Buller, on gaining the high plateau which forms the summit of the Inhlobana mountain, found it to have the large area of about 3 miles in length by a mile and a half in breadth.* Some 2,000 head of cattle which had been placed here for safety were now collected, and the Zulus who had been guarding them dispersed. While this was being done, Lieutenant-Colonel Buller, accompanied by Mr. Piet Uys, examined the plateau and the tracks by which a descent from it might be made. Of these tracks there appeared to be only three, viz., that at the north-eastern end, by which the ascent had been made, and two at the western end, both of which

* This would make it between two and three thousand acres.

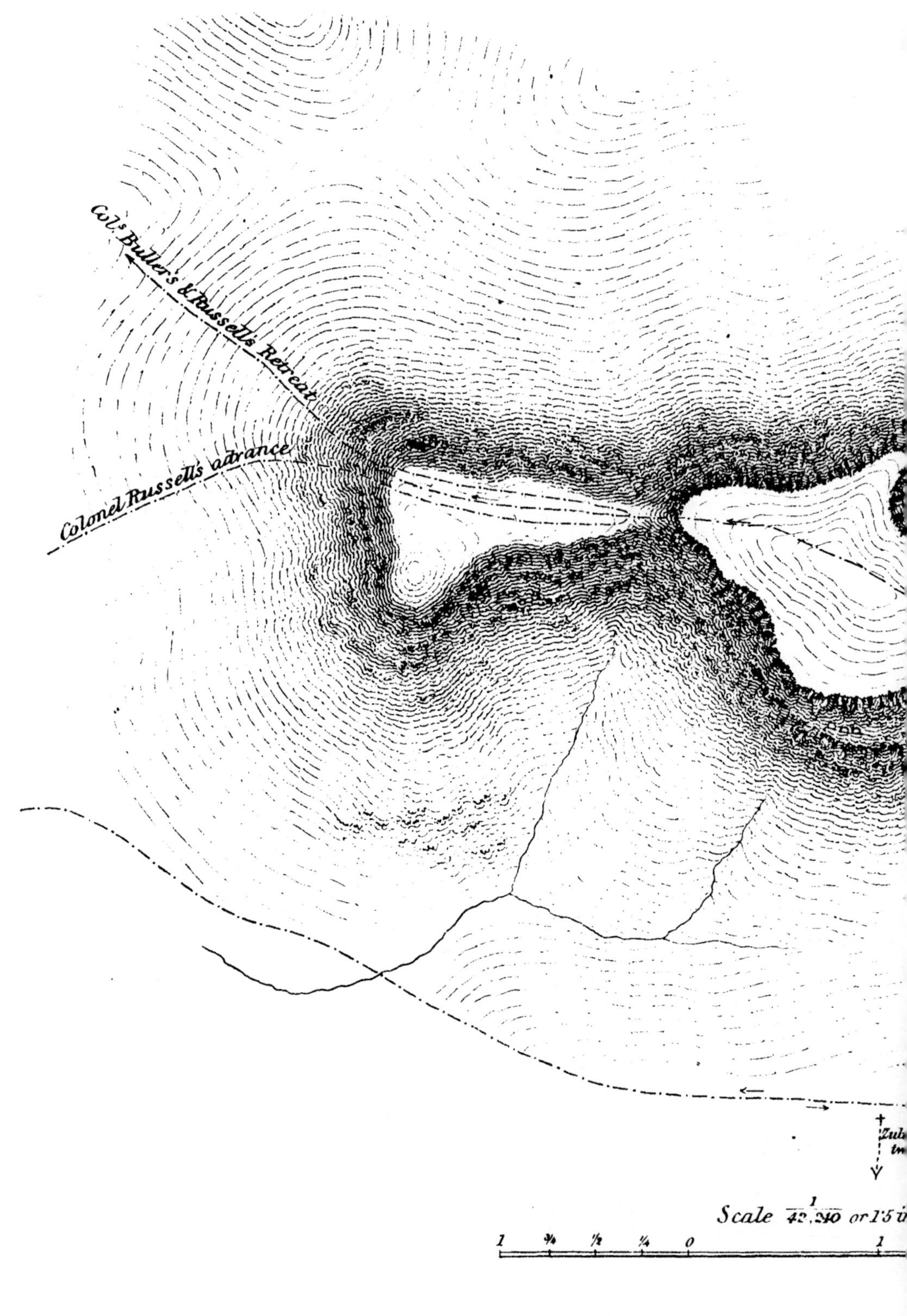

Col^s Buller's & Russell's Retreat
Colonel Russell's advance
Scale 1/42,240 or 1·5 i
1 ¾ ½ ¼ 0 1

To face page 74.

INHLOBANA MOUNTAIN

attacked 28th March 1879.

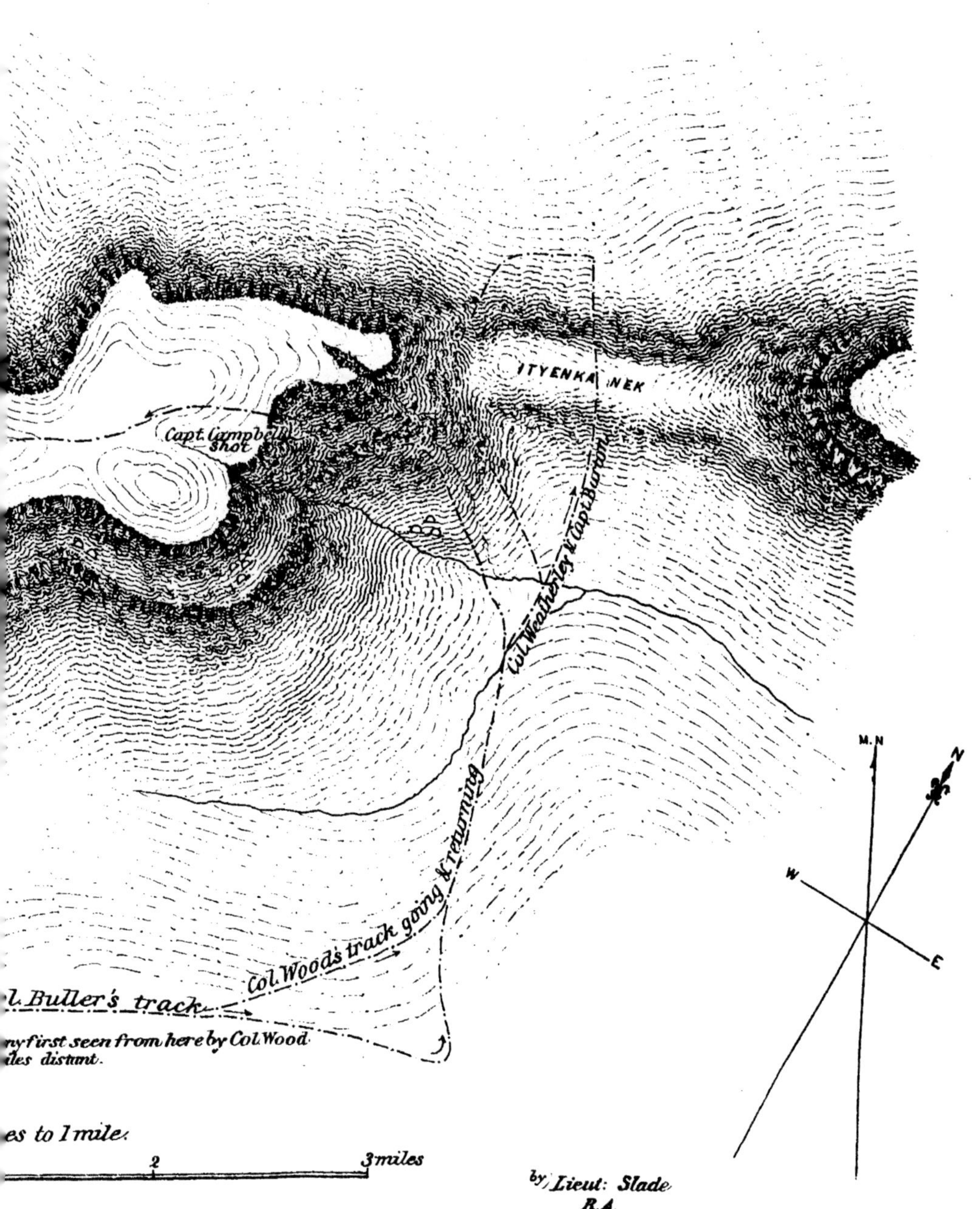

by Lieut: Slade R.A.

Lith^d at the Intelligence Branch Q^r Mr Gen^ls Department. March 1881

presented greater natural difficulties than the one already traversed. The path at the north-western point of the mountain, however, descended nearly at the apex of a salient angle with long faces, and being thus secure from flanking fire, Lieutenant-Colonel Buller determined to use it for the retreat of a portion of his force. 28th March, 1879.

By this time it was nearly 9 o'clock, and Lieutenant-Colonel Buller returning to the east end of the mountain, sent off Captain Barton, his second in command, with a party of 30 men to bury the bodies of the two officers killed during the ascent. All was now quiet on the summit, and Captain Barton was instructed to find Colonel Weatherley, and to return along with him to Kambula by the route south of the Inhlobana mountain which had been followed the day before.

Very soon after Captain Barton's departure, Lieutenant-Colonel Buller saw a Zulu army, estimated at 20,000 strong, approaching the mountain from the south-east. The army was at this time about 6 miles off, and it was calculated that the force on the mountain would thus have about an hour's start. The retreat, however, of that portion of the force ordered back to Kambula by the south of the Inhloblana was seriously threatened by the Zulu advance, and two troopers were therefore sent after Captain Barton, telling him to return "by the right of the mountain," an expression which was intended to convey the idea that his homeward route was to be by the north side, instead of the south as previously arranged. 9.0 A.M.

The captured cattle had by this time been collected by Raaf's Corps and Wood's Irregulars near the western extremity of the plateau which forms the summit of the Inhlobana, and to this point Buller and the force with him now proceeded.

It was considered that a descent by the rugged path at the north-western angle of the mountain previously reconnoitred, would allow the scattered troops on the summit to be united and withdrawn in comparative safety, while they would thus gain the support of Lieutenant-Colonel Russell's force, which, as already mentioned, had been directed on this end of the mountain.

To the west of the Inhlobana, and forming a continuation of the same range, is another and smaller plateau about 150 feet below the main plateau occupied by Buller, and on this lower plateau, to which the above-mentioned path descended, Russell's force had by about 7 A.M. taken up a position. Viewed from below, this path up the cliffs had appeared so precipitous that Lieutenant-Colonel Russell had considered it totally impracticable for horsemen, and had consequently made no attempt to take his party by it to the upper plateau. The mounted infantry, Schermbrucker's Corps, and the Basutos had therefore been drawn up in support of the natives, who were engaged in capturing some cattle on the slopes of the Inhlobana. 7.0 A.M. Russell's proceedings.

As it was impossible from below to see what was occurring on the summit of the mountain, Lieutenant-Colonel Russell sent

28th March, 1879. Captain Browne with 20 men of the mounted infantry to make their way on foot to the upper plateau, and communicate with Buller's party. Captain Browne arrived at the top without opposition, and after speaking to Major Tremlett, R.A., and Major Leet, 1 | 13th Regiment, returned with a report that all was quiet on the upper plateau, and that the path was almost impracticable even for men on foot.

Colonel Wood, after burying the bodies of Captain Campbell and Mr. Lloyd, returned to the bottom of the mountain, and was proceeding slowly towards its western end to ascertain how Russell's party had progressed, when at about 10.30 A.M. he became aware of the approach of the Zulu army on his left. On this Lieutenant Lysons was despatched with the following

10.30 A.M. order:—"10.30 A.M., 28th March, 1879. Colonel Russell, there is a large army coming this way from the south. Get into position on the Zunguin neck. (Signed) E. W." Colonel Wood with his escort then moved on rapidly to this place, the name of which is more correctly written "Zungen nek."

9.0 A.M. At about 9 A.M., however, Lieutenant-Colonel Russell had himself seen the Zulu army in the distance, and had immediately sent a report, addressed to Colonel Wood, to the upper plateau, where he believed him to be at that time.*

10.0 A.M. At about 10 A.M., in consequence of the rapidity with which the Zulus were approaching, Lieutenant-Colonel Russell had issued orders for his men to abandon the cattle which they had collected, and to secure their own retreat to the open country below. The descent from the lower plateau was safely accomplished, and Lieutenant-Colonel Russell, sending his native troops back towards Kambula, proceeded to draw up his mounted men on some rising ground near the foot of the Inhlobana, to cover the retreat of Buller's force, whom he expected to find falling back towards this point. Before the formation was completed, the order above quoted was received, and Lieutenant-Colonel Russell consequently prepared to move his force to the Zungen nek.

10.45. There was some doubt, however, as to the spot which bore this name, and Lieutenant-Colonel Russell, after consultation with his officers, came to the conclusion that the point to which the order directed him to proceed, was that at which the track from Kambula crosses the western portion of the Zungi mountain. To this point, therefore, he moved as rapidly as possible.

The point, however, to which Colonel Wood had gone, and where he intended Lieutenant-Colonel Russell to join him, was at the eastern end of the Zungi mountain, about 6 miles from the spot to which the mounted infantry were now hastening.

Buller's proceedings. The appearance of the Zulu army had not been unperceived by the inhabitants of the Inhlobana mountain, who soon came out from their hiding places, and in constantly in-

* This report was received by Lieutenant-Colonel Buller about 9.20.

creasing numbers harassed Buller in his movement towards the western end of the plateau. 28th March, 1879.

When the top of the path leading down the cliff was reached, the serious difficulties of the descent became apparent, while a glance at the lower plateau showed that no support from Russell's party could be counted on, as they had already withdrawn. Buller and his men, however, had no alternative but to continue the retreat to which they were committed, and the descent to the lower plateau was undertaken. The path, as stated above, had been reported to Lieutenant-Colonel Russell as barely practicable for men on foot, and it could only be considered passable by horses by reason of the fact that the rocks of the encircling precipice here presented some appearance of regularity, and formed a series of ledges from 8 to 12 feet wide, on which an insecure foothold could be obtained, the drop from one ledge to the next being about 3 or 4 feet. 10.0 A.M.

The Native portion of Lieutenant-Colonel Buller's force went down first, their retreat being covered by the mounted men. These then began to descend, the Frontier Light Horse, who formed the rear guard, for a while successfully keeping in check the enemy, who were constantly endeavouring to press closer. Much time, however, was occupied in the descent, and before the bulk of the force had reached the lower plateau the rear guard unfortunately ceased firing, thinking that the approaching Zulus were some of their own natives. The enemy, profiting by this mistake, promptly occupied the rocks close to the line of descent, and poured a hot fire at short range into those who were endeavouring to get their horses over the almost impassable natural obstacles in their way. The casualties, which up to this had not been of much importance, now became serious, as the Zulus succeeded in closing with the assegai on the scattered members of the party. One officer and about 16 men were lost, and at this spot fell Mr. Piet Uys, the gallant leader of the Boer Contingent, who had rendered such valuable services to Colonel Wood's column.

The lower plateau was at last reached, but Buller's force was by this time in a very disorganised condition. Many of the men were dismounted, their horses having been lost by falling over the rocks, and if the fears which were entertained of an attack by the main Zulu army had been realised, a very serious loss must have ensued. No attack, however, was made by this army, and Buller, having to some extent rallied his men, withdrew towards the Zungi mountain, unmolested except by the Zulus of the Inhlobana, who followed and fired on his party from long range.

Captain Barton, as mentioned above, had been warned of the approach of the enemy's force, and directed to withdraw "by the right of the mountain." When Captain Barton received this message he was facing the east, and unfortunately came to the erroneous conclusion that he was meant to retreat by the south of the mountain. Having, therefore, been joined by

28th March, 1879. Colonel Weatherley and his party, they proceeded together towards Kambula, till they found themselves within a short distance of the Zulu army, which had by this time approached the Inhlobana so closely as to leave no outlet between its right flank and the mountain. From this critical position they at once sought to extricate themselves by turning about and endeavouring to pass the Ityenteka Nek, in order to gain the safe line of retreat by the north side of the Inhlobana.

It appears that a small portion of the main Zulu army turned aside to pursue them, but the principal opposition was caused by a number of the enemy who descended from the Inhlobana, and barred the pass over the Ityenteka Nek. Through these they endeavoured to cut their way, but hampered by the difficulties of the ground, and greatly outnumbered, their efforts were unsuccessful. Colonel Weatherley, his son, and all the Border Horse except eight were slain, and Captain Barton* with 18 of the Frontier Horse likewise perished. Those who survived reached Kambula late the same evening, being brought in by Lieutenant-Colonel Buller, who, on hearing of what had happened, started again from the camp with a party to render assistance.

10.30 A.M. Colonel Wood, after ordering Lieutenant-Colonel Russell to the Zungen nek, went himself to this place, viz., the low ground at the eastern end of the Zungi mountain. Finding that he was not joined by this officer and his party, Colonel Wood sent a fresh order, directing him to move eastwards from the point to which he had gone, in order to cover the retreat of the natives

About 12.0 noon. belonging to Buller's force, who were suffering heavy loss at this time.

Before this order was delivered to Lieutenant-Colonel Russell, he had already, in consequence of the mistake as to the meaning of the term "Zungen nek," taken up his position at the western end of the Zungi mountain, and before he could come to the assistance of the native troops they had been cut off almost to a man, and the Zulus had withdrawn from the pursuit. Russell's force then returned to Kambula, where it arrived between 4 and 5 P.M., unmolested by the Zulu army.

The casualties this day were heavy. Out of Buller's force of 400 Europeans, 92 were killed and 7 wounded, 12 of the former being officers. A heavy loss also occurred among the native troops, but the number has not been ascertained, as with the exception of about 50 the whole of Wood's Irregulars† deserted the same night.

29th March. On the morning of the 29th March a party of Raaf's Corps who had been sent out at daylight to reconnoitre, returned to Kambula, bringing one of Uhamu's men, whom they had met on the Umvolosi, some 10 miles from the camp.

This man appears to have found himself on the 28th close to the Zulu army, and to have joined some acquaintances in

---

* *See* page 160.

† This corps had been about 800 strong.

its ranks who were ignorant that he had attached himself to the British. From these Zulus he learned that it was intended that the army should attack Kambula on the 29th, "about dinner time," and having afterwards separated himself from his friends, was carrying this intelligence to Colonel Wood, when he fell in with Raaf's party. 29th March, 1879.

This, however, was not the only source of information available, for spies were constantly passing, and Colonel Wood on his return to camp on the evening of the 28th, had received a detailed statement of the enemy's force from a Zulu messenger, who had reached Kambula on the evening of the 27th.

When this report as to the hour selected for the attack was received, two companies of the 1 | 13th were absent from camp, bringing down wood from the 'Ngabaka Hawane mountain in rear. As fuel was urgently required, Colonel Wood. trusting to the accuracy of the information, determined not to recall these companies till this duty had been completed, and it was satisfactorily carried out before the enemy appeared.

The position taken up at Kambula was on the ridge of a spur running eastwards from the 'Ngabaka Hawane mountain. A wagon laager had been formed on this ridge, and the crest of a small knoll which at about 150 yards to the eastward rose above the general level of the spur, was the site of a redoubt capable of holding three companies. On the southern side of the ridge, between the redoubt and the laager, there was a cattle kraal or enclosure, formed of wagons, within which the oxen of the column were now collected.

The ground to the north of the position thus occupied sloped gently down, but to the south some abrupt ledges afforded a considerable amount of cover, and left a large area comparatively close at hand unseen by the defenders.

At about 11 A.M. the Zulus were reported to be in sight of the camp. They were then moving in dense masses from the direction of the Zungi mountain, and, as on the previous day, their advance was made in five columns. 11.0 A.M.

At 12.45 P.M., dinners being over, the tents were struck, the men were posted, and boxes of reserve ammunition were opened and placed in convenient spots. This was done rapidly and without confusion, as similar preparations for defence had been previously practised. 12.45 P.M.

The enemy's columns were meanwhile drawing near, but the point on which they were directed was not at first apparent. It seemed that this Zulu army was about to pass by, and that, neglecting the Kambula camp, it would march on the town of Utrecht, which, though provided with a strong stone fort in which the inhabitants could find safety, offered a somewhat tempting object for a hostile raid.

The local authorities at this place had, since the Isandhlwana disaster, been urgent that Colonel Wood should withdraw his force from Kambula, and garrison their town. With this

29th March, 1879. request Colonel Wood had refused to comply, as he considered that Utrecht was effectually covered by his force at Kambula, and he had accordingly remained in his advanced position in spite of the entreaties of the townspeople. Now, however, it seemed for a time as though their forebodings would be realised, and that Wood's force might be powerless to protect them.

The general line of advance of the Zulu army was at this time towards the west, but when their columns had reached a point nearly due south of the Kambula camp a change of direction was made, and while one portion of the army moved to its right and circled round towards the north side of the camp, the other continued its advance for some distance, and then wheeled up against the western side. The latter portion was still on the march when the right horn of the Zulu army, having a shorter distance to go, had reached the position from which it was to attack, and here it halted in sight of the camp, but out of range of the guns.

1.30 P.M. At 1.30 P.M. Colonel Wood directed some of the mounted men under Buller and Russell to move out against this right horn, and the action commenced by their riding up to within range, dismounting and opening fire. Zulu discipline, though good, was not strong enough to restrain a column some 2,000 strong, when attacked by about a hundred men, and the result was that the whole of the right horn sprang up, and charged the little party of horsemen. These speedily remounted, and fell back on the camp, holding a running fight with the enemy who pressed on eagerly. The mounted men now retired within the laager, and fire was opened by the artillery and infantry from their strong defensive position. As the ground to the north of this position was open with a gentle fall this fire was very effective, and obliged the enemy to halt about 300 yards from the camp, and eventually to fall back on some rocks to the north-east.

From this point they kept up a fire on the camp and its defenders, but made no further attempt to assault the position.

The premature attack of the Zulu right having been thus checked, Colonel Wood was now able to direct his attention mainly to repelling the onset of the centre and left columns.

2.15 P.M. By 2.15 P.M. their attacks were developed, the Zulu left having worked round to the west of the camp, while the centre advanced against the southern face. Taking advantage of the cover which the steepness of the ridge on this side afforded, they assembled in large numbers in this dead ground, and assaulted the cattle kraal so vigorously that a company of the 1 | 13th posted in it was obliged to withdraw, after suffering somewhat heavily.

Encouraged by this success a Zulu column, 1,000 or 1,500 strong, was now formed up on the west of the cattle kraal, where they were sheltered from the fire of the main laager. A serious assault on this was evidently contemplated, but before it was delivered, Colonel Wood ordered a counter attack to be made

SKETCH SHOWING MODE OF ATTACK ON C(

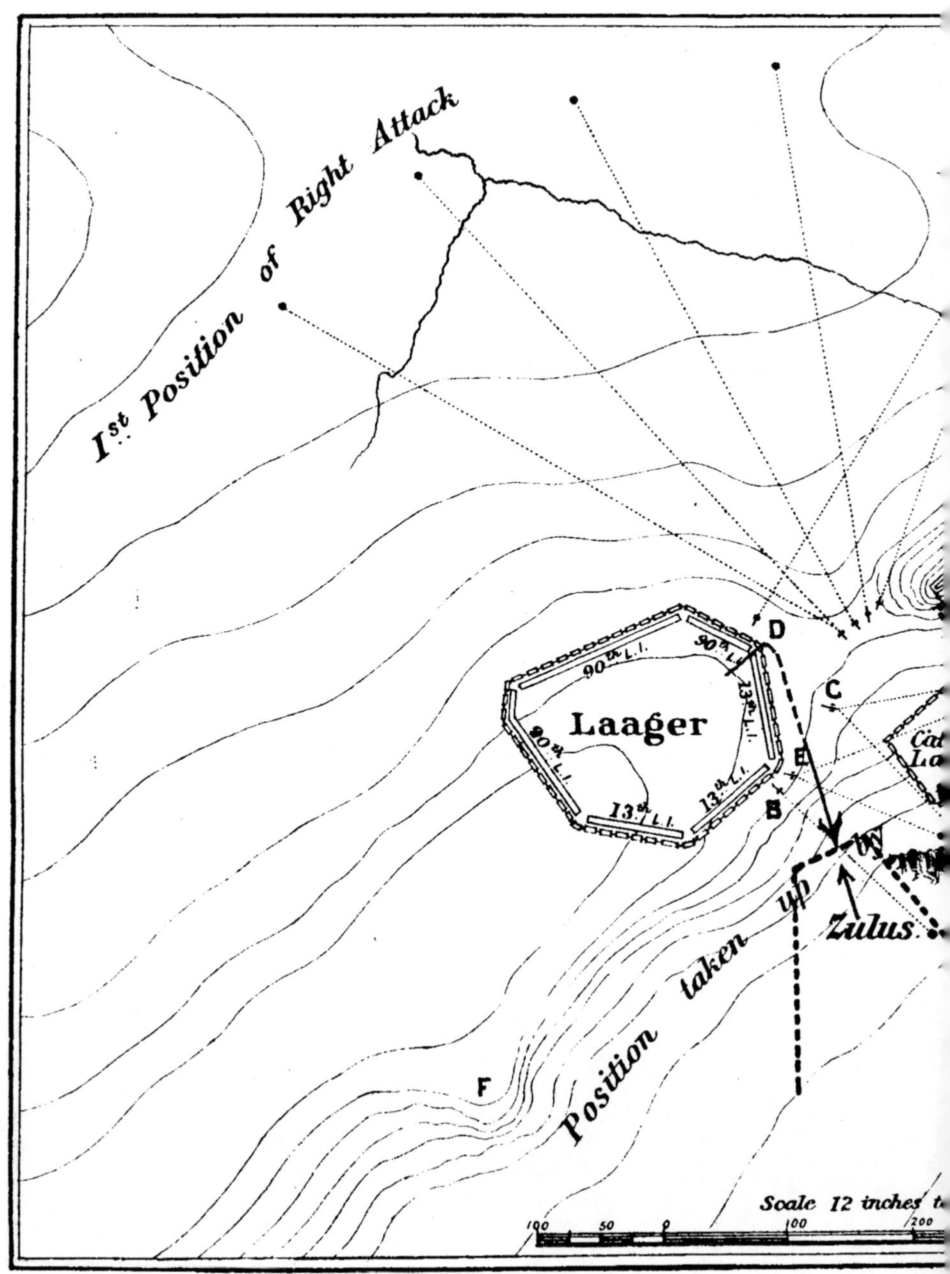

To face page 80.

ONEL WOOD'S CAMP MARCH 29th 1879.

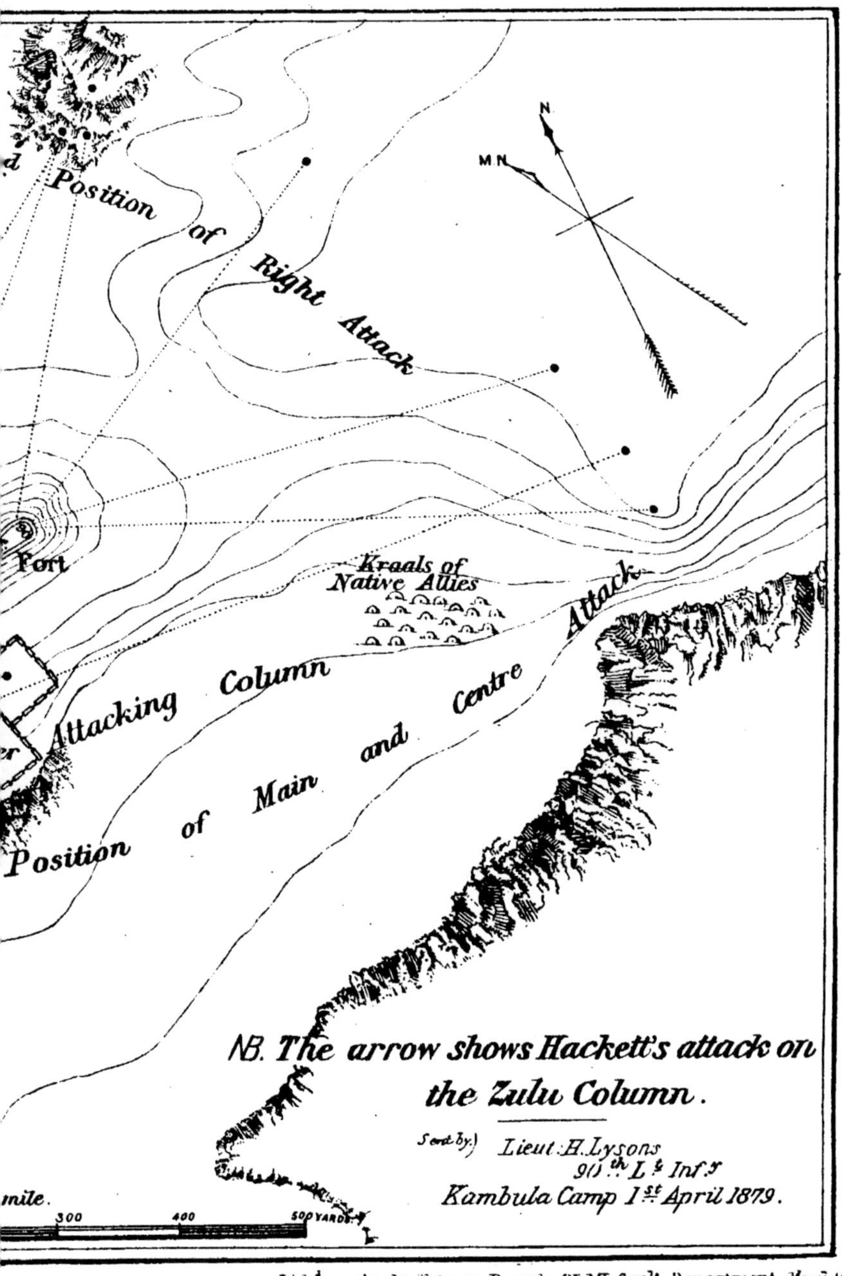

Lithd at the Intelligence Branch Qr Mr Genls Department. March 1881

on the column by two companies of the 90th under Major Hackett, and these issuing from the laager forced the enemy to retire. The two companies, however, became exposed to such a severe enfilade fire from a number of Zulus posted on a spur to the westward, that they were recalled, and again took post within the laager. 29th March, 1879.

Those Zulus who had occupied the cattle kraal failed to remove any of the oxen; but as the position now held by the defenders consisted merely of the main laager and the redoubt, the enemy's forces were able to assemble below the rocks and steep ground, within 200 yards of the laager, and hence to assault it. This was done several times with great determination, but the steady fire of the infantry in the laager and the redoubt, and the coolness with which the guns outside were served drove them back on each occasion with enormous loss.

The action was a long one; but in the end the Zulus were forced to recognise the impossibility of passing the open space which separated them from the laager. By about 5.30 P.M. the vigour of the attack had so evidently slackened, that Colonel Wood ordered a company of the 1 | 13th to retake the cattle kraal, while a company of the 90th advanced on their right to the edge of the rocks, and poured a heavy fire into the mass of Zulus below, who were now beginning to fall back. The mounted men, who, after having placed their horses within the laager, had been assisting in the defence, now remounted, and were sent against the retreating enemy. The retreat speedily became a rout, and the horsemen, following for a distance of about 7 miles, smote down the fugitives almost with impunity till darkness obliged them to desist. 5.30 P.M.

The Zulu army which fought this day at Kambula had been assembled at Ulundi, and was specially detailed for the duty of attacking Colonel Wood's camp. The right horn was composed of the 'Nkobamakosi regiment, which, in consequence of its losses at Isandhlwana was specially eager for distinction, and suffered very severely in its premature commencement of the action. The main attack was made by the 'Mbonambi and Nokenke regiments, the latter forming the force which occupied the cattle kraal. Both of these regiments also suffered heavily, and, including the number killed in the pursuit, the loss inflicted on the Zulus this day is estimated at nearly 2,000.

The British force engaged numbered in all 1,998 and its casualties amounted to 18 non-commissioned officers and men killed, and 8 officers and 57 non-commissioned officers and men wounded.*

The Zulu army which attacked Kambula dispersed immediately after the action, and during the period which followed all was quiet in this district.

---

* Many of the latter died of their wounds, and a considerable number of casualties also occurred among the non-combatants.

IX. Arrival of Reinforcements and General Situation, 4th to 15th April.

It had been determined by Lord Chelmsford that the position occupied at Etshowe should be abandoned immediately after the garrison blockaded there had been relieved, and the evacuation of the fort was accordingly commenced on the morning of
4th April, 1879. the 4th April. All stores of any value were collected and placed on wagons, and at 1.30 P.M. the head of the column moved off. Much delay, however, occurred, and it was late in the day before the end of the train of wagons, 120 in number, got clear of Etshowe. The route taken was that which Colonel Pearson had followed on his arrival in January, as the new track was greatly cut up by the advance of the relief column the previous day.

Colonel Pearson and the relieved garrison bivouacked on the night of the 4th April on the same ridge where they had passed the night after the action of the Inyezane, and on the following
5th April. morning again moved forward. The original plan had been for this column to proceed to Gingihlovo, but in the course of the day, while on the march, Colonel Pearson received orders to move direct to the Lower Tugela by the old road. Colonel Pearson's force accordingly crossed the Inyezane, and encamp-
6th April. ing between that river and the Amatikulu, moved on the 6th to
7th April. within 4 miles of the frontier. Next day the Tugela was reached, and the force encamped on the Zulu side of the stream.

The relieving column did not leave Etshowe till the 5th
4th April. April, and on the 4th Lord Chelmsford accompanied a patrol, which destroyed a kraal of Dabulamanzi's on the Entumeni hill some 8 miles away. When Etshowe was evacuated on the
5th April. 5th April the buildings were immediately burnt by the Zulus.

Lord Chelmsford's column, being lightly equipped, overtook Colonel Pearson while on the march, but the two forces soon separated, as Lord Chelmsford was returning to Gingihlovo while Colonel Pearson's lengthy convoy was now proceeding to the Tugela.

The position near the Imfuchini mission station, where Lord Chelmsford's column bivouacked this night,* was the scene of a false alarm, which had serious results. At 3.30 A.M. on the
6th April. morning of the 6th April, a sentry of the 91st Regiment, fired a shot at what he took to be a party of the enemy. A piquet of the 60th Rifles, which was on the opposite side of the entrenched enclosure, on hearing this shot, hastily fell back, as did some of Mr. John Dunn's scouts, who had been still further in advance.

---

* The 5th April was excessively hot, and the troops with Lord Chelmsford suffered much from fatigue and want of water.

The main body of the 3 | 60th, who were within the entrenchment, opened fire on the party, thus hastening towards them, and the result was that 5 of the 60th, and 9 of the native scouts were either shot or bayonetted. Of these 1 man of the 60th was killed on the spot, and 2 of the natives died of their wounds shortly afterwards.

From this bivouack the column marched on the 6th, and passing by the Gingihlovo laager, formed a new entrenched camp about a mile to the southward. The force which had been left in the original laager moved to this new entrenchment on the 7th.

Lord Chelmsford, accompanied by his staff, and Commodore
Richards, now hastened back to Natal, and at noon on the 7th **7th April,**
April reached the Tugela, where Colonel Pearson's force was at **1879.**
that time arriving.

Leaving Fort Pearson on the 8th, Lord Chelmsford got to **8th April.**
Durban on the 9th, and found the bulk of the reinforcements **9th April.**
already disembarked.*

The conveyance to Natal of these reinforcements had been marked by only two misadventures worthy of notice. Of these, one happened to the "City of Paris," which ran aground in Simon's Bay, on the 23rd March, and was consequently obliged to transfer her troops, &c., to Her Majesty's ship "Tamar," and the other befell the "Clyde," which was totally wrecked near Dyer's island, some 70 miles to the eastward of Simon's Bay.

The "Clyde," which was taking out large drafts for the
1 | 24th Regiment, appears to have run aground about 4.30 A.M.,
on the 3rd April, on a reef between Dyer's island and the main **3rd April.**
land. At 6.20 A.M. the first boats, with the sick, were despatched to a spot on the shore of the latter, some 3 miles distant from the vessel, and, as the sea was fortunately calm, successive trips were made without difficulty till 11.30 A.M., by which time all the troops had been landed, with the exception of a working party. This party remained on board, saving baggage and other property up to 1.30 p.m., when the vessel was abandoned, as she appeared to be sinking.

In consequence of the exceptionally calm weather, the whole of the troops and crew were thus landed without any casualty, but as the "Clyde" sank during the following night, the large supplies of warlike stores which she contained were totally lost.

Those who had first reached the shore had selected a convenient camping ground, about 2 miles inland, and the men's provisions were conveyed from the beach to this place in the wagon of a neighbouring farmer.

Shortly before 8 A.M. the Chief Officer of the "Clyde" had started in one of the ship's boats for Simon's Bay, and on his arrival there at 10.30 P.M. the same evening, he reported to the Senior Naval Officer that the vessel had run ashore.

---

* See Appendix B.

Her Majesty's ship "Tamar" was immediately despatched to render assistance, and at about 9 A.M. the next morning arrived at the wreck, of which only the masts and funnel were now visible.

6th April, 1879.

The work of re-embarking the troops was carried on rapidly, and was nearly complete by 1.30 P.M., when Her Majesty's ship "Tenedos," which had followed the "Tamar," reached the anchorage. Both vessels arrived at Simon's Bay, on the 5th, and on the 7th the "Tamar" proceeded to Durban with the troops.

The arrival of the reinforcements and of the general officers who had accompanied them, rendered it necessary for Lord Chelmsford on his return from Etshowe to reorganise his forces, which were now so largely increased. The old designations were at first retained, and the command of No. 1 Column, now to consist of two brigades, was given to Major-General H. Hope Crealock, C.B. Colonel Pearson, with the local rank of Brigadier-General, was appointed to one of these brigades.

8th April.

Columns Nos. 2 and 3 had ceased to exist, but No. 4 (Wood's column) was likewise to be brought up to a strength of two brigades, of which one was to be formed by the troops now at Kambula, under Wood (also made a Brigadier-General), and the other by the new arrivals under Major-General Newdigate.

The cavalry brigade, consisting of the 1st Dragoon Guards and 17th Lancers, was under the command of Major-General Marshall, and was directed to join the northern column.

Major-General the Honourable H. Clifford, V.C., C.B., was appointed Inspector-General of the Lines of Communication and Base, and established his Head-quarters at Durban.

13th April.

On the 13th April a different arrangement of the forces was made. No. 1 Column was now styled No. I Division, South African Field Force, under the command of Major-General Crealock; Wood's force was to remain independent, under the title of "Brigadier-General Wood's Flying Column," and the remainder of the troops in the Utrecht district were to constitute No. II Division, of which the command was given to Major-General Newdigate.

The infantry on landing were sent forward immediately, but the mounted troops were encamped near Durban for about a week after disembarkation, in order to get the horses into condition.

During the first fortnight in April few movements took place among the troops which had been occupying defensive positions on the frontier. Helpmakaar and Rorke's Drift were still garrisoned by the 2 | 24th, and the two remaining companies of the 1 | 24th, and a considerable force of natives was maintained at Fort Cherry. On the Transvaal side, two companies of the 2 | 4th went to Luneberg, relieving five companies of the 80th, who reached Utrecht on the 11th April, and thus materially increased Wood's available force. This force had remained undisturbed at Kambula, after the action of the 29th March, its

11th April.

operations being confined to the sending out of various patrols of mounted men. In an expedition of this kind, a small party from Luneberg, under Captain Prior, of the 80th, met a number of Zulus, on the 5th April, near the Intombi, and had a skirmish with them, in which one of their number, who proved to be the celebrated chief Umbelini, received a wound, from the effects of which he died a few days later.

14th April, 1879. On the 14th April fresh ground was taken up by the greater portion of the force at Kambula. While the redoubt was still occupied, a new entrenched camp was this day formed, some 600 or 700 yards to the westward of the old one, the site of which it had now, for sanitary reasons, become desirable to vacate.

15th April. On the 15th April the general position of the Army in South Africa was as follows:—Lord Chelmsford's Head-quarters were at Durban, in the neighbourhood of which place the Cavalry Brigade and the artillery were encamped. The 2nd Brigade, Ist Division (57th, 3 | 60th, and 91st Regiments) with a portion of the Naval Brigade and the mounted infantry, was still at Gingihlovo, in the camp occupied on the 6th April. The 1st Brigade of this Division (2 | 3rd, 88th, and 99th Regiments), with the remainder of the Naval Brigade, was encamped on the Lower Tugela, principally on the left bank of the stream.

The infantry of the IInd Division (2 | 21st, 58th, and 94th Regiments) were on the march up country, the place named for their concentration being the Doornberg, a wooded mountain in the angle between the Buffalo and Blood rivers.

Wood's Column, consisting of the 1 | 13th and 90th Regiments, with Tremlett's battery* (11 | 7 R.A.), No. 1 Squadron Mounted Infantry, the Frontier Light Horse, and other Colonial troops, was still occupying the entrenched position at Kambula, and drew its supplies from Utrecht, which was now held by the 80th Regiment.

Fort Pearson and Dundee† were the main depôts for the Ist and IInd Divisions respectively, and to these places supplies were being forwarded as rapidly as the means of transport would permit.

---

* Four 7-pr. guns.

† The selection of this place instead of Helpmakaar was due to its being nearer to the Orange Free State whence supplies were obtainable, and to the fact that the road to it *viâ* Ladysmith was remote from the Zulu frontier. The principal supplies which the country afforded consisted of bullocks and Indian corn for the troops, and oat hay for the horses.

X. Operations of the Ist Division—16th April to 17th June.

16th April, 1879. On the 16th April, Major-General Crealock left Durban to assume command of his Division, and on the 18th his Headquarters were established at Fort Pearson.

18th April. By Lord Chelmsford's instructions* to General Crealock, the work to be performed by the Ist Division was to be as follows:—The Emangwene and Undi military kraals north of the Umlatoosi river were to be burnt; a strong permanent post was to be formed on the Inyezane, and two months' provisions for the Division stored in it, and an intermediate post was to be constructed half way between this and the Tugela. The operations against the two kraals were to be undertaken with as little delay as possible, and on their completion the further movements of the Division were to be at General Crealock's discretion. General Crealock was informed that Ulundi would be the objective of the northern force, and it was suggested that in support of this force an entrenched post and supply depôt should eventually be established by the Ist Division, in the neighbourhood of the St. Paul's mission station.

21st April. On the 21st April a convoy of 110 wagons, containing three weeks' supplies for the 2nd Brigade, left the Lower Tugela in charge of an escort of about 1,000 men and 2 guns. An empty convoy, with an escort from the 2nd Brigade, was met on the
22nd April. 22nd at the Amatikulu, and the convoys having been exchanged, the escort of the 2nd Brigade returned to Gingihlovo, where it
23rd April. arrived on the 23rd. The escort of the 1st Brigade remaining for a day on the Amatikulu, constructed an entrenched post there, called Fort Crealock, and returned to the Tugela on the
24th April. 24th April.

25th April. On this day and the following the 2nd Brigade moved to a new position lower down the Inyezane river, on the right bank
29th April. of which a fort was commenced on the 29th April, to which the name of Fort Chelmsford was given.

These two posts having been established in accordance with Lord Chelmsford's instructions, all efforts were now directed to the collection of two months' supplies for the Division at Fort Chelmsford. The base authorities delivered these supplies at
Fort Pearson to Fort Chelmsford, 20. the depôt at Fort Pearson, and their conveyance from this point had to be undertaken by the divisional transport. This transport was composed almost entirely of ox wagons, of which about 250, with some 3,500 oxen, were available when the Division was formed.

The convoy despatched on the 21st April was followed by others, at intervals of about a week,† the average number of

---

* Dated 12th April.

† The dates of starting from the Tugela were as follows: 21st, 29th April: 5th, 10th, 14th, 19th, 23rd, 28th May; 4th, 10th, 13th, 17th June.

wagons in each convoy being 100. No attempt was made by the enemy to interfere with the movements of these convoys, which usually took three days to reach Fort Chelmsford. While supplies were thus being sent to the front, the two brigades remained in their positions on the Tugela and Inyezane, furnishing the necessary escorts, and strengthening the defences of the posts. Fort Tenedos, which had been constructed on the advance of Colonel Pearson's column in January, was found to be capable of considerable improvement, and the alteration of this work, as well as certain changes in the defensive arrangements on the Natal side of the river, was undertaken by the 1st Brigade. 21st April, 1879.

After much delay, caused by the difficulty of transporting the materials from Durban, a pontoon bridge across the Tugela was completed on the 7th May, and on the 11th June this was 7th May. replaced by a semi-permanent trestle and pontoon bridge. Among other works which were carried out during this period was the extension of the telegraph to Fort Chelmsford. This was completed on the 30th May. 30th May.

The low lying coast region in which the Ist Division was encamped proved to be extremely unhealthy, and the amount of sickness was very large, the most serious disease being enteric fever. The 2nd Brigade, though its camp at Fort Chelmsford was free from the sanitary objections to which the Gingihlovo position was open, suffered severely, and 18 officers and 479 men of the regular troops were sent back sick from Forts Chelmsford and Crealock, between the 16th April and the 17th June. During the same period 3 officers and 68 men of the Division died.

The transport difficulties of the Division did not diminish as time went on. By the passage of the convoys the grass near the road and round the halting places was consumed or trampled down, and the oxen, which were thus obliged to travel farther for their food, fell off in condition, and became unfit for hard work. No others, however, were available, and the result was that large numbers of animals perished, the average daily loss being 10.* At the beginning of June the Natal Government directed the magistrates of the different districts to use their influence to induce owners to part with their cattle, and 674 which were thus bought† to some extent supplied the deficiencies in the divisional transport.

Great difficulty was also experienced in obtaining the services of natives to drive the oxen, but at length their numbers were made up, and the requisite two months' provisions having been accumulated at Fort Chelmsford, the Division was ready to move forward.

The month of June, however, was well advanced before this was accomplished, and it was on the 13th June that the first 13th June.

---

* These oxen were hired, and for each ox that died or was lost in Zululand, an indemnity of £20 had to be paid by the British Government.

† The average price was £15 1*s.* 1*d.*

movement was made. On this day, with a view to the concentration of the Division at Fort Chelmsford, a portion of the 1st Brigade, consisting of the 2 | 3rd Regiment, Lonsdale's Horse,* and 2 guns, marched from the Tugela. This was followed on the 17th June by the second section of the Brigade, consisting of the 88th Regiment and the Naval Brigade, and on the 19th, 3 companies of the 99th Regiment, with a battery of artillery (M | 6 R.A.) and various drafts formed the third section of the troops moving up from the frontier.

17th June, 1879.

19th June.

On the 17th June General Crealock's Head-quarters were still at Fort Pearson, and the Ist Division, for which two months' provisions had been stored at Fort Chelmsford, was now in process of concentration at that place, preparatory to an advance.

---

* Raised by Commandant Lonsdale in the Cape Colony in February, 1879. *Vide* Appendix D.

NOTE.—The operations of the Ist Division are continued in section XIII.

XI. Operations of the IInd Division—16th April to 17th June.

On the 16th April the infantry regiments of the IInd Division were on the march towards the north of Natal, the 2 | 21st and 94th Regiments taking the route by Greytown, the remainder that by Estcourt and Ladysmith. 16th April, 1879.

The mounted troops began to leave their camp near Durban, on the 17th April, and proceeded by marches averaging 10 miles, 17th April. with a halt every third or fourth day. Two companies of the Army Service Corps had landed about the same time as the cavalry, and for the march up country one of these companies was at first attached to each cavalry regiment, for regimental transport. This arrangement, however, was modified on the arrival of the cavalry brigade at Pietermaritzburg, and from this point on, the cavalry were accompanied merely by detachments of the Army Service Corps.

Lord Chelmsford moved his Head-quarters from Durban to Pietermaritzburg, on the 17th April, and was accompanied by the Prince Imperial, who had reached Durban on the 1st April. Before leaving England, the Prince had sought permission to serve with the British troops in Zululand, but as this was not sanctioned, he had proceeded to South Africa as a spectator. The Prince was the bearer of a letter from the Commander-in-Chief to Lord Chelmsford, requesting that assistance might be rendered him to see as much as possible with the columns in the field, and with this view Lord Chelmsford now attached him to his personal staff.

During the few days which Lord Chelmsford spent in Pietermaritzburg, he endeavoured to bring about such a change in the existing laws of Natal as would enable the military authorities to impress carriage, as at this time no transport was forthcoming, the owners holding back in hopes of a further advance in the already enormous prices offered. The Government of Natal, however, was not disposed to take any step in this direction, and the requisite power was not obtained till a much later date.

Another difficulty which now became apparent was the want of native drivers and leaders for the wagon teams. The Isandhlwana disaster had caused such widely felt apprehensions among the class from whom these men were usually obtainable, that, on a fresh advance into Zululand being about to take place, desertions became numerous, and most of those who now undertook these duties stipulated that their engagement should terminate on reaching the frontier.

On the 22nd April, Lord Chelmsford left Pietermaritzburg 22nd April. for Dundee, and on his departure Major-General Clifford moved to Pietermaritzburg from Durban.

General Newdigate, who had started a week earlier, had

employed the time during which his Division was on the march in paying a visit to General Wood, at Kambula, and now returned to meet Lord Chelmsford at Dundee. This place was the main depôt for the IInd Division, and from it supplies were afterwards sent forward to Landman's Drift and Conference hill.

29th April, 1879. 1st May. On the 29th April the 2 | 21st and 94th Regiments reached Dundee, and by the 1st May the remainder of the infantry had arrived. The cavalry brigade, the artillery, and the ammunition column were still on the march.

2nd May. On the 2nd May Lord Chelmsford left Dundee for Kambula, and the same day the infantry of the IInd Division moved up to Landman's Drift, on the Buffalo river. Here an entrenched camp was formed, in which the bulk of the Division remained for some time stationary, awaiting the completion of the arrangements for its advance.

10th May. On the 10th May the Division occupied the following positions:—General Newdigate's head-quarters were at Landman's Drift, where the troops present consisted of the 58th Regiment,* and three companies of the 2 | 21st;† N | 5 R.A.‡; Bengough's battalion of natives; and Shepstone's Horse. The 94th Regiment§ was at Conference hill, whither it had gone as escort to a convoy; three companies of the 2 | 21st were at the Doornberg cutting firewood, and the cavalry brigade was at Dundee, where N | 6 R.A. and two companies of the 1 | 24th were also encamped. The drafts for the 1 | 24th, amounting to five companies,|| having been delayed in consequence of the wreck of the "Clyde," were still on the road, as were a half battery (10 | 7 R.A.) and the ammunition column.

12th May. On the 12th May the right wing of the 17th Lancers and N | 6 R.A. moved up to Landman's Drift. The 1st Dragoon Guards, who had been informed on the 6th that they were to proceed to Standerton in the Transvaal, remained still at Dundee, with the other wing of the Lancers and the 24th.

Conference hill was to be a depôt for Wood's force as well as for the IInd Division, and during the month of May large quantities of stores were forwarded to this place. Great difficulty was at first experienced in inducing the wagon drivers to cross the Buffalo, but, as the country was found to be quite deserted by the enemy, confidence was eventually restored.

It had been ascertained that a route suitable for the advance of Wood's column led from Conference hill to Ibabanango, but as yet no other track had been found by which the IInd Division could join in the advance. Hopes were, however, entertained that this long détour might be avoided by the discovery of a more direct line from Landman's Drift, and on the arrival of the

---

* Minus 1 company at Durban and one at Ladysmith.

† 2 companies were at Pietermaritzberg.

‡ 4 guns, 7-pr. The two lost at Isandhlwana had not yet been replaced.

§ Minus 2 companies at Greytown.

|| 1 company of the 1 | 24th was at St. John's river, Pondoland.

cavalry some reconnaissances of the country beyond the frontier were undertaken. On the 16th May a squadron of Lancers left **16th May, 1879.** Landman's Drift, and, after bivouacking near the Vecht Kop, reached the Itelezi hill the next morning. **17th May** Here they met a detachment of Bettington's Horse, which had ridden out from Conference hill, but no Zulus were seen, and the Lancers, recrossing the Buffalo at Robson's Drift, returned to the Landman's Drift camp at 8 P.M.

On the 20th May General Marshall, with the 1st Dragoon **20th May,** Guards and the left wing of the Lancers, marched from Dundee for Rorke's Drift.

This force, after bivouacking on the eastern side of the Biggarsberg, continued its march the next day, being joined on the road by the right wing of the Lancers and 2 guns of Harness's battery, which had started from Landman's Drift the same morning. The united force reached Rorke's Drift at half-past 3 P.M., and bivouacked near Fort Melvill,* the object being to visit the battlefield of Isandhlwana the next day.

Isandhlwana had been visited on the 15th May by a small party of officers and others, under Lieutenant-Colonel Black,† but with this exception the ground had been untrodden by Europeans since Lieutenant-Colonel Black's previous visit on the 14th March, and those who had fallen on the 22nd January still lay unburied.

At 4 A.M., on the 21st May, Colonel Drury-Lowe, with a **21st May,** force consisting of a wing of the King's Dragoon Guards, a wing of the Lancers, and 10 of the Natal Carabineers, crossed the Buffalo, and proceeding up the Bashee valley, past Sirayo's stronghold, worked round over the hills, and eventually descended to Isandhlwana from the heights to the north of it.

General Marshall, with the remainder of the mounted force, consisting of the other wings of the cavalry regiments, police, and Volunteers, with the 2 guns, started from Rorke's Drift at 5.30 A.M., and proceeded by the direct track to Isandhlwana. Four companies of the 2 | 24th marched out as far as the Bashee river, and occupied the heights on the eastern side of that stream.

The two cavalry columns arrived at Isandhlwana about 8.30 A.M. and found the battlefield, as well as the whole of the surrounding country, entirely deserted. Vedettes were posted and many of the dead were buried, but the bodies of all 24th men were left untouched at the express request of Colonel Glyn, who desired that they should be interred by their own comrades. A great many of the remains were still recog-

---

* This fort had been constructed about a mile from the mission station.

† Among other relics found by this party was a Letts' diary belonging to Lieutenant Pope, in which he had made the following entry on the 22nd January:—"Four A.M., A, C, D, E, F, H, 1 and 2 | 3 N.N.C., mounted troops, and four guns off. Great firing. Relieved by 1 | 24th. Alarm. Three columns Zulus and mounted men on hill E. Turn out. Seven thousand more E.N.E., four thousand of whom went round Lion's Kop. Durnford's Basutos arrive and pursue with rocket battery. Zulus retire everywhere. Men fall out for dinners."

nisable, and various small articles of value were recovered for transmission to the friends of those who had fallen.

Of the wagons and carts which had now been standing on this ground for exactly four months, about forty were removed to Rorke's Drift by horses which had accompanied General Marshall's column. The whole force returned to Rorke's Drift the

23rd May, 1879. same evening and reached Landman's Drift on the 23rd May.

Reconnaissances made in the month of May by Lieutenant-Colonel Harrison, A.Q.M.G., had established the fact that the Ibabanango mountain could be reached from Landman's Drift by a fairly practicable track leading by the Itelezi hill. This line was accordingly chosen for the advance of the IInd Division, which was now to enter Zululand at Koppie Allein, and to

24th May. this place Bengough's battalion of natives was sent on the 24th May.

On the evening of this day Lord Chelmsford arrived at Landman's Drift from Utrecht, where his Head-quarters had been since his return from Kambula on the 5th.

Up to this time the transport of the IInd Division had been employed in pushing up supplies from Landman's Drift to Conference hill, and within the earthworks formed at this place very large quantities of stores had now been accumulated. The adoption of the more southern line of advance, however, now necessitated the formation of a depôt at Koppie Allein, and the removal of stores to this place from Conference hill and from Landman's Drift was at once commenced.

The contemplated move of the King's Dragoon Guards to Standerton was found to be unnecessary, but in consequence of the great difficulty of transporting the requisite forage it was decided that the greater part of this regiment should remain on

26th May. the frontier, and on the 26th May the right wing left Landman's Drift for Conference hill and the left wing for Rorke's Drift.

The advance of the Division to Koppie Allein was com-

27th May. menced on the 27th May, when Harness's battery* (N | 5 R.A.) and the 58th Regiment moved forward. Two companies of the 2 | 24th marched from Dundee this day and occupied the post

28th May. vacated by the 58th. Next day both Army and Divisional Head-quarters, with the remainder of the IInd Division (17th Lancers, N | 6 R.A., No. 2 Company R.E., and the 1 | 24th Regiment), moved up from Landman's Drift to Koppie Allein.

29th May. Here they were joined on the 29th by the 2 | 21st Regiment

30th May. from the Doornberg, and on the 30th by the 94th, a squadron of the King's Dragoon Guards, and Shepstone's Basutos from Conference hill. Two infantry Brigades were now formed, of which the 1st, consisting of the 2 | 21st and 58th Regiments, was commanded by Colonel Glyn, and the 2nd, composed of the 1 | 24th and 94th Regiments, was under Colonel Collingwood.

The IInd Division was thus concentrated on the Blood river by the end of May, at which time Colonel Wood's column was

* This battery was now complete, 2 guns sent from England having arrived.

at Munhla hill, some 18 miles distant. The Division had with it supplies for 31 days, about one-fourth of which was carried by the regimental transport.

On the 31st May Major-General Newdigate, with the 1st Brigade and Harness's battery, crossed the Blood river and encamped on its left bank. The country in front had by this time been reconnoitred, and it had been decided that the Division should follow a route by the north of the Itelezi hill and advance thence between the Tombokala and Ityotyozi rivers. The selection of this route, and the choice of camping grounds along it, naturally fell to the Quartermaster-General's department, and the Prince Imperial, who had been attached to this branch of the Staff, had taken part in several of the reconnaissances. **31st May, 1879.**

The IInd Division moved from the Blood river to the Itelezi hill on Sunday, the 1st June, and on the morning of this day the Prince Imperial started in advance of the column to select a camping ground for the Division to occupy at the end of its second day's march and to examine the road to be traversed in that march. It had been arranged that this halting place should be on the banks of the Ityotyosi river, and as the country up to this point had been reconnoitred on the 29th without any Zulus having been seen, the escort detailed this day consisted merely of six troopers of Bettington's Horse and six of Shepstone's Basutos.* **1st June.**

The Prince was accompanied by Lieut. Carey, D.A.Q.M.G., who applied for permission to join the party in order to verify some observations made on a previous reconnaissance, and at 9.15 A.M. they started from the camp at Koppie Allein. A friendly Zulu joined them as a guide, but only the six European troopers of Bettington's Horse reported themselves to Lieutenant Carey as escort, the six Basutos, who had also been ordered to attend, failing to appear. With this small escort they pushed on over a good open grass country and reached the Itelezi hill soon after 10 A.M. At this place, to which the IInd Division was about to move, Lieutenant-Colonel Harrison, A.Q.M.G., was met, and the Prince and Lieutenant Carey spent some little time here discussing with him the question of the water supply available. Having afterwards become separated from Lieutenant-Colonel Harrison, the Prince moved on with his eight companions to carry out the reconnaissance on which he was engaged.

At about half-past 12 o'clock the party reached a flat-topped hill, on the summit of which they dismounted while the Prince made a rough sketch of the surrounding country. After spending nearly an hour on this hill the party moved on along the ridge between the Tombokala and Ityotyosi rivers, and about 2.30 P.M. descended from the high ground towards a kraal some 200 yards from the latter stream. This kraal was of an ordinary

---

* Wood's column was advancing this day from Munhla hill towards the Ityotyosi.

1st June, 1879.

native type, and consisted of a circular stone enclosure about 25 yards in diameter, outside which five huts were built. These huts were unoccupied, but as some dogs were prowling about, and as fresh remains of such food as is commonly eaten by Zulus could be seen, it was evident that the inhabitants had only recently gone away. The whole of the level ground near the kraal was covered with coarse grass and Indian corn, growing to a height of 5 or 6 feet, and closely surrounding the circle of huts on all sides except the north and north-east. Here the ground was open for about 200 yards, but at that distance from the kraal there was a donga or dry watercourse some 6 or 8 feet deep by which, in the rainy season, the storm waters found their way into the Ityotyosi.

On arriving at the kraal, about 3 P.M., the Prince ordered the escort to offsaddle and knee-halter the horses for grazing. This was done, and the men made some coffee and remained resting till 10 minutes to 4, when the native guide reported that he had seen a Zulu come over the hill. The horses, which had been feeding close by, were now caught and saddled, and the order "Prepare to mount" was given by the Prince. At this time the men of the escort, whose Martini-Henry carbines had not been loaded, were standing by their horses in different places near the kraal, and all were quite unconscious of danger. The Prince gave the word "mount," and as this was uttered a volley was fired at the party by a number of Zulus who had crept unobserved through the long grass to within 15 yards of the huts. Though no one was hit by this volley the surprise was complete, and the troopers, not yet settled in their saddles, could hardly control their horses, which, terrified by the shots and by the yells of the Zulus, bore them across the open ground towards the donga. The Prince himself was in the act of mounting when the volley was fired, but his charger becoming exceedingly restive, he appears to have failed to get into the saddle and to have run alongside the animal which followed the horses of the escort. The Prince, who was extremely active, now endeavoured to vault on to his horse while thus in rapid motion, but his efforts seem to have been foiled by the tearing of the wallet which he had seized, and on this giving way he fell to the ground and his horse broke away from him.

As the escort were galloping away from the kraal the Zulus kept up a fire by which one trooper was hit in the back and fell. The native guide and another trooper, who had not mounted along with the rest, were left behind at the kraal, and neither was again seen alive. The remainder of the party, consisting of Lieutenant Carey and four troopers, crossing the donga at different points, galloped on for several hundred yards. Lieutenant Carey, who after crossing the donga had only been accompanied by one man, was presently joined by the other three who had escaped, and learnt that the Prince was not of the party, and that he had been last seen between the kraal and the donga, dismounted, and pursued by the Zulus.

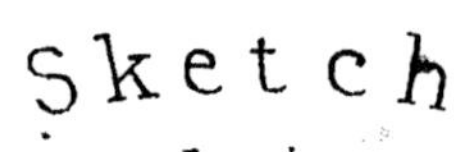

showing
position of Kraal
near which
PRINCE LOUIS NAPOLEON,
Prince Imperial
of
France*, was *killed
1st. June 1879.

TALL GRASS

ITYOTYOZI RIVER

MEALIES

M.N.

N.

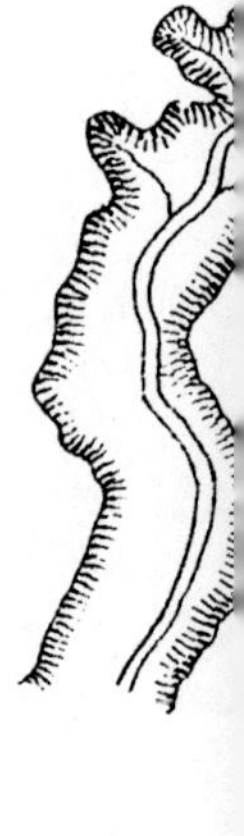

To face page 94.

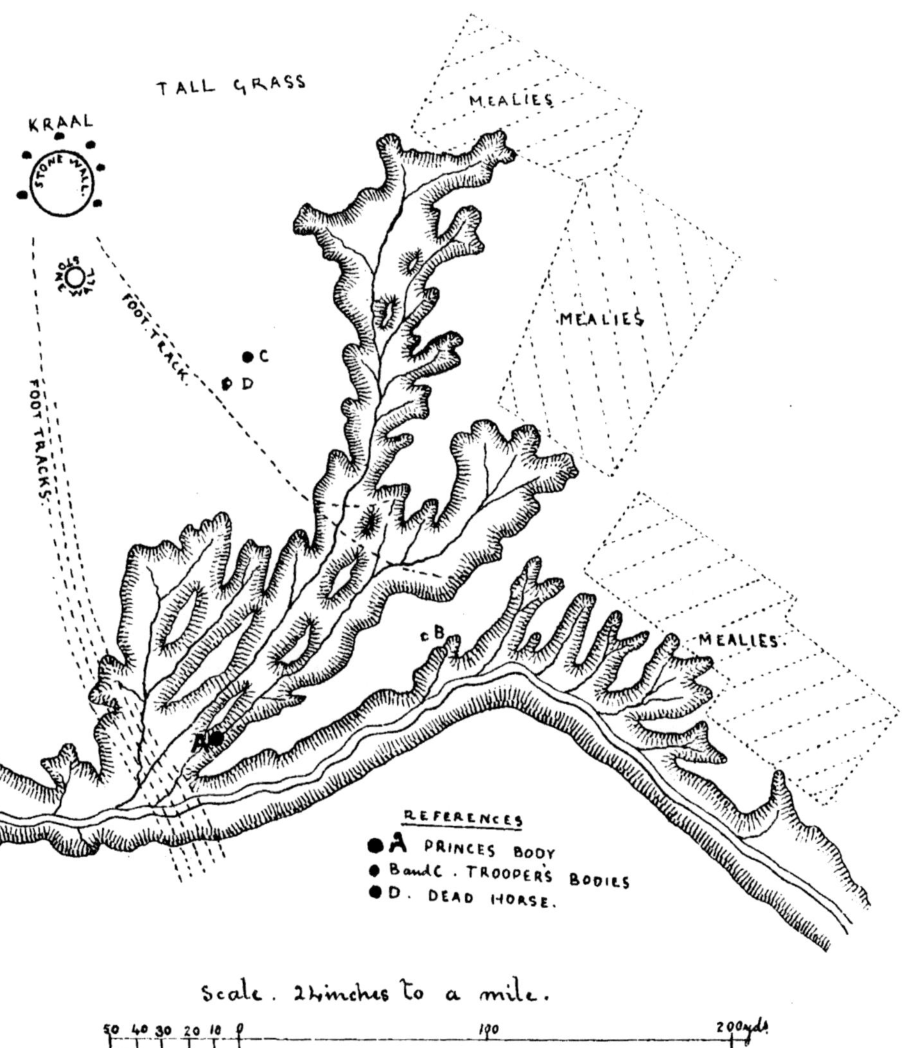

Lith[d] at the Intelligence

Many of the enemy being already on this ground, and the Prince's horse being seen galloping riderless at some little distance, Lieutenant Carey came to the conclusion that the Prince must by this time have fallen, and that it would be useless for the few survivors to return. The party accordingly proceeded in haste to bear the news to the camp of the IInd Division, which was now established at the Itelezi hill. **1st June, 1879.**

To avoid the Zulus Lieutenant Carey and his party crossed to the north side of the Tombokala, and after riding about 4 miles fell in with General Wood and Lieutenant-Colonel Buller, who were reconnoitring the track for the next advance of the Flying Column which had marched from Munhla hill that morning.* After informing them of what had happened, Lieutenant Carey proceeded to rejoin the IInd Division, and on reaching the Itelezi hill camp at about 7 P.M. made his report to Lord Chelmsford.

By this time it was dark and nothing could be done towards ascertaining the fate of the Prince, but on the following morning strong parties were sent out from General Wood's camp, as well as from the camp of the IInd Division, to visit the kraal where the reconnoitring party had been surprised. All doubts as to the fate of those who were missing were soon set at rest. The dead bodies of the two troopers were first found, one in the donga, the other between it and the kraal, and soon afterwards the body of the Prince was discovered in the donga, whither he had made his way on foot after losing his horse. Being overtaken here he had evidently turned on his pursuers, but after emptying his pistol his sword had been of little use against the assegais of the enemy, and he had fallen where he stood. **2nd June.**

The body, which bore 16 wounds all in front, was placed on a bier formed of lances and a blanket, and was carried to an ambulance on which it was conveyed to the Itelezi hill camp where the IInd Division remained halted this day. After such preservative measures as were possible under the circumstances had been taken by the medical officers, the body was sent back to Natal, a detachment of cavalry escorting the ambulance in which it was borne. This was despatched the same afternoon, and proceeding by Koppie Allein, Landman's Drift, and Dundee, reached Pietermaritzburg on Sunday, the 8th June. The remains of the Prince were here received with all possible honour, and after being removed to Durban were there embarked on the 11th June on board Her Majesty's ship "Boadicea" and conveyed to Simon's Bay, whence they were taken to England in Her Majesty's ship "Orontes," which had been specially prepared for their reception. The "Orontes" anchored at Spithead on the 10th July, and the coffin containing the Prince's body reached its resting place in the mortuary chapel at Chislehurst on the 12th July, 1879.

On the 3rd June the IInd Division resumed its advance and encamped near the junction of the Tombokala and Ityotyosi **3rd June. Itelezi hill to Ityotyosi, 10.**

---

* *Vide* section XII.

rivers, within half a mile of the spot where the Prince had been killed. Wood's column, which had marched on the 2nd, was now on the left front of the Division, on the farther side of the Ityotyosi.

4th June, 1879. Ityotyosi to Inshalwan hill, 2½. Inshalwan hill to Nondweni river, 3½.

On the 4th the IInd Division moved across the Ityotyosi and occupied the camping ground just vacated by Wood, whose column moved to the farther bank of the Nondweni river.

News having been received on the evening of this day that a considerable force of the enemy was a few miles in front of Wood's camp, General Marshall, with the cavalry attached to the IInd Division, started at 4.30 A.M. on the 5th June, and, proceeding by the camp of Wood's column which had not yet commenced its march, reconnoitred the track in advance as far as the valley of the Upoko* river. Here a junction was effected with a reconnoitring party from the Flying Column under Lieutenant-Colonel Buller, who had found some 300 Zulus collected near some kraals on the eastern side of the Upoko, and had obliged them to retire into some thorn bush on the lower slopes of the Ezunganyan hill. This ground, proving impracticable for mounted men, Buller's party, after having burnt the kraals, were withdrawing with a loss of two men wounded, when General Marshall's force arrived.

5th June.

Colonel Drury-Lowe now advanced with three troops of the 17th Lancers, and, on coming under the fire of the Zulus, who were in the broken ground, dismounted some of his men and opened fire in reply. In the skirmish which now ensued it seemed that little effect was produced on the enemy, who were well concealed among the long grass and bushes,† and General Marshall moved forward with a squadron of the King's Dragoon Guards to support the Lancers, who were ordered to withdraw.

These fell back steadily, but as they commenced to retire, their adjutant, Lieutenant Frith, was killed by the enemy's fire.

The two reconnoitring parties now returned to their respective columns, which during the day had occupied new camping grounds, the IInd Division marching from the Inshalwan hill to the right bank of the Nondweni river.

Three Zulu envoys had presented themselves at the outposts of Wood's camp on the evening of the 4th, and Lord Chelmsford, who had happened to be at this camp when the chiefs came in, had then had an interview with them. This interview was resumed on the evening of the 5th at the camp of the IInd Division on the Nondweni, when the conditions demanded by the British were explained, and the probability of their being accepted was discussed.

5th June.

Various communications had previously passed between the British authorities and messengers purporting to be the bearers of peaceful proposals from Ketchwayo, but most of

---

* Also called the Teneni.

† The bodies of 25 dead Zulus were found in this bush on the 3rd August by a party cutting firewood for Lieutenant-Colonel Baker Russell's column.

these messengers had been regarded as impostors, and up to this time the original ultimatum was the only definite statement of the British demands which had been announced. These envoys, however, though not of the highest rank, appeared to have been really sent by the Zulu King, and they were desired to return and inform him that before any terms of peace could be discussed the following conditions must be complied with:—1st. The restoration of the oxen at the King's kraal, and of the two 7-pr. guns captured at Isandhlwana. 2nd. That a promise should be given by Ketchwayo that all arms taken during the war should be collected and surrendered. 3rd. That one Zulu regiment, to be named by Lord Chelmsford, should come under a flag of truce and lay down its arms at a distance of 1,000 yards from the British camp.

A written statement of these conditions was given to the envoys, who were then dismissed.

On the 6th June the IInd Division remained halted on the **6th June, 1879.** Nondweni river, and wagons containing provisions for a fortnight were here unloaded in order that they might be sent back to the frontier for a further supply. For the protection of the stores here deposited, two stone forts were this day commenced, and the post was named Fort Newdigate. The ordinary arrangements for security at night were that the camp was surrounded by groups of infantry with supports in rear, small parties of natives being stationed between these groups. At 9 P.M. on the 6th June, the natives forming one of these parties thought they saw a Zulu creeping towards them, and fired three shots, which was the recognised signal that the camp was attacked. The groups of the 58th Regiment, who were on either side of this party of natives, ran in on their supports, the officer in charge of which, after ordering two volleys to be fired, instantly retired with his men into one of the unfinished forts. The tents were immediately struck, and the troops manned the wagon laager to receive the expected attack. Fearing that the piquets might be shot, General Newdigate now ordered the "close" to be sounded, and very soon afterwards the troops opened fire from all faces of the laager, and two rounds were fired by the artillery. Orders were promptly issued for this firing to cease, but, as all the outposts had not been withdrawn, two sergeants and three men received gunshot wounds. Order having been restored, the bright moonlight showed that there was no enemy near the camp, and shortly afterwards the tents were again pitched.

Leaving two companies of the 2 | 21st, two Gatlings, and a company of the Native Contingent as a garrison for Fort Newdigate, with a squadron of the King's Dragoon Guards to keep open the communications, the IInd Division moved forward on the 7th June, and encamped on the left bank of the Upoko river **7th June.** near the scene of the skirmish of the 5th.

The duty of furnishing an escort for the large convoy of empty wagons now about to return to the frontier, was entrusted to General Wood's Flying Column, which this day moved back from its advanced position to Fort Newdigate. Half the regular cavalry of the IInd Division joined the Flying Column, and during its absence on escort duty, Buller with his mounted men was attached to the IInd Division.

This remained halted on the Upoko from the 7th till the 17th June, and during this period reconnaissances were made and cattle captured, but no large numbers of Zulus were seen.

8th June, 1879. On the 8th June communications were opened with Rorke's Drift, a squadron of the King's Dragoon Guards stationed at that place arriving unmolested at the camp on the Upoko, and returning the following day.

13th June. On the 13th June the following changes in the organization of the Division were announced. On the next advance of the IInd Division, the general defence of the frontier, as well as the charge of the line of communications from the frontier up to the army, was to be undertaken by General Marshall. Colonel Collingwood was placed in command of Fort Newdigate and of a post* to be constructed about 5 miles in front of the present camp, for which a garrison was to be furnished by the four remaining companies of the 2 | 21st Regiment. The 2nd Brigade being thus broken up, the remainder of the infantry, consisting of the 1 | 24th, 58th, and 94th Regiments with Bengough's natives, were to form a brigade under Colonel Glyn.

The force of regular cavalry which was to accompany the IInd Division in its advance, was to consist of two squadrons, and the remainder were to be distributed along the line of communications, a squadron being left at each important post.

The delays which had occurred in the progress of the Zulu war, and the manifest want of harmony between the civil and military authorities in Natal, had led Her Majesty's Government, on the 28th May, to place the chief military and civil command in the eastern portion of South Africa in the hands of Lieutenant-
16th June. General Sir Garnet Wolseley; and on the 16th June a telegram announcing this appointment reached Lord Chelmsford's Headquarters on the Upoko.

17th June. On the 17th June Wood's column returned with the convoy of laden wagons, and, passing by the camp of the IInd Division, took up a position about a mile in advance.

---

* This post was named Fort Marshall.

NOTE.—The operations of the IInd Division are continued in section XIV.

XII. Operations of Brigadier-General Wood's Flying Column—16th April to 17th June.

The most important business in General Wood's command after the change of camp at Kambula on the 14th April, was the organisation of transport and the necessary preparations for the advance which was now impending. Stores were accordingly collected at Utrecht and Balte Spruit, and between these places and Kambula, convoys passed unmolested by the enemy.

Utrecht to Balte Spruit, 20.
Balte Spruit to Kambula, 25.

16th April, 1879.

On the 16th April a Frenchman named Grandier was brought into the Kambula camp, having been found in the open country almost naked. This man belonged to Weatherley's Horse, and, having been missing since the action at the Inhlobana on the 28th March, was supposed to have perished on that occasion, but from the statement which he now made, the following appear to have been the circumstances of his escape.

When Weatherley was endeavouring to take his force across the Ityenteka Nek,* through the midst of the Zulus who barred the passage, Grandier was with him, but was on foot, having put a comrade on his horse. Being thus one of the last of the party he was captured, and instead of being at once killed, like so many of his comrades, was taken to Umbelini's kraal, which was situated on a ledge on the south side of the Inhlobana. After having been examined by Umbelini, he was on the following day taken before Manyanyana, by whose orders he was on the 30th March sent to Ketchwayo. Arriving at Ulundi in charge of an escort of four men on the evening of the 3rd April, Grandier was taken before Ketchwayo at noon on the 4th, and questioned as to the name of the Commander of the British army, the object of the invasion, and the whereabouts of Uhamu.

The two guns captured at Isandhlwana were seen at Ulundi by Grandier, who was kept there as a prisoner for about ten days.

News having arrived that Umbelini had died of his wounds,† Ketchwayo determined to send his prisoner back to Umbelini's tribe to be slain by them, and Grandier was accordingly removed from Ulundi on the 13th April, escorted by two Zulus. At midday Grandier seized an assegai and killed one of them, on which the other ran away. Being now free, Grandier endeavoured to make his way out of Zululand, and shaping his course by the stars during the nights, and lying hid by day, he eventually on the morning of the 16th April fell in with a small party of mounted men who were on escort duty, and was taken to Kambula by them.‡

---

* *Vide* section VIII, p. 78.
† *Vide* section IX, p. 85.
‡ This statement made by Grandier has been much questioned. It is asserted

The supply of very indifferent fuel which the neighbourhood
21st April, 1879. Kambula to Potgieter's Farm, 30. of Kambula afforded being nearly exhausted, two companies of infantry* were sent away on the 21st April with 28 wagons to obtain coal from a seam close to the surface at Potgieter's farm, on the Pivan, or Bevan, river.

22nd April. On the 22nd April Major-General Newdigate arrived at Kambula, and after joining General Wood in a reconnaissance
24th April. to the Zungi mountain on the 23rd, started on the 24th for Dundee.

The supply of fuel being still a matter of serious difficulty,
26th April. two companies of the 80th were sent on the 26th April from Balte Spruit to the Doornberg to cut firewood, and about the same date coal was obtained from a seam which was discovered in the neighbourhood of Kambula.

29th April. On the 29th April a detachment of Royal Artillery and two companies of the 2 | 4th Regiment arrived at Utrecht, where three companies of this regiment had previously been in garrison. One of these companies was now ordered to Potgieter's farm, where a fortified post had been commenced on the 26th, and the remaining companies of the regiment were stationed at Newcastle and Luneberg.

30th April. On the 30th April Lieutenant-Colonel Buller started on a reconnaissance in the direction of Bemba's Kop, and examined the country as far as Munhla hill, without finding any traces of the enemy.

Lord Chelmsford with his Staff, and accompanied by the
3rd May. Prince Imperial, arrived at Kambula on the 3rd May, and on the
4th May. following day rode out with General Wood to view the country from the top of the Zungi mountain. On his return to Kambula the alarm was sounded, tents were struck, and all the usual preparations for defence were practised.

The plan originally entertained of an independent advance on the part of Wood's column by the Inhlazatye mountain, had been by this time relinquished, and in order to co-operate with the IInd Division when this should advance from Conference hill, a movement to the southward was made by Wood's force on
5th May. the morning of the 5th May, and the position occupied at Kambula since the 31st January was finally abandoned.

Lord Chelmsford, who started about the same time as the column moved off, proceeded this day to Conference hill, and thence the day after to Utrecht, where he established his Head-quarters.

The distance by road traversed by Wood's column on the 5th May was about 15 miles, and the camping ground reached was a spot known as Segonyamana hill, some 10 miles due south of Kambula. At this point the column was nearer its base

---

by the Dutch trader Vijn (who was at Ulundi, but did not see Grandier) that Grandier was well treated, and that it was Ketchwayo's intention to set him at liberty at the close of the war. Vijn regards the fact that he himself was left alive as conclusive that Grandier did not kill a Zulu as stated.

* One of the 1 | 13th, and one of the 90th.

than it had been at Kambula, and during the week that it remained here stores were being brought up from Balte Spruit.

On the 12th May an advance was made to Wolf hill, an 12th May, 1879. Segonyamana hill to Wolf hill, 3.
eminence overlooking the Magwechwana stream, and from the entrenched camp formed here various reconnaissances were undertaken.

In one reconnaissance which set out on the 14th May, the 14th May.
Prince Imperial accompanied Lieutenant-Colonel Buller and Lieutenant-Colonel Harrison, A.Q.M.G., and proceeded with them as far as the Ngutu mountain, whence they returned by the eastern side of Munhla hill, and reached the camp of the Flying Column on the 16th May. 16th May.

On the 18th, Buller again left camp to reconnoitre the 18th May.
country to the south-east, and reaching the Ityotyosi the same day, he examined the Nondweni valley on the 19th, and pushed 19th May.
beyond it to a point within 6 miles of the Ibabanango mountain, where a trader's wagon track, said to lead to Ulundi, was found.

In all this region the kraals were deserted, and the party returned to the Wolf hill camp on the 20th, without having been 20th May.
molested in any way.

While this reconnoitring party was out, General Wood himself headed another expedition on the 20th, and proceeding to the ground below the Inhlobana mountain, found and buried the bodies of Lieutenants Williams and Potter, who had fallen on the 28th March.

The reconnaissances having shown the practicability of the route by the Ibabanango mountain, it was decided to adopt this line for the advance on Ulundi.

While it was plain that the Transvaal frontier would thus be less secure against Zulu raids than if the original plan of moving by the valley of the White Umvolosi had been adhered to, it was considered that no serious risk was incurred, and that the inhabitants of Northern Zululand, who had shown little enterprise since the death of Umbelini, would be sufficiently restrained by the fort on the Pivan and the other posts which had been established.

On the 25th May Wood marched southwards to Munhla hill, 25th May. Wolf hill to Munhla hill, 12.
and as he had heard that Ketchwayo had ordered his troops in future only to attack the British columns when on the march, an alarm was practised this day while the troops were on the move. Two wagon enclosures were formed, about 500 yards apart, in which the draught animals were secured, and it was found that the time necessary for the completion of this work was only 35 minutes. This result was satisfactory, as, in case of an attack, longer notice than this might always be counted on.

The site of the new camp was on a ridge between the Munhla and Incanda hills, and here on the 28th May Wood's 28th May.
force was joined by five companies of the 80th, who marched in from Conference hill and the Doornberg, and on the 29th 29th May.

May by Owen's battery of four Gatlings (10 | 7 R.A.), which came up from Landman's Drift.

The Flying Column was now complete, and consisted of the 1 | 13th, 80th,* and 90th Regiments, 11 | 7 R.A. with 4 guns,† and 10 | 7 R.A. with 4 Gatlings, No. 5 Company R.E., 740 mounted men and some 700 natives, making a total of about 3,400 combatants and 650 non-combatants. Supplies for six weeks were conveyed in 260 ox wagons, of which 100 were for regimental transport.

1st June, 1879. Munhla hill to Umyamyene, 8.

The camp at Munhla hill was occupied till the 1st June, when the Flying Column, marching at 7 A.M. in a southerly direction, encamped about mid-day on the right bank of the Umyamyene river. In the afternoon General Wood rode out with Lieutenant-Colonel Buller to examine the country in front, and, as already mentioned, learnt from Lieutenant Carey the fate of the Prince Imperial.

2nd June. Umyamyene to Ityotyosi, 10.

On the 2nd June Wood continued his advance, and encamped on the left bank of the Ityotyosi, near its junction with the Tombokala.

3rd June. Ityotyosi to Inshalwan hill, 2½.

The following day was spent in crossing the Ityotyosi,‡ and an advance of only 2½ miles was made, which enabled the IInd Division to come up and encamp within about 3 miles of the Flying Column. This on the 4th June advanced to the farther side of the Nondweni river, and from here Buller's patrol started next morning for the Ezunganyan hill, as mentioned previously. While this patrol was out the Flying Column moved southwards about 6 miles, and encamped on the right bank of the Nondweni, near the Matyanhlope hill.

4th June. Inshlwana hill to Nondweni, 3½. 5th June.

6th June.

The column remained halted here on the 6th June, as orders were received that it was to furnish the escort for the empty wagons returning to the frontier to be refilled.

7th June.

On the 7th June the Flying Column retraced its steps to the camping ground on the Nondweni vacated this day by the IInd Division, and deposited the contents of most of its wagons in Fort Newdigate. The Flying Column with the empty wagons then moved across the Nondweni, and encamped on the left bank, where it was joined by 240 wagons belonging to the Commissariat Train of the IInd Division.

Two squadrons of the 17th Lancers, one squadron of the King's Dragoon Guards, and four companies of the 1 | 24th Regiment also joined the column this day from the IInd Division.

8th June.

At 4 A.M. on the 8th June the convoy moved off, and crossing the Ityotyosi about 8·30 A.M. below its junction with the Tombokala, encamped on the right bank of the latter about 2 P.M. On this day the Army Service Corps wagons and mule wagons which had accompanied the convoy were pushed on to

* 5 companies.

† The other 2 guns of this battery were with the Ist Division.

‡ The bed of this stream was soft and sandy, and was made passable by laying down grass, which bound with the sand.

Koppie Allein, being escorted by the squadron of the King's Dragoon Guards, and having two companies of the 1 | 24th carried in the wagons.

On the 9th the main body of the convoy moved from the right bank of the Tombokala, and crossing the Itelezi hill reached the left bank of the Blood river near Koppie Allein about 2·30 P.M. 9th June, 1879.

On the 10th June the ox-wagons were sent away in successive detachments of 50 each, those belonging to the Flying Column proceeding to Conference hill, and those belonging to the IInd Division to Landman's Drift, where the advanced convoy of Army Service wagons had arrived on the 9th. The 17th Lancers escorted the ox-wagons which went to Landman's Drift, and the two remaining companies of the 1 | 24th those which went to Conference hill. 10th June.

During the 11th and 12th June, the main body of the Flying Column was halted near the Blood river, and working parties were sent out to improve the track near the Itelezi hill, where, during its march on the 9th, the convoy had been much delayed. 11th June.

By the evening of the 12th, the whole of the wagons with their escorts had returned from the depôts, and the total number of loaded wagons now amounted to 660.* 12th June.

On the 13th June this convoy left the Blood river and encamped on the Itelezi ridge. 13th June.

The Tombokala was reached the following day, and by 2 P.M. on the 15th the column had re-occupied the camping ground on the left bank of the Nondweni, from which it had started on the morning of the 8th. 14th June. 15th June.

The 16th June was employed in re-adjusting the loads of the wagons, and on the 17th the column, marching about $10\frac{1}{2}$ miles, occupied a camping ground about a mile higher up the valley of the Upoko than that of the IInd Division. 16th June. 17th June.

The Flying Column thus resumed the leading position which it had previously occupied, and the troops which had been temporarily attached having rejoined their respective columns, these were now ready for a combined advance.

---

* 24 of these were mule wagons of the Army Service Corps.

NOTE.—The operations of Wood's Flying Column are continued in section XIV.

XIII. Operations of the Ist Division—18th June to 8th July, 1879.

18th June, 1879. On the 8th June Major-General Crealock, attended by his personal Staff and accompanied by Commodore Richards, R.N., left Fort Pearson and proceeded to Fort Crealock.

19th June. The Staff of the Division accompanied the 3rd section of the 1st Brigade, which, under the command of Brigadier-General Rowlands, V.C., marched next day from the Tugela to Fort Crealock.

Major-General Crealock arrived at Fort Chelmsford early on the 19th June, and rode out the same afternoon to reconnoitre the Umlalaz river some 6 miles in advance. A camping ground
20th June. and a point of crossing were chosen, and on the 20th June a column* under Major Bruce, 91st Highlanders, was sent forward in this direction. The difficulties of the track, however, caused considerable delay, and this column was obliged to encamp about a mile short of the ground which had been selected.

21st June. On the 21st June the remainder of the Division moved forward in two detachments. The leading detachment,† under Lieutenant-Colonel Parnell, 3rd Regiment, reached the selected site near the Umlalaz, where Major Bruce's advanced column had this day established itself, but the rear detachment,‡ under Lieutenant-Colonel Clarke, 57th Regiment, failed to traverse the whole distance, and halted for the night about 2 miles short of the position taken up by the leading troops.

22nd June. On the 22nd June the passage of the Umlalaz by a portion of the force was effected without opposition, a pontoon bridge being thrown across about 9 A.M. at a point where the river was 35 yards wide and 8 or 10 feet deep.

Clarke's column moved up this day, but did not arrive till the afternoon, four hours being consumed in traversing the distance which separated its halting-place from the camp.

The hill, on the right bank of the Umlalaz, where the Ist Division was now assembled received the name of "Napoleon Hill," and from this camp a convoy of empty wagons was sent
23rd June. back to Fort Chelmsford on the 23rd, escorted by the 2 | 3rd Regiment. Major-General Crealock and Commodore Richards this day accompanied a reconnaissance made by the mounted men to the eastward of Napoleon hill. The reconnoitring party approached the coast, and having ascertained that the true

---

* 91st Highlanders, 2 guns (11 | 7 R.A.), a detachment R.E., and half the 4th Battalion N.N.C.

† The Naval Brigade, with its armament of 3 9-pr. guns, 4 Gatlings, and 4 24-pr. rocket tubes, and the 2 | 3rd Regiment.

‡ 57th Regiment, 3 | 60th Rifles, M | 6 R.A., and 200 men of the 4th Battalion N.N.C.

Fort Chelmsford was at this time held by 4 companies 88th Regiment, and half the 5th Battalion N.N.C. Fort Crealock by 3 companies of the 99th.

position of Port Durnford was about five or six miles north of the mouth of the Umlalaz, instead of being at the estuary of that river as had previously been believed, returned to camp along the coast ridge.

Port Durnford itself was visited by a similar reconnoitring party on the following day, and was found to be merely an open sandy beach, where, for some reason as yet unexplained, the surf breaks with less than its usual violence. Soundings of the adjoining coast had been previously taken by Her Majesty's Ship "Forester," and this vessel was now seen at anchor at no great distance from the shore, and signals were exchanged. **24th June, 1879.**

It was considered that a landing-place near the mouth of a small stream* was practicable, and the "Forester" was ordered by the Commodore to return at once to Durban with instructions for transports which had been already detailed, to be at Port Durnford on the 29th June.

General Crealock returned with the reconnoitring party to the camp at Napoleon hill the same evening, his retreat on this occasion, as well as on the previous day, having been secured by a force† under Brigadier Clarke, which had moved in support to the left bank of the Umlalaz. No hostile force, however, was encountered, the only Zulus who were met being some old men, women, and children.

A fort to hold one company was commenced on the 25th June on the left bank of the Umlalaz. It occupied the crest of a hill covering the bridge, and this work, which was called Fort Napoleon, was occupied on the 26th. The mounted men made an expedition this day towards the Ungoya hills, supported by a force under Brigadier Clarke,‡ while a column§ under Brigadier Rowlands, V.C., moved in the direction of Port Durnford, and encamped for the night about 2 miles beyond the Umlalaz. **25th June.** **26th June.**

Messengers from Ketchwayo with proposals for peace reached General Crealock's Head-quarters this day. They carried a large elephant's tusk as a proof that their mission was genuine, and were received by Major-General Crealock in person. They were informed, however, that all communications on this subject must be made to Lord Chelmsford.‖

The main body of the Division moved forward on the 27th and reached a camping ground some 3 miles beyond the Umlalaz, the time occupied being 10½ hours. Brigadier Rowlands' advanced column marched about 4 miles this day and encamped at a spot called "Five Kraal Hill," having been joined while on the march by Major-General Crealock, the Divisional Headquarters, and the mounted men. **27th June.**

---

* This stream had been mistaken for the Umlalaz previously. Port Durnford is in Lat. 28° 55′ S., Long. 31° 52′ E.

† A battalion and 2 guns.

‡ 3 | 60th with 2 guns, and 200 natives.

§ Naval Brigade with armament, 2 | 3rd Regiment and 200 natives.

‖ The elephant's tusk was retained by Major-General Crealock, and was eventually sent home to the Secretary of State for the Colonies.

28th June, 1879. On the 28th June both columns advanced and reached a camping ground on a plain about a mile from the coast, and close to the stream which enters the sea at Port Durnford. To the southward lay the coast range of sandy hills through which this stream makes its way, and on the other three sides of the plain large marshes extended. Although the weather had been comparatively dry, the passage of the marsh which had thus to be traversed by the Division was very tedious, and it was 8 P.M. before the rear-guard got into camp.

29th June. A track leading from the camp to the landing-place was commenced on the 29th June, and on the 30th Her Majesty's
30th June. ship "Forester," with the transports "Natal" and "Tom Morton," a tug, and two surf boats,* anchored off Port Durnford.

The Naval Brigade and other troops were sent down to the beach to assist in landing the stores, and to clear a place on which the surf boats could be drawn up.

The first operation was to take ashore and make fast the ends of two strong hawsers, the other ends of which were moored some 400 yards out to sea, as the surf boats were to be warped backwards and forwards along these hawsers. This was satisfactorily accomplished, and, the weather being fine, about 18 tons of stores were landed in the course of the day.

A reconnaissance was made this day by Major-General Crealock with the mounted men and two guns, as far as the Umhlatoosi River, and a practicable route for an advance having been selected, and a number of large kraals destroyed, the party returned to Port Durnford the same afternoon.

1st July. The earlier part of the 1st July was favourable for landing stores, and about 60 tons of supplies and 30 mules were put on shore, while 2 officers and 14 men were embarked. The ammunition column and No. 1 field hospital arrived this day from the Tugela, and various detachments and drafts also marched in. These troops were accompanied by mule transport, and were but little delayed on the way.

The Division was at this time encamped by Brigades, the 1st, under Brigadier Rowlands, being nearest to the sea, and the 2nd, under Brigadier Clarke, about half a mile further inland. A fort was this day commenced between the camp of the 1st Brigade and the sea, and to this work the name of Fort Richards was given.

2nd July. The 2nd July was wet and stormy, and the surf was so heavy that communication with the vessels at the anchorage was impossible. Among these vessels was Her Majesty's ship "Shah," which, having left Durban the day before with His Excellency Sir Garnet Wolseley and his Staff, had arrived off Port Durnford at 8.30 A.M. this day.

Sir Garnet Wolseley, who had reached Durban from England

---

* Decked vessels, one of 25, the other of 30 tons. The anchorage was about 1,500 yards from the beach.

on the morning of the 28th June, had proceeded at once to Pietermaritzburg, and had been sworn in at 5 P.M. the same day. After holding an interview on the 30th June with a number of the most influential native chiefs of Natal, Sir Garnet Wolseley had returned to Durban on the 1st July, and had embarked on board the "Shah" with the object of joining the Ist Division.

During the whole of the 2nd and 3rd July the "Shah" remained at the anchorage off Port Durnford, but the surf was too high to render a landing possible, and on the 4th, as the weather showed no sign of improvement, the vessel returned to Durban with Sir Garnet Wolseley. 4th July, 1879.

The transports were also obliged to put to sea, and it seemed possible that the Division, whose supplies were now running short, might become entirely dependent on the depôt at Fort Chelmsford. The whole of the horse and mule transport available was therefore sent back this day to bring up stores from Fort Chelmsford, to which place a large convoy of empty ox wagons had also been despatched on the 3rd.

The Emangwene military kraal was burnt on the 4th July by the mounted men of the division and 200 of Dunn's scouts, the party being commanded by Major Barrow. This kraal lay some 9 miles beyond the Umhlatoosi river, and showed no signs of recent occupation. About 200 Zulus were seen a few miles beyond, and the party having captured some cattle and made a few prisoners, returned to camp the same evening without any casualty.

Since the Division had crossed the Umlalaz, many Zulu refugees had come into camp, and the number of these people, who consisted principally of women and children, now amounted to about 1,400. Their presence did not increase the healthiness of the camp, and the sick list, which had been comparatively small when the Division first occupied the Umlalaz plain, now showed a steady increase.

On the 5th July the surf moderated and some stores were landed. The destruction of the old Ondine kraal having been determined on, a supporting force* under Brigadier Clarke left camp at 3.30 P.M. this day and bivouacked at the lower drift of the Umhlatoosi, where it was joined by the mounted men under Major Barrow and by Major-General Crealock and his Staff. This party made but a short halt, and pushing on by the light of the moon, arrived at a deserted Norwegian mission station about 2 A.M. on the 6th. From this Major-General Crealock returned to the bivouack at the lower drift, and Barrow's force, starting again at 4 A.M., recrossed the Umhlatoosi by the middle drift, and reached the Ondine military kraal at 9.45 A.M. This kraal, consisting of 640 huts, was found to be unoccupied and was burnt, a few Zulus, who were discovered in the neighbourhood, being made prisoners. 5th July. Fort Richards to Umhlatoosi, 7. 6th July.

---

* A battalion of the 2nd Brigade, a Gatling, and a 9-pr. gun, Naval Brigade, and 500 natives.

After an unsuccessful attempt to discover a track leading to the St. Paul's Mission Station, the party retraced their steps, and reached the bivouack at the lower drift of the Umhlatoosi about 9 P.M. without any casualty. This bivouack was now occupied merely by the Native Contingent, as the European portion of Clarke's force had returned during the day along with Major-General Crealock.

7th July 1879. On the morning of the 7th July, Barrow's force and the Native Contingent returned to the camp near Port Durnford, where the landing of stores was this day continued, some sick officers and men being embarked. At 5 P.M. Sir Garnet Wolseley rode into camp, having left Durban on the 5th. On the night of the 7th very heavy rain fell, and this continued during the

8th July. 8th, when communication with the transports was again interrupted.

NOTE.—The operations of the Ist Division are concluded in section XV.

XIV. Combined Operations of the IInd Division and Wood's Flying Column—18th June to 8th July, 1879.

On the 18th June Major-General Marshall left the front to take up his duties on the line of communication,* and a combined forward movement of the IInd Division and the Flying Column was commenced. The latter led the way, and both moved up the valley of the Upoko and encamped near its head waters. The Flying Column crossed this stream, but the bulk of the IInd Division remained halted on its left bank. A wing of the 2 | 21st Regiment, however, was sent forward and commenced a fort close to the camp of the Flying Column. This fort, which was constructed for the purpose of covering the junction of the road from Rorke's Drift, was called Fort Marshall,† and the charge of it and of Fort Newdigate was entrusted to Colonel Collingwood, 2 | 21st Regiment. 18th June, 1879.

The march was resumed on the 19th June, and the ascent of a steep spur of the Ibabanango mountain having been accomplished, the Flying Column encamped on the left bank of the Ibabanango Spruit with the IInd Division a short distance in rear. 19th June. Fort Marshall to Ibabanango Spruit, 5.

On the 20th June the IInd Division remained halted, while the Flying Column marched about 5 miles and encamped between two branches of the Umhlatoosi river. A small number of Zulus had been seen on the 19th, and during this day's march a skirmish took place in which a few of the enemy were killed by men belonging to Baker's Horse. As a rule, however, the kraals near the line of march were deserted, but as they contained large supplies of corn, it appeared that the occupants had only recently left them. 20th June.

The Flying Column made a short march of about 3 miles on the 21st June, and crossed to the left bank of the eastern branch of the Umhlatoosi, the IInd Division coming up from the Ibabanango Spruit, and encamping opposite on the right bank. 21st June. Ibabanango to Umhlatoosi, 8.

On the 22nd June the Flying Column moved on about 4 miles, the IInd Division remaining at the Umhlatoosi. Detachments from the Flying Column,‡ and from the IInd Division§ were sent forward, and began the construction of a work called Fort Evelyn, near the ground where the Flying Column encamped on its arrival. Lieutenant-Colonel East joined Lord Chelmsford's staff this day from England as Deputy Quartermaster-General. 22nd June. Umhlatoosi to Fort Evelyn, 4.

---

* *Vide* section XI.

† The garrison of Fort Marshall consisted of 4 companies 2 | 21st Regiment, 2 7-pr. guns (N | 5 R.A.), and a squadron 17th Lancers.

‡ 2 companies 90th.

§ 2 companies 58th, 2nd company R.E., and Bengough's natives.

23rd June, 1879. The Flying Column remained halted on the 23rd, engaged in building Fort Evelyn,* and the IInd Division marched up and encamped close by.

24th June. Fort Evelyn to summit of Jackal Ridge, 4. On the 24th June the Flying Column marched to the top of the Jackal Ridge, the IInd Division following it to the base of the hill and encamping about a mile in rear. While patrolling in front of the column this day, the mounted men under Lieutenant-Colonel Buller came on and dispersed a number of Zulus who were burning the grass along the line of advance, and large bodies of the enemy were seen in and near the military kraals lying in the valley north of the ridge along which the army was to move.

25th June. An advance of about 6 miles was made by the Flying Column on the 25th June, and early in this march a stream with steep banks and a soft muddy bed had to be crossed. The latter difficulty was overcome by laying down grass mats found in the deserted Zulu kraals, but as there was only one crossing place, the passage caused much delay, and the IInd Division following in rear got no further than the eastern bank of this stream, which it took seven hours to cross.

26th June. On the 26th June the Flying Column remained halted, and the IInd Division closed up to within a mile and a half of its camp.

The advance of the British troops had now brought them within reach of some of the Zulu military kraals observed on the 24th, and while the Flying Column was halted this day, Brigadier-General Wood led a force, consisting of two squadrons 17th Lancers, Buller's mounted men, two 9-pr. guns (N | 6 R.A), and two companies of Bengough's natives, against those kraals in the 'Mpembene valley, which lay about 5 miles north of his camp. On the approach of Wood's force, these kraals were evacuated by the Zulus, who set three† of them on fire, and the remaining kraals,‡ which they had left uninjured, were burnt by the British troops, who suffered no loss in a slight skirmish which took place.

27th June. Camp to Entonjaneni, 8. On the 27th June, both columns marched to the Entonjaneni hill, where a convenient camping ground had previously been selected. A party under Lieutenant-Colonel Buller who were out this day reconnoitring the country between Entonjaneni and the White Umvolosi, met three messengers from Ketchwayo who bore two elephant's tusks, and were accompanied by a herd of about 150 cattle, which had been captured at Isandhlwana. These messengers were taken to the camp at Entonjaneni, and handed to Lord Chelmsford a letter written on behalf of Ketchwayo by a Dutch trader named Vijn, who, having been in Zululand at the outbreak of the war, had since remained among the Zulus. This letter was in reply to Lord Chelmsford's communi-

---

* The garrison of Fort Evelyn consisted of 2 companies 58th Regiment, 2 7-pr. guns (N | 5 R.A.), a detachment N.N.C., and 1 troop Natal Light Horse.

† Lixepeni, Dugaza, and Kanghla.

‡ 'Ngwekweni and Dubakani.

cation of the 5th June,* and was to the effect that the cattle sent were all that could be collected, the rest having died of lung sickness, that the arms demanded could not be surrendered, as they were not in the king's possession, that the two 7-pr. guns were on their way, and that the English troops must now retire.

The Zulu messengers returned on the following day, carrying back the elephant's tusks, and bearing a written reply from Lord Chelmsford.† In this Ketchwayo was informed that, as the conditions demanded had not been complied with, the British army would still advance, but that as some cattle had been surrendered, this advance would be delayed until the evening of the 29th, to allow time for the fulfilment of the remainder of the conditions. **28th June, 1879.**

In this note Lord Chelmsford expressed his willingness to make peace, and modified the preliminary conditions by stating that the surrender of such of the arms, captured at Isandhlwana, as were in the possession of Zulus now with the king, would be accepted; and that a body of Ketchwayo's retainers to the number of a regiment (1,000) might make submission by laying down their arms, instead of this being done by a named regiment.

During the 28th and 29th June the whole force remained halted on the Entonjaneni hill. On the afternoon of the 28th, Lord Chelmsford received a telegram‡ sent by Sir Garnet Wolseley from the Cape Colony, announcing his assumption of the command in South Africa, and requesting information as to the position of the troops and the plan of the campaign, and to this telegram a reply was despatched on the 29th. **29th June.**

Ulundi lay not more than 16 miles distant, and Lord Chelmsford decided that the troops moving on it from Entonjaneni should march lightly equipped, without kits or tents, and with rations for ten days only. These supplies were carried in ox-wagons, which were the only transport vehicles accompanying the force, except the mule carts for the regimental reserve ammunition.

The mule wagons of both columns were sent back on the 29th June to Fort Marshall to bring up more supplies, and the remainder of the ox-wagons were formed into a large defensible laager on the Entonjaneni hill, for the protection of the stores left behind.§

These arrangements were completed by the evening of the 29th, and on the 30th June both columns moved down from Entonjaneni into the valley of the White Umvolosi, and **30th June.**

---

* *Vide* section XI.

† It appears that four messengers bearing a note similar in tenor to the above had presented themselves at Fort Marshall a few days previously, but it had not been received, and this was the first document which reached Lord Chelmsford.

‡ There was telegraphic communication up to Landman's Drift, whence this was taken to the front by Captain Stewart, Brigade Major of Cavalry.

§ This post had a garrison of 2 companies, 1 | 24th Regiment, and 1 non-commissioned officer and 2 privates from each company in both columns.

Entonjaneni to Emakeni bivouack, 5.

bivouacked by a small stream, known to be the only watering place in the sandy bush-covered flat which extends from the base of the Entonjaneni heights to the banks of the Umvolosi.

During the advance a report was sent in from the front that a large force of the enemy was moving from Ulundi towards the Umvolosi, but as the Zulus did not cross the river, no collision occurred.

About mid-day two messengers from Ketchwayo were received by Lord Chelmsford. They brought the sword of the late Prince Imperial, and another letter written by the Dutchman Vijn on behalf of the king. This letter merely promised that the two 7-pr. guns and some more cattle would be sent the following morning, and the messengers were directed to return to Ulundi with another written communication from Lord Chelmsford to Ketchwayo.

By this document the conditions demanded as a preliminary to peace negociations were still further modified, as it was intimated that on the two guns and the rest of the cattle being given up, the surrender by the Induna Mundula of 1,000 rifles taken at Isandhlwana would be accepted instead of the act of submission of 1,000 men previously required.

As the water at the present camp was scarce, Lord Chelmsford stated his intention of moving on to the Umvolosi, but consented to go no further than the banks of that river before noon on the 3rd July, in order to give time for the fulfilment of the conditions demanded. Meanwhile, if the Zulus made no opposition to his advance to the river, and refrained from acts of hostility, Lord Chelmsford promised that his troops should desist from burning Zulu kraals.

On the departure of the Zulu envoys, Lord Chelmsford telegraphed to Sir Garnet Wolseley the terms which he had offered, and gave a brief sketch of the situation, adding an inquiry as to the position of the Ist Division, from which he had received no recent intelligence.

1st July, 1879.

Emakeni to White Umvolosi, 9.

Next day both columns advanced through a difficult country covered with long grass, cactus, and mimosa bush, and arrived without opposition at the White Umvolosi. About 1.30 P.M., while Wood's column, which was leading, was taking up its position near the river, a large force of the enemy was seen advancing on the opposite side of the stream, and as an immediate attack was apprehended, the IInd Division, then about a mile in rear, formed a laager on its leading wagons, instead of occupying ground beside the bivouack of the Flying Column. The Zulus, however, did not cross the river, and neither column was attacked. The IInd Division remained in the position thus taken up till the following day, when it moved forward and parked its wagons beside those of the Flying Column, so as to form one double laager. The whole of the 2nd July was employed in making this laager defensible by clearing away the bush on all sides, and in building a small stone fort on a rising ground close by.

2nd July.

This day passed without any Zulu force being seen, and no further message arriving, Ketchwayo's intentions remained unknown. A herd of white cattle* which were observed in the course of the day coming from the direction of Ulundi, appear, however, to have been sent by the king as a peace offering, but before they reached the river they were driven back by the Zulu troops, who were indignant at the prospect of these cattle being surrendered. 2nd July, 1879.

The defensive preparations at the fort and laager were continued during the 3rd July, undisturbed by the enemy. At noon this day, when the time allowed by Lord Chelmsford for the receipt of a reply expired, no answer had been received from Ketchwayo, and this silence was regarded as a rejection of the proposals which had been sent to him.† As the Zulus on the high ground on the left bank of the river constantly fired on the watering parties, negociations were regarded as at an end, and the cattle surrendered on the 27th June, having been driven back across the Umvolosi, a reconnaissance in force was undertaken at 1 P.M. by Lieutenant-Colonel Buller and the mounted men of the Flying Column. Sending a portion of his force by the ford of the wagon track, Buller with the main body crossed at another ford lower down, and moved against the southern end of the hill overlooking the river between these two fords. This hill, which had been occupied by the enemy's skirmishers, was promptly evacuated, and when Buller's party emerged from the bush bordering the left bank of the river, a number of Zulus were seen hastening over the open country in front. These were pursued to a distance of nearly 3 miles from the Umvolosi, when Buller's party suddenly came under a heavy fire from a force of about 5,000 Zulus who were concealed in the valley of the 'Mbilane stream. Numbers of the enemy also appeared on both flanks of the reconnoitring party, pushing boldly forward with the object of encircling them and cutting off their retreat. In this attempt they were unsuccessful, and Buller ultimately withdrew his party, having lost three men killed and four wounded. The retreat was covered by the mounted men who had been left on the hill mentioned above, and by two 9-prs. and some infantry which had been sent out from the camp, but which had not crossed the river. 3rd July.

By this reconnaissance information was gained as to the nature of the country between the Umvolosi and Ulundi, and as to the strength and position of the enemy's forces.

---

* The white cattle were the peculiar property of the King.

† It is stated ["Cetshwayo's Dutchman," p. 148] that the messengers who visited Lord Chelmsford on the 30th June, were falsely informed on their return to Ulundi that Vijn had gone away, and no other translator being available, it appears that the letter which they bore was never delivered to the King, but remained unopened in the possession of one of them till the 18th October following. The purport of this communication, however, had been explained to the messengers before leaving Lord Chelmsford's camp, and might have been conveyed orally to Ketchwayo in the period between the 30th June and the 3rd July.

3rd July, 1879. During the 3rd July a telegram, sent by Sir Garnet Wolseley from Durban on the 1st July, was received by Lord Chelmsford. In this Sir Garnet Wolseley acknowledged the receipt of Lord Chelmsford's memorandum of the 28th June, and ordered him, if compelled to fall back, to retire on the Ist Division viâ Kwamagwasa and St. Paul's. Sir Garnet Wolseley, as he strongly objected to the separation of the columns, further desired that measures might be taken for uniting the force with Lord Chelmsford to General Crealock's Division now at Port Durnford.*

Lord Chelmsford in reply announced the movements which he proposed to make on the following day, and reported his intention of subsequently marching by Kwamagwasa and St. Paul's.

During the night of the 3rd July the noise of the Zulus singing in Ulundi and the surrounding kraals could be plainly heard, and a night attack on the British entrenchments was anticipated, but none was made.

4th July. At 6 A.M. on the 4th July the mounted men of the Flying Column crossed the Umvolosi by the lower drift and occupied the hill commanding the upper or wagon drift. The river was here forded at 6.45 A.M. by a combined force comprising the greater part of Wood's Flying Column and the IInd Division, and having a total strength of 4,166 European and 958 native troops, with 12 guns and 2 Gatlings.

Five companies of the 1 | 24th Regiment and 1 company R.E., with detachments from other regiments and corps, was left to hold the entrenched camp. This force was commanded by Colonel Bellairs, and had a strength of 529 European and 93 native troops.

The mounted men under Buller pushed on ahead of the column, which made its way unopposed through the rough and bushy ground east of the Umvolosi, and reached the open country beyond at about 7.30 A.M.†

A hollow rectangle was now formed as shown below, the

---

* The text of this telegram was as follows :—

" *Durban, Tuesday, July 1st*, 1879.

"Your letter and enclosures of 28th June received. If compelled to fall back retire on First Division viâ Kwamagwasa and St. Paul's Mission Station, bringing with you the troops and stores from Entonjaneni post, and if possible Fort Evelyn. [If] not possible [to] bring troops and stores from Fort Evelyn; in case of falling back order its garrison to retire to Fort Marshall. Wish you to unite your force with the First Division, as I strongly object to the present plan of operations with two forces [acting] independently of each other, and without possibility of acting in concert. * * * * * * * * * *

* Am now starting, 4 P.M., and join First Division at Port Durnford by sea to-morrow. As soon as I can get things in order there I intend to force my way to St. Paul's Mission Station. Communicate news to me daily through Marshall. Send messages in the cypher which you use with Crealock by native messenger across country to First Division. I shall endeavour to communicate with you the same way. Acknowledge receipt of this message immediately by flashing to General Marshall. If you have no cypher with Crealock, send message in French."

† The order of march was as follows :—80th Regiment, 4 7-pr. (11 | 7 R.A.),

interior being occupied by the Native Contingent, the ammunition and tool carts, and the Bearer Company.* 4th July, 1879.

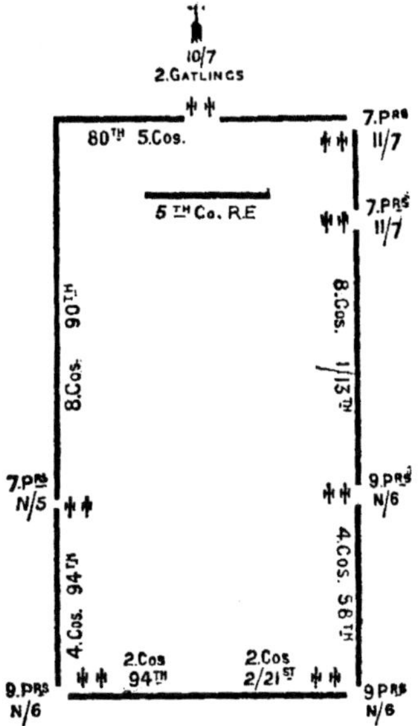

The troops in the sides of this rectangle were in fours, those in the front and rear faces being deployed, and in this formation the force moved forward shortly before 8 A.M., covered by the cavalry. The general direction of the march was towards the north-east, between the Undabakaombi and Nodwengu kraals, and was continued for about half a mile past the latter when, having reached a favourable position, previously reported on by Lieutenant-Colonel Buller, Lord Chelmsford wheeled the rectangle half-right and halted it with its front facing towards Ulundi, which lay due east, and about a mile and a half away.

8.0 A.M.

8.30 A.M.

The Zulus, who had begun to assemble on the surrounding heights soon after the British troops got clear of the bushy ground, were now seen advancing from all sides, and at about 8.45 A.M. came into collision with those mounted men of the flying column who were in front and on the right flank. These were soon forced to fall back, and by about 9 A.M. the whole of the mounted men had retired within the rectangle formed by

8.45 A.M.

9.0 A.M.

---

2 9-pr. (N | 6 R.A.), 2 Gatlings (10 | 7 R.A.), 90th and 1 | 13th Regiments, 94th and 58th Regiments, 2 7-pr. (N | 5 R.A.), 4 9-pr. (N | 6 R.A.). Bengough's natives with the 2 | 21st Regiment in rear, covered by 3 squadrons of the 17th Lancers.

* When the battle commenced, the artillery came into action in line with the infantry, maintaining the same relative positions as when on the march, except 2 guns of N | 6, which were moved up from the left rear angle to the left front angle.

4th July, 1879. the infantry, which afforded ample space for their accommodation.

When their front was clear the artillery opened fire on the advancing enemy, and the ground being almost entirely free from bush the effect of this arm was very destructive. The Zulu movements, however, were not checked, and their great circle gradually contracting to within musketry range, the firing soon became general. The casualties among the British troops, collected as they were in a dense mass on open ground, and exposed to a converging attack, must have been very serious if the enemy's fire had been at all accurate, but as it was, the loss was comparatively small. The Zulus, firing wildly, pressed forward in their usual loose order, and sought to close with the British troops, but the steady and well-sustained fire of the infantry supported by the Gatlings and artillery, rendered this impossible, and at no point did they succeed in approaching nearer than 30 yards. A large force of the enemy came up from near the Nodwengu kraal, and, having failed to make any impression on the right face of the rectangle, extended to its left with the object of outflanking the troops immediately opposed to it. Finding, however, that on all sides a similar solid line of infantry met them, the Zulus lost heart and began to falter. A want of concert in their action was perceptible, and the large reserves which were on the ground not being brought up, the check which the advanced portions received was speedily taken
9.25 A.M. advantage of. At 9.25 A.M. Lord Chelmsford ordered the 17th Lancers to engage the enemy, and Colonel Drury-Lowe, leading out his men through an opening made in the rear face of the rectangle, charged the Zulus who were near the Nodwengu kraal, and dispersed all who were on the open ground. Leaving a number of the enemy who had taken refuge in a ravine to be dealt with by the mounted natives, the Lancers pushed on after those who were now flying towards the hills, and in this pursuit the efficacy of the lance as a cavalry weapon was abundantly proved.

The mounted men of the Flying Column, under Lieutenant-Colonel Buller, issued from the front of the square after the Lancers had gone out, and pursued various scattered parties of the enemy, whose flight now became general. Comparatively little opposition was attempted after the Zulus had commenced to fall back, and the very heavy losses which they suffered in their flight were inflicted almost with impunity. The pursuit ceased at the base of the hills, and some of the enemy who remained on the crests above were soon dispersed by a few shells from the 9-prs. Shells were also thrown into the great kraal of Ulundi,* and this, as well as the other military kraals in the neighbourhood, was burnt by the mounted men.

After the wounded had been cared for, the troops of the

* Ulundi, or Ondine, was similar to the other military kraals, but of unusual size. It was elliptical in shape, the major axis being 700 yards, and the minor 550.

Flying Column and IInd Division, still in the rectangular formation, moved about a mile nearer Ulundi and halted on the banks of the 'Mbilane stream. Here the men rested and dined, and at about 2 P.M. the force started to return to the bivouack on the Umvolosi, which was reached about 4 P.M.* 4th July, 1879.

The British loss this day amounted to 12 killed and 88 wounded, and that of the Zulus, whose force is set down at 20,000, was estimated at not less than 1,500.

By this action the Zulu military power was completely broken, and a conviction was brought home to the fighting men whom Ketchwayo had assembled, that their superiority of numbers was of no avail against the weapons and discipline of British troops, even when these were on the open ground and unprotected by entrenchments.

Ketchwayo himself left the neighbourhood of Ulundi the day before the battle,† and his army, after its defeat, at once melted away, all the people returning to their own kraals.

The British troops passed the night of the 4th at the laager by the Umvolosi river, the garrison of which had not been attacked during the absence of the main body, and on the following day a movement for effecting a junction with the Ist Division was commenced, both the IInd Division and the Flying Column marching back to the camping ground, below the Entonjaneni Heights, which had been occupied on the night of the 30th June. Here the Flying Column bivouacked, the IInd Division being ordered to ascend the heights and encamp at the fortified laager above. 5th July.

The Flying Column marched up on the 6th and encamped beside the IInd Division, and the defensible laager in which the supplies had been stored was now broken up. 6th July.

Lord Chelmsford had on the evening of the 5th received a further communication from Sir Garnet Wolseley, brought by native runners sent up by General Crealock from Port Durnford, and on the 6th a reply was sent notifying the movements which were about to be undertaken.

These were the return of the IInd Division, with all the wounded, to Fort Newdigate, and a march of the Flying Column to join Sir Garnet Wolseley by way of Kwamagwasa and St. Paul's.

On the night of the 6th July a storm of bitterly cold wind and rain began, which lasted with more or less violence during the whole of the 7th and 8th, and rendered all movement for the time impossible. Both horses and oxen suffered from the severity of the weather, and the mortality, especially among the latter, was very considerable. 8th July.

News of the victory at Ulundi had reached Sir Garnet

---

* The wounded had to be carried on stretchers, and the march was consequently very slow.

† A brother of Ketchwayo was present, and this gave rise to a report that the King was a spectator of the action.

8th July, 1879.

Wolseley at Fort Pearson on the 5th July,* and his congratulations telegraphed from that place were received by Lord Chelmsford on the 8th. On the evening of the same day copies of the general orders issued by Sir Garnet Wolseley on the 28th June arrived at Entonjaneni, and Lord Chelmsford decided to resign his command and return to England as early as possible.

---

* This news was conveyed by a telegram from Mr. A. Forbes, *Daily News* correspondent. Lord Chelmsford's telegram reached Sir G. Wolseley on the 6th at Fort Chelmsford.

NOTE.—The operations of the IInd Division are concluded in section XVII, those o Wood's Flying Column in section XVI.

XV. Operations of the Ist Division—9th July to 23rd July.

The severe storm, which had lasted on the coast of Zululand as well as at Entonjaneni for about 60 hours, abated on the morning of the 9th July, and the surf having moderated, the landing of supplies at Port Durnford was recommenced this day. 9th July, 1879.

The news of Lord Chelmsford's victory on the 4th, which had reached Sir Garnet Wolseley on his way to Port Durnford, led to a modification in the programme of operations for the Ist Division. This force it was now decided should be supplied exclusively from Port Durnford,* its line of communications by Forts Chelmsford and Napoleon being abandoned.

The line, however, from the Lower Tugela to Fort Chelmsford was not to be given up, but was to be extended by Etshowe to St. Paul's, whither Sir Garnet Wolseley had, on the 8th July, ordered Lord Chelmsford to move with the IInd Division.

Wood's Flying Column, which was at the same time ordered to remain at Entonjaneni, was to draw its supplies by the old line through Fort Newdigate and Landman's Drift.

The connection between the Ist Division and the troops left in garrison at Forts Crealock and Chelmsford was thus severed, and on the 10th July orders were issued transferring these troops to the command of General Clifford, whose authority now extended over the whole of the lines of communication instead of being confined to those portions which lay within the frontiers of Natal.

On the 10th July a convoy of 50 empty wagons left Port Durnford with an escort of three companies of the 88th Regiment, one company of the 2 | 3rd Regiment, and a troop of the Natal Horse, and proceeded to Fort Napoleon. Three companies of the 88th Regiment, which had been in garrison at this post were to join the escort, their place being taken by the company of the 2 | 3rd Regiment, and the convoy, moving on to Fort Chelmsford, was there to be loaded with seven days' supplies for 5,000 men and 1,200 horses, and was directed to proceed to the Umlalaz river, north of Etshowe, and there await the arrival of the IInd Division. Colonel Rowlands, V.C., was detailed to command at Fort Chelmsford, and moved to this place on the 11th July. The Ist Division was thus reduced by two battalions (88th and 99th), two guns (8 | 7 R.A.), one troop of Lonsdale's Horse, and one troop of Natal Horse. 10th July.

Her Majesty's ship "Forester," with the transport "Natal," arrived at the anchorage on the 11th, but the heavy surf 11th July.

---

* 120 tons of supplies could be landed daily in fine weather, so it was calculated that if landing could be carried on one day in the week, the division would not want for supplies.

12th July, 1879. rendered communication impossible, both this day and the next.

13th July. On the 13th the weather moderated, and Brigadier-General Colley, Chief of the Staff, and Lieutenant-Colonel Baker Russell, 13th Hussars, were put ashore from the "Natal."

A column, consisting of about 1,600 combatants with two
14th July. Port Durnford to Umhlatoosi Drift, 7. guns,* marched on the 14th July from Port Durnford to the lower drift of the Umhlatoosi river, carrying supplies for ten days, and Sir Garnet Wolseley moved with his Staff to this
15th July. camp the same evening.

From here Sir Garnet Wolseley with his Staff, escorted by the mounted men under Major Barrow, rode on the 15th to the
Umhlatoosi Drift to St. Paul's, 29. St. Paul's Mission Station, where he found that Lord Chelmsford with Wood's Flying Column had just arrived. Sir Garnet Wolseley had, on the 12th, received a communication from Lord Chelmsford, by which he had learnt that the Flying Column was moving southwards and not the IInd Division, the orders as to the march of the latter, and the halt of the Flying Column at Entonjaneni, not having been received by Lord Chelmsford till after the movements proposed by him had been already commenced.

16th July. After inspecting the Flying Column on the 16th, Sir Garnet
17th July. Wolseley rode back on the 17th July to the camp on the Umhlatoosi, accompanied for a part of the way by Lord Chelmsford and his personal Staff.

The country which was thus traversed between the Umhlatoosi and St. Paul's, was found to be in a very peaceful condition, the people having returned and resumed their usual avocations, but it was not certain that resistance on the part of Ketchwayo and the northern chiefs was at an end, and on the
18th July. 18th July Sir Garnet Wolseley determined to re-occupy Ulundi, and from that place to dictate the terms of settlement of the country.

Notices had been sent to all the important Zulu chiefs who could be communicated with, directing them to meet Sir Garnet
19th July. Wolseley at his camp on the Umhlatoosi on the 19th July, and a large number accordingly presented themselves this day, and surrendered arms and cattle belonging to the king. These chiefs, however, all belonged to the coast tribes, and no sign of submission had as yet been made by the more warlike inhabitants of the inland districts.

The chiefs who tendered their submission this day were informed by Sir Garnet Wolseley that the war had not been waged against the Zulu people, but against Ketchwayo, who should never again rule over them, and that it was not the intention of the British Government to annex any portion of Zulu-

---

* 57th Regiment, detachment C Troop, R.E., 30th company R.E., mounted infantry, Dunn's scouts, 2 companies 4th N.N.C., 2 companies 5th N.N.C., Jantzi's natives, Mafunzi's natives, with 2 guns of 11 | 7 R.A., all under Lieutenant-Colonel Baker Russell.

land. The total abolition of the military system, and the partition of the country into a number of independent chieftainships, were also announced, as well as the proposed re-occupation of Ulundi, and the measures to be taken for compelling the submission of Ketchwayo. 19th July, 1879.

Sir Garnet Wolseley considered that for the steps which he proposed to take, no very large military force would be required, and he accordingly proceeded to reduce the number of troops who were in the field. A battalion of Marines,* sent out in response to a request for reinforcements made by Lord Chelmsford in April, had been detained at Simon's Bay by Sir Garnet Wolseley, and was now ordered to return to England, while the greater part of the Naval Brigade attached to the Ist Division was directed to embark immediately at Port Durnford. The Naval Brigade was inspected on the 21st July by Sir Garnet 21st July. Wolseley, who returned this day to Port Durnford from the camp on the Umhlatoosi, and as the weather was fine, the embarkation was completed before evening. This brigade was composed of men from Her Majesty's ships "Active" and "Shah," and was about 400 strong. It was conveyed from Port Durnford in the transport "City of Venice," in which Sir Garnet Wolseley and his Staff also embarked to return to Durban.†

On the 22nd July all the European troops of the Ist Division 22nd July. at Port Durnford were inspected by Major-General Crealock, who took leave of them on relinquishing the command of the Division. This ceased to exist after the 23rd July. 23rd July.

---

* 44 officers, and 1,082 non-commissioned officers and men Royal Marine Artillery and Royal Marine Light Infantry in Her Majesty's ship "Jumna." This force was detailed at the suggestion of Sir Garnet Wolseley before he left England.

† The landing of stores at Port Durnford was discontinued early in August. While this port was used, 2,000 tons of stores were landed, and 500 tons were shipped, besides large numbers of sick.

XVI. Operations of Wood's Flying Column—9th July to 31st July.

9th July, 1879.

On the afternoon of the 9th July, the Flying Column and the IInd Division parted company, the former making a march of about 3 miles from Entonjaneni in the direction of Kwamagwasa. At this place it was intended that a fort should be constructed, and two companies of the 94th Regiment, with two 9-pr. guns from N | 6 R.A., were detached from the IInd Division to garrison the proposed work.

10th July.

The march of the Flying Column was resumed on the 10th July, and a distance of about 9 miles was traversed. At the camp reached this day, the Flying Column was joined by Lord Chelmsford and his Staff who had left Entonjaneni about the same time as the IInd Division marched off towards Fort Newdigate.

11th July. Entonjaneni to Kwagmagwasa, 17.

On the 11th July the Flying Column moved on about 5 miles, and reached the deserted mission station of Kwamagwasa, near which the construction of a fort was at once commenced.

Before leaving Entonjaneni on the 9th, Lord Chelmsford had despatched a message to Sir Garnet Wolseley announcing the projected movements of the IInd Division and Flying Column, and it was not till his arrival at Kwamagwasa this day that Sir Garnet Wolseley's instructions as to the distribution of the troops were received.

12th July. 13th July. 14th July. 15th July. Kwagmagwasa to St. Paul's, 20.

The Flying Column remained halted at Kwamagwasa during the 12th July, and, having left here a company of Wood's Irregulars and 106 mounted men of Buller's force, in addition to the troops detached from the IInd Division, proceeded on the 13th towards St. Paul's. The distance marched this day was about 9 miles, and on the 14th an advance of some 6 miles more was made. St. Paul's Mission Station was reached on the 15th July, after a severe march of some 5 miles, and on the evening of the same day Sir Garnet Wolseley with his Staff arrived from the Umhlatoosi camp as already mentioned.

16th July. 17th July.

On the 16th July the Flying Column was inspected by Sir Garnet Wolseley,* and on the following day Lord Chelmsford, whose resignation had been accepted, started to return to Natal. Lord Chelmsford accompanied Sir Garnet Wolseley for a short distance, till their tracks separated, the latter returning to the Umhlatoosi, and the former making his way back to the frontier by Etshowe. Lord Chelmsford, who reached Durban on the 20th July, proceeded on the 21st to Pietermaritzburg, and after having been received with enthusiasm by the inhabitants, re-

* On this occasion the Victoria Cross was presented to Major Chard, R.E., for the defence of Rorke's Drift post on the 22nd January, 1879.

turned to Durban on the 26th, and embarked for Cape Town next day on his way to England.

Brigadier-General Wood and Lieutenant-Colonel Buller, who
were both returning to England on medical certificate, took
leave of the Flying Column at St. Paul's on the 18th July, and 18th July,
the command of the column devolved on Colonel Harrison, R.E. 1879.

On the 19th July the Frontier Light Horse started for Land- 19th July.
man's Drift, and Baker's Horse for Fort Tenedos, as both these
corps were about to be disbanded. Wood's Irregulars also
marched for Utrecht, being joined on the way by the company
which had been left at Kwamagwasa.

The Flying Column which now remained stationary at St.
Paul's was employed in improving the tracks and in reconnoitring the surrounding country. Its strength was reduced on
the 26th July by the departure of Raaf's Horse and the 1st 26th July.
squadron of mounted infantry, which, along with two companies
of the 90th Regiment, proceeded to Kwamagwasa with Lieutenant-Colonel Baker Russell, who was about to form a new
Flying Column to operate in the northern part of Zululand. On
this day a party of 1,000 native carriers arrived from Port Durnford with supplies, and this mode of transport was worked successfully on the stage system till the troops were withdrawn.*
Convoys of supplies also reached St. Paul's from the Tugela by
way of Etshowe, so that a considerable quantity of stores was
accumulated here, and for the protection of these stores a fort
was commenced on the 28th July. 28th July.

On the 30th July Lieutenant-Colonel Clarke's Column arrived 30th July.
from Port Durnford, and on its departure on the 1st August, the 1st August.
force at St. Paul's was still further reduced by the 80th Regiment, the Gatling battery and the Natal Pioneers being placed
under his command.

On this day the 1 | 13th Regiment, being under orders for England, started to return to Natal, accompanied by four guns of 11 | 7 R.A., so that Wood's Flying Column now ceased to exist.

---

* There were 2,000 carriers in all, of whom 500 were at St. Paul's, 500 at Port Durnford, and 1,000 at half-way station on the Umhlatoosana. From these points they worked towards each other. Compared with ox wagons on a fair road, this mode of transport was not found to be ecomonical, but it answered well for the rough and difficult country on this line.

XVII. Operations of the IInd Division—9th July to 27th July.

The IInd Division remained at Entonjaneni one day longer
10th July, 1879. than the Flying Column, and on the 10th July commenced to march back by the track followed during the advance. The distance traversed was about 7 miles, and it was found that the sick and wounded, who numbered nearly 100, bore the journey well.*

11th July. On the 11th the Division marched to Seguine Spruit, and on the 12th reached the left bank of the Umhlatoosi river. Halting
12th July. here during the 13th, the Division marched on the following
14th July. day to the Ibabanango Spruit, and on the 15th, passing Fort
15th July. Marshall, encamped about 4 miles lower down the Upoko.

The Division remained at this camp for a week, during which time the horses and oxen improved considerably in condition.†
18th July. The convoy of sick and wounded was sent away on the 18th July, escorted by two companies of the 2 | 21st, and two companies of the 1 | 24th, with 200 of Bengough's Natives as bearers.

This convoy proceeded by Fort Newdigate, where the companies of the 1 | 24th were relieved by two of the 2 | 21st, who had been in garrison at that post, and moving by the Ityotyosi and Koppie Allein, eventually reached Ladysmith, where a convalescent hospital had been established.

It had been determined by Sir Garnet Wolseley that the column which he had ordered to reoccupy Ulundi should draw its supplies from the depôt at Landman's Drift, and telegrams on the subject of the despatch of a convoy to meet this column at Entonjaneni were received by General Newdigate on the
21st July. 20th and 21st July.

22nd July. On the 22nd July the Division moved to a new camping ground, some 2 miles lower down the Upoko, where it remained till it was broken up.

While the Division was encamped on the Upoko, many officers visited Isandhlwana, where traces of the action of the 22nd January were still to be seen. Those of the 24th Regiment who had fallen here on that day had, before the end of the previous month, received burial at the hands of their comrades. Parties of the 2nd Battalion stationed at Rorke's Drift had, on the 20th, 23rd, and 26th June marched from that place to Isandhlwana, under Lieutenant-Colonel Black, and had worked at the interment of the bodies, which were scattered over a wide extent of country. These parties had not been molested by the

* About 25 had to be carried in stretchers and cots by native bearers (4 men to a stretcher, 6 to a cot), a hospital orderly accompanying each patient. A company was told off daily to strike and pitch the hospital tents.

† The horses were now getting 10lbs. of oats daily.

Zulus, and had on each occasion returned to Rorke's Drift the same day.*

The break up of the IInd Division was commenced on the 26th July, by the departure of one troop of the 17th Lancers, the 2nd Company R.E., and four companies of the 94th Regiment† for Fort Newdigate, whence they were to proceed into the valley of the White Umvolosi, and construct a work to be called Fort Cambridge. 26th July, 1879.

On the 27th July Major-General Newdigate took leave of the remaining troops of the IInd Division, whose subsequent distribution was as follows:—The 17th Lancers were ordered to Koppie Allein, and, having handed over their horses to the King's Dragoon Guards, were to proceed thence, dismounted, to Durban, for embarkation for India. Harness's battery (N | 5 R.A.) was to form part of Lieutenant-Colonel Baker Russell's Flying Column, and Le Grice's Battery‡ (N | 6 R.A.) was to move to Dundee, and eventually to form part of the force which was to be employed in the Transvaal. Of the infantry, the 2 | 21st had left previously with the sick and wounded, and the 1 | 24th was now ordered to Landman's Drift, and so to Durban for embarkation. The escort for the convoy moving up to Entonjaneni was to be furnished by the remaining battalion, the 58th, which on the completion of this duty was to find garrisons for Forts Evelyn, Marshall, Newdigate, and Koppie Allein. 27th July.

---

* All the bodies were not found till later, as many were hidden by the long grass. Several parties were subsequently employed burying remains which were afterwards discovered, and the work was finally accomplished in March, 1880, by a party of the 60th Rifles. This party was accompanied by the Rev. J. M. Ritchie, Chaplain to the Forces, who performed the funeral service at two places on the battle-field. The following is an extract from Mr. Ritchie's report to the Chief of the Staff, dated 29th March, 1880:—

"I beg to state that, in my opinion, speaking both as a clergyman and also as one who lost a very near connection and many intimate friends in the engagement, all has now been done that the most sensitive relative of any of the deceased could desire."

† 2 companies of this regiment had been detached to Kwamagwasa, and 2 had remained at Grey Town when the Division advanced in May.

‡ 2 guns belonging to this battery were at Kwamagwasa.

XVIII. Operations of Lieutenant-Colonel Clarke's Column —24th July to 12th August.

21st July, 1879.

Before leaving Port Durnford, on the 21st July, Sir Garnet Wolseley had arranged that when the Ist Division was broken up, a column, formed mainly of troops which had belonged to that Division, should move northwards from Port Durnford and reoccupy Ulundi, and that this column should be commanded by Lieutenant-Colonel Clarke, 57th Regiment.

The submission or capture of Ketchwayo was considered to be essential to a permanent settlement of Zululand, and the movement of this column was part of a general plan, of which the remaining features were as follows:—A flying column, under Lieutenant-Colonel Baker Russell, was to be assembled on the White Umvolosi, north of Fort Newdigate, and was to operate thence towards the Black Umvolosi. Uhamu* with his tribe was to advance from Luneberg, and, assisted by some Burghers, was to resume the occupation of his original district between the Black Umvolosi and the Pongola. A force of Swazies, which had previously been ordered to assemble on the Pongola, was to make a demonstration in the north, and the circle was completed by taking measures to prevent the escape of the king, if he should seek to make his way through the country of the Amatonga.

24th July. Port Durnford to Umhlatoosi, 7½.

Lieutenant-Colonel Clarke's Column commenced its march at 10 A.M., on the 24th July, and moved from Port Durnford to the left bank of the Umhlatoosi. The 57th Regiment, which had been encamped at the crossing place of this river since the 14th July, joined the column on its arrival, as well as the mounted men under Major Barrow.

25th July. Umhlatoosi Lower Drift to Empangeni stream, 5¾.

On the 25th July, Lieutenant-Colonel Clarke's Column left the Umhlatoosi lower drift, its composition being as follows:—57th Regiment, 3 | 60th Rifles, 4th Battalion N.N.C., Lonsdale's Horse, Natal Horse, and the mounted infantry. The column was accompanied by a field hospital, and a supply train of 106 wagons, which were to be filled up on arriving at St. Paul's.† The point reached by the column on the 25th July was the left bank of the Empangeni stream, and on the following day the force arrived at the Umhlatoosi middle drift, and crossing the river encamped on its right bank.

26th July. Empangeni to Umhlatoosi middle drift, 3.

27th July. Umhlatoosi middle drift to Carrier Station, 4½.

The march was continued on the 27th to the carrier station on the Umhlatoosana, and on the 28th the column advanced about 10 miles, passing near the site of the Ondine Kraal which

* Or Oham. This chief had surrendered in March, 1879 (see section VIII), and had been living since that time near Utrecht.

† This depôt was to be refilled by the Carrier Corps from Port Durnford, and by mule train from Fort Chelmsford.

had been burnt by the mounted men of the Ist Division on the 6th July.

28th July, 1879. Carrier Station to Camp near Ondine, 10.

29th July. Camp near Ondine to Idongo stream, 5½.

On the 29th July the column once more crossed the Umhlatoosi river, by the ford known as the Upper Drift, and encamped at the Idongo stream which flows at the base of the Inkwenkwe hill.

30th July.

Early on the 30th July a convoy of 56 wagons came up 'rom Etshowe and Fort Chelmsford, and as this convoy contained supplies for his column, Lieutenant-Colonel Clarke sent it forward at once up the steep hill on which the buildings of the St. Paul's Mission Station were situated. The difficulties of this ascent, however, were so great that it was 2 P.M. before the convoy was clear of the road, and 11.30 P.M. before the last wagon of Clarke's Column arrived at St. Paul's.

Idongo stream to St. Paul's, 3½.

31st July.

At this station Clarke's Column was joined by the five companies of the 80th Regiment, the Natal Pioneers, and the two Gatlings (10 | 7 R.A.) which had formed part of Wood's Flying Column, and on the 31st July, while the main body of the column remained halted at St. Paul's, these troops were sent on towards Kwamagwasa as escort to 70 wagons of supplies.

1st August. 2nd August. 3rd August. St. Paul's to Kwamagwasa, 20.

The main body followed next day, and joined the leading section at its camp about 7 miles from St. Paul's. From here both portions of the column* moved forward on the 2nd, and by the evening of the 3rd August the entire force was encamped about a mile beyond the fort at Kwamagwasa.†

4th August. 5th August. 6th August.

Two 9-pr. guns (N ¦ 6 R.A.) here joined the column, which on the 4th August proceeded to the junction of the Fort Evelyn road, by which the convoy from Landman's Drift‡ came up this day, and passed on direct to Entonjaneni. Heavy rain prevented all movement on the 5th, but on the 6th August Clarke's Column marched to Entonjaneni, and encamped beside the convoy.

7th August. Entonjaneni to Fort Victoria, 4.

On the 7th August the column descended from the Entonjaneni heights and re-occupied the camping ground where Lord Chelmsford's force had halted on its march to Ulundi, and near this spot a site was chosen for a fort, which received the name of Fort Victoria. During the afternoon Sir Garnet Wolseley arrived at this camp escorted by a squadron of the King's Dragoon Guards.

After leaving Port Durnford Sir Garnet Wolseley had proceeded by Durban to Pietermaritzburg, which he had reached on the 26th July, and where he had remained till the 30th.

---

* The total strength of the column, including drivers, leaders, &c., now amounted to 2,159 whites, and 1,257 blacks. It was accompanied by 198 wagons, 54 carts, and 6 ambulances, and had supplies for 14 days.

† This fort was at first called Fort Robertson, but was afterwards named Fort Albert.

‡ See section XVII.

From here he had ridden to Rorke's Drift, and pushing on thence by Isandhlwana and Fort Marshall to Entonjaneni, came up with Clarke's Column at Fort Victoria.

8th August, 1879. 9th August. A very severe storm of wind and rain commenced on the evening of the 7th August, and lasted throughout the two following days. During the continuance of this storm, movement was impossible, and the cold weather caused a very serious loss of oxen, of which 452 belonging to Clarke's Column perished within sixty hours.*

10th August. Sir Garnet Wolseley had announced his intention of being at Ulundi on the 10th August, and accordingly proceeded thither this day, accompanied by a squadron of mounted infantry. The weather had improved, and Clarke's Column also moved forward to the White Umvolosi, and encamped on its right bank.

11th August. On the 11th August, Clarke's Column crossed the river, and joined the Head-quarters camp at Ulundi. Neither at this nor at the other military kraals had any thing been done in the way of rebuilding, and it appeared from the reconnaissances made by the mounted men that there was no armed force of Zulus in the surrounding districts.

While Clarke's column was moving up from the White Umvolosi to Ulundi, the mounted men pushed on towards the Black Umvolosi, and reached a kraal belonging to Ketchwayo, named Mayizekanye. (Ulundi to Mayizekanye, 8.) This place, which had been supposed to be a formidable stronghold for the protection of Ketchwayo's arsenal, was found to be merely an ordinary military kraal, about 100 yards in diameter, which had been already destroyed by the Zulus. Some rockets and 7-pr. shells were found at Mayizekanye, and in a ravine about a mile short of the kraal, the two 7-pr. guns, captured by the Zulus at Isandhlwana, were discovered. An attempt had been made to render these guns serviceable by screwing ordinary gun nipples into their vents, but they were otherwise uninjured. They were now mounted on their carriages which were standing close by, and brought to Ulundi by the mounted men.

12th August. On the 12th August Mayizekanye was again visited. On this occasion the patrol, which was accompanied by Sir Garnet Wolseley, found and recovered a number of rockets and other stores, and blew up a large quantity of powder which had been collected in some caves within a short distance of the kraal.

---

* In addition to these, 195 sick oxen were left behind at Fort Victoria, with 54 wagons.

XIX. Operations of Lieutenant-Colonel Baker Russell's Column—26th July to 2nd September.

26th July, 1879.
St. Paul's to Kwamagwasa, 20.

On the 26th July Lieutenant-Colonel Baker Russell marched from the camp at St. Paul's with a force composed as follows:—Two companies 90th Regiment, the 1st Squadron Mounted Infantry, the Transvaal Rangers (Raaf), and one troop of Lonsdale's Horse*.

27th July.
28th July.
29th July.
Kwamagwasa to Jackal Ridge, 18.
1st August.

At Kwamagwasa, which was reached on the 27th, the two companies of the 90th were left, their place in the column being taken by the two companies of the 94th, which had been detached to garrison this post. Marching from Kwamagwasa on the 28th, the column arrived at the Jackal Ridge on the 29th, and, halting here on the 30th, reached Fort Evelyn on the 31st. From this the march was continued on the 1st August, the column being joined this day by two 7-pr. guns (N | 5 R.A.), which had been at Fort Evelyn.

2nd August.
3rd August.

On the 2nd August the column arrived at Fort Marshall, and on the following day, having been joined by two more 7-pr. guns (N | 5 R.A.) from this post, moved down the valley of the Upoko to the Erzunganyan hill, where parties engaged in cutting firewood discovered the bodies of 25 Zulus, who appeared to have fallen in the skirmish of the 5th June.

4th August.
Fort Newdigate to Fort Cambridge, 13.
5th August.

The column, on arriving at Fort Newdigate on the 4th August, was joined by Lieutenant-Colonel Harness and the two remaining guns of his battery, and also by some drafts for the 94th Regiment. The Head-quarters and four companies of this regiment, with the 2nd Company Royal Engineers, were at this time at a new post called Fort Cambridge, whither they had gone on the 26th July, and on the 5th August Baker Russell's Column moved on to this place.

7th August.

Here the column remained for three days, being joined on the 7th by three companies of the Native Contingent under Major Bengough.

9th August.
10th August.
Fort Cambridge to Fort George, 11.

On the 9th August† the infantry, artillery, and train moved eastwards across the White Umvolosi, while the cavalry pushed on and reconnoitred the country as far as Bethel, a deserted German mission station. On the following day the column reached the Enlongana Mission Station, and on a site adjoining this a new fort was commenced, to which the name of Fort George was given.

13th August.

Leaving the infantry, artillery, and all the wagons at this post, Lieutenant-Colonel Baker Russell started at daybreak on the 13th August with a force of about 340‡ mounted men, and

---

* This troop, about 50 strong, had escorted Lieutenant-Colonel Baker Russell from the camp on the Umhlatoosi near Port Durnford.

† The garrison left at Fort Cambridge consisted of 1 company 94th Regiment, 200 of Bengough's natives, and 12 of Lonsdale's Horse.

‡ 80 of these were natives.

13th August, 1879.

proceeded eastwards beyond the Black Umvolosi. The steep and rugged country now traversed was found to be occupied by the Zulus, who at one point seemed disposed to resist the advance of the patrol. They withdrew, however, on the approach of the advanced guard, and by the evening of the 13th the party had arrived unmolested at Rheinstorf's Mission Station.

Fort George to Rheinstorf's Mission Station, 27.

The immediate object of this expedition was to reach Umkondo, where Ketchwayo was believed to be; but it was now ascertained that 35 miles of difficult country would have still to be traversed to reach this place. During the night of the 13th the only native guide who had remained with the party deserted, and as many of the horses were greatly exhausted by the march from Fort George, Lieutenant-Colonel Baker Russell decided to go no further, but to make his way back by a different road.

14th August.

On the 14th August, therefore, the force moved westwards, and crossing the head-waters of the 'Mkusi river, bivouacked some 10 miles to the east of the sources of the Black Umvolosi.

15th August.

At daylight on the 15th the march was resumed, and Fort George was reached the same afternoon.

While this party was away many Zulus had arrived at Fort George, surrendering their arms and the cattle belonging to the king, and during the week that followed, reconnaissances made through the surrounding country secured the submission of those chiefs who were not disposed to tender it voluntarily. This was accomplished without a shot being fired, and on the completion of this duty Lieutenant-Colonel Baker Russell's Column was directed to move towards the northern district of Zululand.

25th August. 26th August. Fort Cambridge to Inseke mountain, 12. 27th August.

A garrison of two companies of the 94th and some native troops being left at Fort George, the column accordingly moved on the 25th August towards Fort Cambridge and halted on the White Umvolosi. Ascending the valley of this stream the column reached the Inseke mountain on the 26th, and remained halted here on the following day, while 200 of the mounted men pushed forward to the Zungen Nek.

29th August.

The column moved up to this place on the 28th, and on the 29th advanced to the neighbourhood of the Inhlobana mountain, which was this day patrolled by the mounted men without any hostile natives being discovered.

30th August.

At this halting place, near the Inhlobana mountain, a fort was constructed which was called Fort Piet Uys, and here the column remained during the 30th August, while a party of the mounted men patrolled the track towards the Dumbi mountain, and discovered and buried the remains of many of those who had fallen in the action of the 28th March.*

News having been received on the 30th that Ketchwayo had been captured, a party of mounted men was despatched on the

* These belonged to Weatherley's and Barton's parties.

31st to communicate with Lieutenant-Colonel Villiers, who was at this time with Uhamu's people beyond the Pongola, where he had effected a junction with the Swazies who had been assembled by Captain Macleod. 31st August, 1879.

Leaving one company of the 94th as garrison for Fort Piet Uys, Lieutenant-Colonel Baker Russell's Column marched on the 1st September to the Pivan river, and crossing this next day, entered the Transvaal and moved in the direction of Luneberg. 1st Sept. 2nd Sept.

XX. The Pursuit and Capture of Ketchwayo—13th August to 2nd September.

Consequent on the movements of Clarke's and Baker Russell's columns, a considerable number of Zulu chiefs had tendered their submission by the date of Sir Garnet Wolseley's arrival at Ulundi. There were good grounds for hoping that Ketchwayo himself was about to act in a similar manner, for the Dutchman Vijn, who has been mentioned as having acted in the capacity of secretary to Ketchwayo, had presented himself on the 10th August at the British Head-quarters established that day on the site of the King's kraal. This man had brought a verbal message from Ketchwayo to the effect that, his army being dispersed, he was collecting his cattle and was about to surrender them.

A personal surrender on the part of the king had not been touched on in this message, and Vijn had, at Sir Garnet Wolseley's request, returned on the morning of the 11th with the object of inducing Ketchwayo to submit, his safety and good treatment being guaranteed.

13th August, 1879. At noon on the 13th August, however, Vijn once more presented himself at Ulundi and reported that his mission had been unsuccessful. A party of mounted men was promptly detailed to proceed, under the guidance of Vijn, to the kraal where Ketchwayo had been the day before, and if possible to effect his capture. This party was under the command of Major Barrow, 19th Hussars, and consisted of a troop of the King's Dragoon Guards and 60 mounted infantry, with some natives, making a total of about 300.

Starting at 3 P.M. the Black Umvolosi was reached about midnight, and after halting here for about an hour the march northwards was resumed. The difficulty of keeping the force together while moving along a narrow path through bush, caused great delay in its progress during the dark hours, and

14th August. it was not till 1 P.M., on the 14th August, that the party rode up to and surrounded the kraal where Ketchwayo had been on the 12th. This kraal was now deserted, but as it was ascertained that Ketchwayo had only left it the previous afternoon, Major Barrow decided to push on in pursuit. The King's Dragoon Guards were left at this kraal, and the remainder of the party starting again shortly after 3 P.M. soon reached another kraal, where the king had slept the previous night. This too was unoccupied, but information was received from some natives here which caused the party to move on to another kraal, which was reached at sunset. Bivouacking here the search was con-

15th August. tinued on the 15th, and resulted in the discovery of an old man who was recognised by Vijn as one of the king's personal

16th August. attendants. This man was induced on the 16th to guide the party to the spot where the king had passed the night of the 14th, but here all direct traces were lost. 16th August, 1879.

This day's march brought Major Barrow and his followers back to the Black Umvolosi somewhat below the original point of crossing, and here the party divided. Only three days' provisions having been taken out, Major Barrow, with the main portion of the force, started on the 17th to return to Ulundi, 17th August. while a small detachment, under Lord Gifford, moved eastwards down the valley of the Umvolosi. As it was asserted by the natives that it was the king's intention to make his way to the rugged country, known as the Incanda forest, which lies south-west of Kwamagwasa, Lord Gifford's detachment moved southwards on the 17th across the White Umvolosi. At a kraal on the high ground, south of this river, a servant of Ketchwayo's was captured bearing a handsome express rifle, which was believed to be the king's property. Though it was ascertained that the king himself was still near the Black Umvolosi, it appeared probable that he might try to escape by the same path by which he had sent his property, and therefore while Lord Gifford returned to search the country north of the Black Umvolosi Sir Garnet Wolseley, on learning the circumstances, detailed a force of the King's Dragoon Guards to patrol the district near Kwamagwasa.

Sir Garnet Wolseley, who was encamped at Ulundi, had in the mean time received the submission of many important Zulu chiefs. Among these were Umnyamana, Ketchwayo's prime minister, and Tshingwayo, the commander of the Zulu army at Isandhlwana, both of whom reached Ulundi on the 15th August.

Ketchwayo's reported movement towards the Incanda forest led to the despatch, on the 17th August, of a party of officers under Captain Stewart, 3rd Dragoon Guards, to intercept him. This party moved in a south-easterly direction, but failed to find the king, and various other expeditions which were sent out during the latter part of August were equally unsuccessful.

Ketchwayo still remaining at large, a force of infantry consisting of the 3 | 60th Rifles and two companies of Barton's Natives, marched on the 23rd August from Ulundi and encamped on the Black Umvolosi to guard the crossing places of this river. Lieutenant-Colonel Clarke, who was in command of this force, received information from the Chief of the Staff, during the night of the 26th August, that Ketchwayo was 26th August. believed to be moving towards the 'Ngome forest, and ordered Major Marter, K.D.G., to start on a reconnaissance in this direction the following morning.

Major Marter, accompanied by an interpreter,* accordingly started on the morning of the 27th August, his force consisting 27th August. of a squadron of the King's Dragoon Guards, a company of the

* Mr. Oftebro, junr.

Native Contingent, and an officer and 10 men of mounted infantry and Lonsdale's Horse.

Moving by the 'Ndaza kraal and thence up the valley of the Ivuna river, Major Marter and his party reached the top of the Nenge mountain the same evening and bivouacked near Umgojana's kraal. Starting again at 6 A.M. on the 28th August the party arrived about 10 A.M. at a stream which flows westwards into the Ibululwana, and while halted here, a native appeared who, after speaking on indifferent subjects, remarked, "I have heard the wind blows from this side to-day," pointing towards the 'Ngome forest, "but you should take that road until you come to Nisaka's kraal."

Camp on Black Umvolosi to Umgojana's kraal, 24. 28th August, 1879.

It was known that the Zulus were extremely averse to giving direct information about the king, and Major Marter determined to act on the hint conveyed in this speech, and consequently followed the track towards Nisaka's kraal.

While on the way to this kraal, a native messenger was met carrying a note in a cleft stick, and this note was read by Major Marter. It was open, and was addressed to Captain Maurice, R.A., by Lord Gifford.

Lord Gifford who had never returned to camp since he started on the 13th, had got back to the Black Umvolosi on the 20th, on which day provisions for his party had reached him on pack mules, and up to the 26th had been searching the bushy valley of that stream and the country between it and the Umona river. Lord Gifford on the 26th being within 2 miles of Lieutenant Colonel Clarke's camp on the Black Umvolosi, had obtained from it two day's rations for his party, and starting at 10 P.M. the same night had proceeded in a north-westerly direction.

On the morning of the 28th August therefore the two parties commanded by Major Marter and Lord Gifford respectively, were at no great distance apart, but were acting independently, and the note which thus reached Major Marter contained no clue either to the actual position of Lord Gifford or to the hiding place of Ketchwayo, and the messenger was sent on to try and deliver it to Captain Maurice.*

Some information with regard to the king had been obtained by Lord Gifford on the 27th, and on the morning of the 28th his scouts had ascertained that Ketchwayo was at that time in the Kwa Dwasa kraal, some 5 or 6 miles from where his party then was. This kraal being described as closely surrounded by bush on all sides but one, Lord Gifford determined to wait till night before attempting to capture its inmates.

Major Marter meanwhile moved up to Nisaka's kraal, and on asking here for guides, without mentioning the object of the expedition, was supplied with two who conducted his party to the top of the range where the kraal of Umhlungulu, Nisaka's

---

* Captain Maurice had started from Ulundi on the 26th with a third party to visit the kraals in Umgojana's and Umyamana's districts. The note referred to never reached Captain Maurice, but was eventually returned to Lord Gifford, by whom it was destroyed.

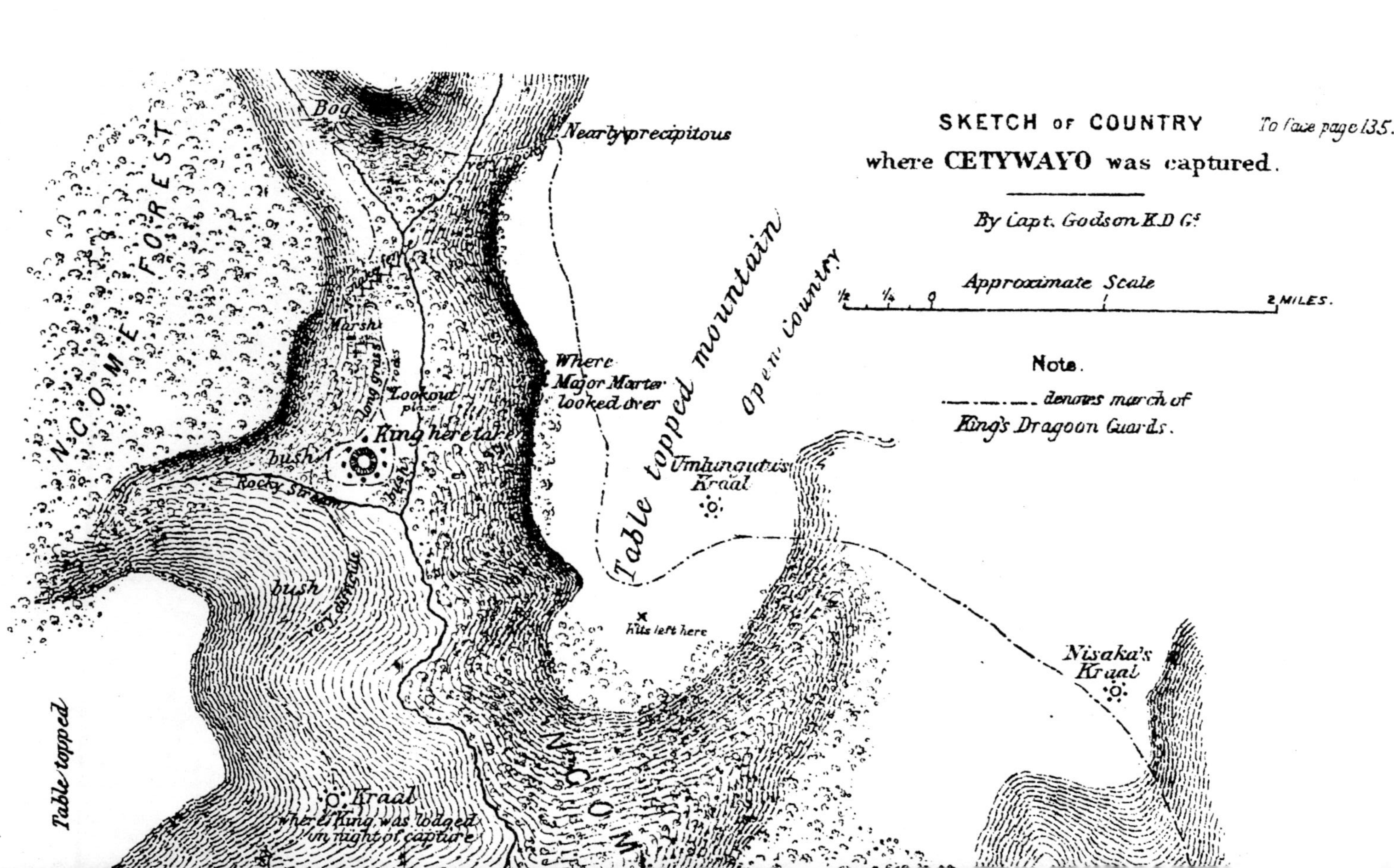

To face page 135.
SKETCH OF COUNTRY
where CETYWAYO was captured.
By Capt. Godson K.D G^s
Approximate Scale
½ ¼ 0 1 2 MILES.
Note.
— · — · — denotes march of King's Dragoon Guards.
Bog
Nearly precipitous
N COME FOREST
Marsh
Long grass
Lookout place
King here taken
bush
Rocky Stream
Where Major Marter looked over
Table topped mountain
Open country
Umhunguti's Kraal
hits left here
Nisaka's Kraal
bush
Kraal where King was lodged on night of capture
Table topped
N COM

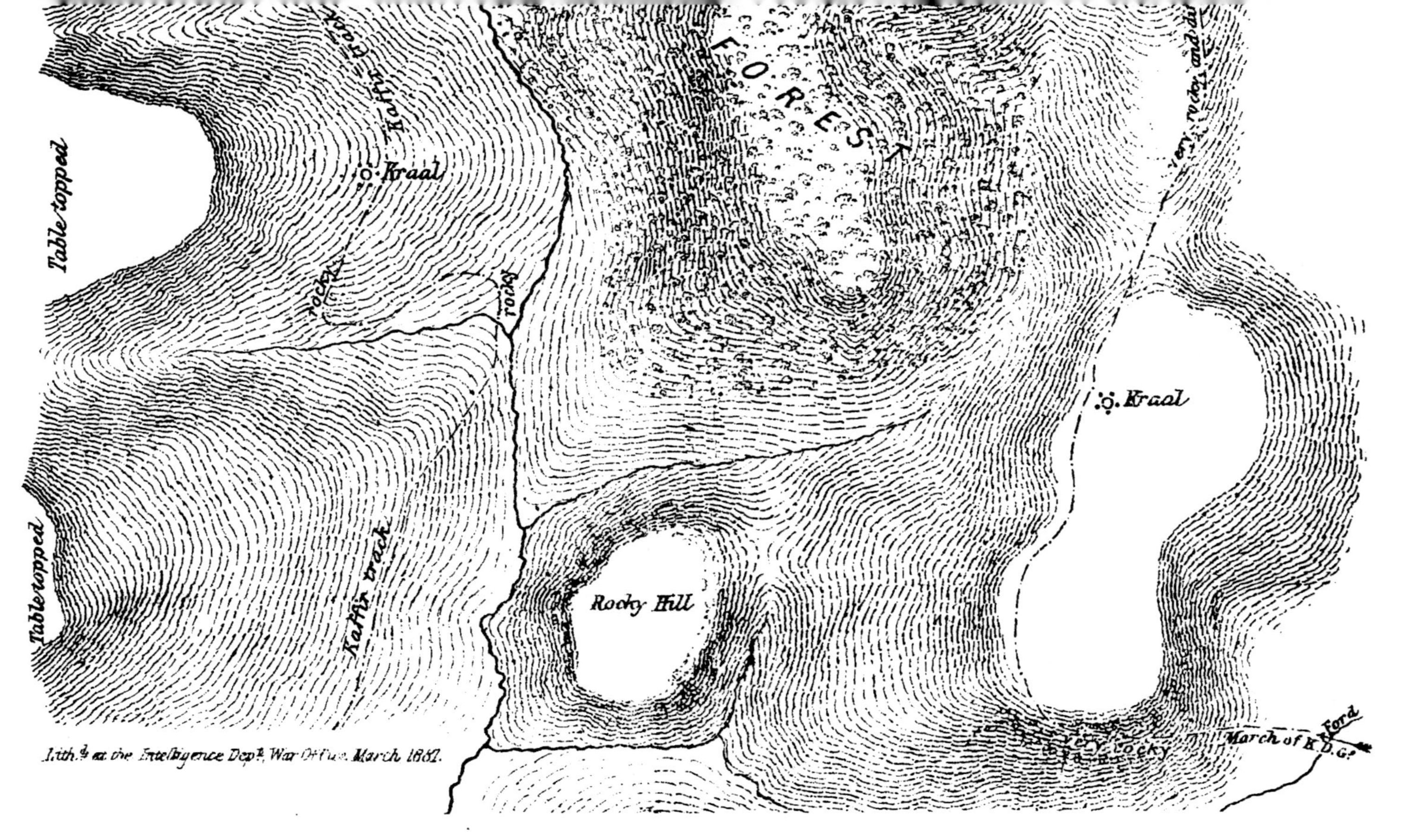
FOREST
Kaffir track
Kraal
rocky
rocky
Table topped
Table topped
Kaffir track
Rocky Hill
Kraal
very rocky
very rocky and dif
March of K.D.G.
Ford
Lith. at the Intelligence Dep. War Office, March 1881.

brother, was situated. The western side of this mountain was precipitous, and Major Marter having dismounted, was desired by the guides to approach the edge of the cliff and to look over into the valley beneath. In the bottom of the narrow valley, nearly 2,000 feet below, a small kraal could be seen, and here it was concluded that Ketchwayo would be found. 18th August, 1879.

This was in fact the Kwa Dwasa kraal which Lord Gifford had at about the same hour discovered to be the king's resting place. Major Marter, however, ignorant of Lord Gifford's intentions, decided on immediate action, and determined to make a descent on the kraal forthwith.

Mounted men, however, could not reach the bottom of the valley without making a considerable circuit, and Major Marter having made his men take off their steel scabbards and all accoutrements likely to rattle, led his squadron northwards along the top of the range till a less precipitous part of the hill side was reached. While a small detachment was left on the mountain in charge of the accoutrements, pack horses, &c., the company of the Native Contingent was directed to make its way down the steep hill side, but to remain concealed in the forest till they saw the cavalry approach from the head of the valley.

At 1·45 P.M. the men of the King's Dragoon Guards began to lead their horses down, and reached the bottom of the valley with considerable difficulty at 3 o'clock. Remounting in a hollow out of sight of the kraal, the Dragoons now galloped up to it and surrounded it, while the Native Contingent formed up across the open ground to the southward.

The occupants of the kraal, being completely surprised, made no resistance, and were all captured. They were found to consist of Ketchwayo, with the chief Umkosana, nine men and a lad, and five women and a girl. One of the men who was too infirm to travel was left behind, but all the rest were removed as prisoners. These, being on foot, moved slowly, and it was dark when the party, which had left the scene of the capture at 4 P.M., arrived at a kraal some 5 miles lower down the valley. The king and the rest of the prisoners were placed in the huts of this kraal for the night, and next morning the party again moved forward. 29th August.

At about 11 A.M. Lord Gifford was met. This officer had heard at 5 P.M. the previous day that the capture had already been effected, and had consequently remained where he was for the night. Having now obtained particulars from Major Marter, Lord Gifford started for Ulundi, and reported the capture of the king to Sir Garnet Wolseley the same evening.

Major Marter, having despatched a message to Lieutenant-Colonel Clarke, asking that a mule cart might be sent out to meet him, moved on to the 'Ndaza kraal, which was reached before dark. Shortly before arriving here, four of the king's attendants (three men and one woman) attempted to escape into the bush, through which the party were making their way in single file. The prisoners had been warned that if they attempted to escape they would be shot, and the escort, acting in obedience to orders, promptly fired on these fugitives, and killed two of the men. The other man and the woman escaped.

30th August, 1879. After passing the night of the 29th at the 'Ndaza kraal, the party moved on the 30th to Lieutenant-Colonel Clarke's camp on the Black Umvolosi, the king and some of the women being carried in the mule cart which had been sent with two companies of the 60th to the 'Ndaza kraal.

31st August. On the 31st the king and the other prisoners were taken to Sir Garnet Wolseley's camp at Ulundi, where they arrived at 10 A.M. At 2 P.M. the same day the king was sent off with his attendants to the coast by way of Kwamagwasa and St. Paul's, and being embarked at Port Durnford on the 4th September, was removed to Cape Town, and on his arrival there on the 15th September* was confined in the castle.

1st Sept. With the capture of Ketchwayo the Zulu war terminated, and all that now remained to be done was to make a political settlement of the country before it was evacuated by the British troops. It had been decided by Sir Garnet Wolseley that Zululand should in future consist of 13 separate districts, ruled by chiefs who should agree to the conditions demanded by the British, and on the afternoon of the 1st September,† a number of the principal men of Zululand attended at Ulundi, and witnessed the acceptance of these conditions by several of the selected chiefs,‡ who either personally or by deputy put their marks to the following agreement:—

I recognise the victory of British arms over the Zulu nation, and the full right and title of Her Majesty Queen Victoria, Queen of England and Empress of India, to deal as she may think fit with the Zulu chiefs and people, and with the Zulu country; and I agree, and I hereby sign my agreement, to accept from Sir Garnet Joseph Wolseley, G.C.M.G., K.C.B., as the representative of Her Majesty Queen Victoria, the chieftainship of a territory of Zululand, to be known hereafter as the , subject to the following terms, conditions, and limitations:—

TERMS, Conditions, and Limitations laid down by General Sir Garnet Joseph Wolseley, G.C.M.G., K.C.B., and assented to by me , as the terms, conditions, and limitations, subject to which I agree to accept the chieftainship of the aforesaid territory:—

1. I will observe and respect whatever boundaries shall be assigned to my territory by the British Government, through the Resident of the division in which my territory is situated.

* The "Natal," in which Ketchwayo was taken to Cape Town, remained in Simon's Bay from the 9th to the 14th September.

† This day was the anniversary of Ketchwayo's coronation at Ulundi by Sir T. Shepstone in 1873.

‡ The names of the 13 chiefs were as follows: Uhamu (Oham), Umgojana, Usibebu, Somkeli, Chingwayo, Umfanawenlela, Umgitywa, Umlandela, Seketwayo, Faku ka Ziningo, Gaozi, Hlubi, John Dunn.

2. I will not permit the existence of the Zulu military system, or the existence of any military system or organisation whatsoever within my territory; and I will proclaim and make it a rule that all men shall be allowed to marry when they choose, and as they choose, according to the good and ancient customs of my people, known and followed in the days preceding the establishment by Chaka of the system known as the military system; and I will allow and encourage all men living within my territory to go and come freely for peaceful purposes, and to work in Natal, or the Transvaal, or elsewhere, for themselves or for hire.

3. I will not import or allow to be imported into my territory, by any person upon any pretence or for any object whatsoever, any arms or ammunition from any part whatsoever, or any goods or merchandise by the sea coast of Zululand, without the express sanction of the Resident of the division in which my territory is situated; and I will not encourage or promote, or take part in or countenance in any way whatsoever the importation into any part of Zululand of arms or ammunition from any part whatsoever, or of goods or merchandise by the sea coast of Zululand, without such sanction; and I will confiscate and hand over to the Natal Government all arms and ammunition, and goods and merchandise so imported into my territory, and I will punish by fine or other sufficient punishment any person guilty of, or concerned in such unsanctioned importation, and any person found possessing arms, or ammunition, or goods, or merchandise knowingly obtained thereby.

4. I will not allow the life of any of my people to be taken for any cause, except after sentence passed in a council of the chief men of my territory, and after fair and impartial trial in my presence, and after the hearing of witnesses; and I will not tolerate the employment of witch doctors, or the practice known as "smelling out," or any practices of witchcraft.

5. The surrender of all persons fugitives in my territory from justice, when demanded by the Governmeut of any British colony, territory, or province in the interests of justice, shall be readily and promptly made to such Government; and the escape into my territory of persons accused or convicted of offences against British laws shall be prevented by all possible means, and every exertion shall be used to seize and deliver up such persons to British authority.

6. I will not make war upon any chief, or chiefs, or people without the sanction of the British Government, and in any unsettled dispute with any chief or people, I will appeal to the arbitration of the British Government, through the Resident of the division in which my territory is situated.

7. The succession to the Chieftainship of my territory shall be according to the ancient laws and customs of my people, and the nomination of each successor shall be subject to the approval of the British Government.

8. I will not sell, or in any way alienate, or permit or counte-

nance any sale or alienation of any part of the land in my territory.

9. I will permit all people now residing within my territory to there remain, upon the condition that they recognize my authority as chief, and any persons not wishing to recognize my authority as chief, and desiring to quit my territory, I will permit to quit it, and to pass unmolested elsewhere.

10. In all cases of dispute in which British subjects are involved, I will appeal to and abide by the decision of the British Resident of the division in which my territory is situated; and in all cases where accusations of offences or crimes committed in my territory are brought against British subjects, I will hold no trial and pass no sentence, except with the approval of such British Resident.

11. In all matters not included within these terms, conditions, and limitations, and in all cases unprovided for herein, and in all cases where there may be doubt or uncertainty as to the laws, rules, or stipulations applicable to matters to be dealt with, I will govern, order, and decide in accordance with ancient laws and usage of my people.

These terms, conditions, and limitations I engage, and I solemnly pledge my faith to abide by and respect in letter and in spirit, without qualification or reserve.

A British Resident* was entrusted with the general supervision of the different chiefs, and the details of the boundaries of their respective districts were arranged by a commission, consisting of three military officers† who went through the country in September and October.

2nd Sept., 1869. On the 2nd September the force assembled at Ulundi was inspected by Sir Garnet Wolseley, and the evacuation of Zululand was at once commenced. Lieutenant-Colonel Clarke, with the 57th Regiment, 3 | 60th Rifles, the Gatling battery, and the Natal Horse, started this day for St. Paul's, whence he was to make his way into Natal by Entumeni and the middle drift of the Tugela, and another column consisting of the 80th Regiment with two 9-pr. guns (N | 6 R.A.), marched off about the same time for Utrecht by the Inhlazatye mountain and Conference hill.

Sir Garnet Wolseley and his Staff remained at Ulundi till the 4th September, when he proceeded to Utrecht, where he arrived on the 9th.

The stores which had been collected in the various posts having been consumed or removed, all these posts were abandoned, and by the end of September, 1879, the last detachment of British troops had left Zululand.

---

* W. D. Wheelwright, Esq.

† Lieutenant-Colonel the Honourable G. Villiers, Grenadier Guards; Captain J. Alleyne, R.A.; and Captain H. Moore, 4th Regiment.

APPENDICES.

A. Staff of the Army, with Composition and Strength at different periods of the Campaign.

B. Table showing despatch of Reinforcements from England.

C. Return of Forces engaged, and Casualties, at the Actions of the Intyezane, Isandhlwana, Rorke's Drift, Intombi, Inhlobana, Kambula, Gingihlovo, and Ulundi.

D. Return of Local Corps called out.

E. Transport in South Africa.

F. Approximate Summary of Cost of War.

Appendix A.

COMPOSITION OF COLUMNS AND DISTRIBUTION OF TROOPS ON 11th JANUARY, 1879.

Lieutenant-General Commanding the Forces	Lord Chelmsford, K.C.B.

Personal Staff.

Assistant Military Secretary ..	Brevet Lieutenant-Colonel Crealock, 95th Foot.
Aides-de-Camp	Brevet Major Gosset, 54th Foot. Captain Buller, R.B. Lieutenant Milne, R.N.

Head-quarter Staff.

Deputy Adjutant and Quartermaster-General	Brevet Colonel Bellairs, C.B. (unattached).
Deputy Assistant Adjutant and Quartermaster-Generals	Brevet Major Spalding, 104th Foot. Brevet Major Grenfell, 60th Foot.
Officer Commanding Royal Artillery	Lieutenant-Colonel Law, R.A.
Commanding Royal Engineers..	Colonel Hassard, C.B., R.E.
Commanding Natal Mounted Police and Volunteers	Major Dartnell, N.M.P.
District Commissary-General ..	Commissary - General Strickland, C.B.
Commissary-General (Ordnance)	Deputy Commissary - General Wright.
District Paymaster	Staff Paymaster Ball.
Principal Medical Officer	Deputy Surgeon-General Woodfryes, C.B., M.D.

No. 1 Column.

Colonel Commanding	Colonel Pearson, 3rd Foot.

Staff.

Orderly Officer	Lieutenant Knight, 3rd Foot.
Principal Staff Officer	Brevet Colonel Walker, C.B., Scots Guards.
General Staff Duties..........	Captain McGregor, 29th Foot.
Transport Duties	Captain Pelly Clarke, 103rd Foot.
Senior Commissariat Officer ..	Assistant Commissary Heygate.
Sub-District Paymaster........	Paymaster Georges.
Senior Medical Officer	Surgeon-Major Tarrant.

Corps.

Royal Artillery, two 7-prs. (mule)	Lieutenant Lloyd.
Royal Engineers, No. 2 Company	Captain Wynne, R.E.
2nd Battalion 3rd Foot........	Brevet Lieutenant-Colonel Parnell, 3rd Foot.
99th Foot (6 companies)	Lieutenant-Colonel Welman.
Naval Brigade	Commander Campbell, R.N.
No. 2 Squad. Mounted Infantry	Captain Barrow, 19th Hussars.
Natal Hussars................	Captain Norton.
Durban Mounted Rifles........	Captain Shepstone.
Alexandra Mounted Rifles	Captain Arbuthnot.
Stanger Mounted Rifles	Captain Addison.
Victoria Mounted Rifles	Captain Sauer.
2nd Regiment Natal Native Contingent	Major Graves, 3rd Foot.
Staff Officer	Captain Hart, 31st Foot.
1st Battalion	Major Graves, 3rd Foot.
2nd Battalion................	Commandant Nettleton.
No. 2 Company Natal Native Pioneer Corps.	Captain Beddoes.

No. 2 Column.

Commanding	Lieutenant-Colonel Durnford, R.E.

Staff.

For General Staff Duties	Captain Barton, 7th Foot.
For Transport Duties	Lieutenant Cochrane, 32nd Foot.
Senior Medical Officer	Civil Surgeon Cartwright Reed.

Corps.

Rocket Battery (mules)	Captain Russell, R.A.
1st Battalion 1st Regiment Natal Native Contingent	Commandant Montgomery.
2nd Battalion 1st Regiment Natal Native Contingent	Major Bengough, 77th Foot.
3rd Battalion 1st Regiment Natal Native Contingent	Captain Cherry, 32nd Foot.
Sikali's Horse.	
No. 3 Company Natal Native Pioneers	Captain Allen.

No. 3 Column.

Commanding	Brevet Colonel Glyn, C.B., 24th Foot.

Staff.

Orderly Officer	Lieutenant Coghill, 24th Foot.
Principal Staff Officer	Major Clery.
For General Staff Outies	Captain Gardner, 14th Hussars.
For Transport Duties	Captain Essex, 75th Foot.
Senior Commissariat Officer....	Assistant Commissary Dunne.
Sub-District Paymaster	Paymaster Elliot (Hon. Captain).
Senior Medical Officer	Surgeon-Major Shepherd.

Corps.

N Battery 5th Brigade Royal Artillery	Brevet Lieutenant-Colonel Harness.
Royal Engineers, No. 5 Company	Captain Jones, R.E.
1st Battalion 24th Foot	Brevet Lieutenant-Colonel Pulleine, 24th Foot.
2nd Battalion 24th Foot	Lieutenant-Colonel Degacher, C.B., 24th Foot.
No. 1 Squad. Mounted Infantry	Lieutenant-Colonel (loc. r.) Russell, 12th Lancers.
Natal Mounted Police	Major Dartnell.
Natal Carabineers	Captain Shepstone.
Newcastle Mounted Rifles	Captain Bradstreet.
Buffalo Border Guard	Captain Smith.
3rd Regiment Natal Native Contingent	Commandant Lonsdale.
Staff Officer	Lieutenant Hartford, 99th Foot.
1st Battalion	Commandant Lonsdale.
2nd Battalion	Commandant Cooper.
No. 1 Company Natal Native Pioneer Corps	Captain Nolan.

No. 4 Column.

Commanding	Brevet Colonel Evelyn Wood, V.C., C.B., 90th Foot.

Staff.

Orderly Officer	Lieutenant Lysons, 90th Foot.
Principal Staff Officer	Captain Hon. R. Campbell, Coldstream Guards.
For General Staff Duties	Captain Woodgate, 4th Foot.
For Transport Duties	Captain Vaughan, Royal Artillery.
Senior Commissary Officer	Commissary Hughes.
Commissary of Ordnance......	Assistant Commissary Phillimore.
Sub-District Paymaster	Paymaster Macdonald.
Senior Medical Officer	Surgeon-Major Cuffe.

Corps.

Royal Artillery, six 7-prs.	Major Tremlett, R.A.
1st Battalion 13th Foot	Lieutenant-Colonel Gilbert, 13th Foot.
90th Foot	Brevet Lieutenant-Colonel Cherry, 90th Foot.
Frontier Light Horse	Brevet Lieutenant-Colonel Buller, C.B., 60th Foot.
Wood's Irregulars............	Commandant Henderson.

No. 5 Column.

Commanding	Colonel Rowlands, V.C., C.B., h.p., late 34th Foot.

Staff.

Principal Staff Officer	Captain Harvey, 71st Foot.
District Adjutant	Lieutenant Potts, 80th Foot.
Senior Commissariat Officer....	Assistant Commissary-General Phillips.
Commissary of Ordnance......	Commissary Wyon.
Sub-District Paymaster	Assistant Paymaster Burgers.
Senior Medical Officer	Surgeon-Major Johnson.

Corps:

80th Foot	Major Tucker.
Schutte's Corps	Captain Schutte.
Eckersley's Contingent........	Captain Eckersley.
Raaff's Corps.................	Captain Raaff.
Ferreira's Horse..............	Captain Ferreira.
Border Horse	Lieutenant-Colonel Weatherley.
Transvaal Rangers.	
Cape Mounted Rifles.	

One Krupp gun, two 6-prs., Armstrong.

LINE OF COMMUNICATIONS.

Greytown—Helpmakaar.

Commanding	Brevet Lieutenant-Colonel Hopton, 88th Foot.

Staff.

District Adjutant	Lieutenant Morehead, 24th Foot.
Commissariat Officer..........	Commissary Furse.
Commissary (Ordnance)	Commissary Moors.
District Paymaster	Paymaster Bacon.
Senior Medical Officer	Surgeon-Major Ingham.
Commanding General Depôt ..	Brevet Major Chamberlin, 24th Foot.

One company 88th Foot, Fort Napier.

Greytown and Middledrift.

Commanding	Brevet Major Black, 2nd Battalion 24th Foot.

Greytown.

One company 2nd Battalion 4th Foot.

Helpmakaar—Rorke's Drift.

Commanding	Colonel Bray, C.B., 4th Foot.

Four companies 2nd Battalion 4th Foot.

Base of Operations, Durban.

Commanding	Major Huskisson, 56th Foot.

Staff.

For General Duties .... Captain Somerset, R.B.
For Transport Duties .... Captain Spratt, 29th Foot.
Senior Commissariat Officer.... Deputy Commissary Granville.
Commissary of Ordnance...... Assistant Commissary de Ricci.
Senior Medical Officer .... Surgeon Jennings.

One company 99th Foot.

Stanger—Lower Tugela Drift—Stanger.

Commanding .... Brevet Major Walker, 99th Foot.

One company 99th Foot.

Fort Pearson.

Detachment Naval Brigade.

STRENGTH OF COLUMNS.

No. 1.

20 Staff and Departments, 23 Royal Artillery, 4 7-prs., 1 Gatling gun, 2 rocket tubes and 1 trough, 1,517 infantry, 312 cavalry, 2,256 Native Contingent, 622 conductors, drivers, and foreloopers, 3,128 oxen, 116 horses, 121 mules, 384 wagons, and 24 carts. Total, 4,750 officers and men.

No. 2.

5 Staff and Departments, 3,488 Native Contingent, 315 mounted natives, 3 rocket troughs, 63 conductors, drivers, and foreloopers, 480 oxen, 498 horses, 350 mules, and 30 wagons. Total, 3,871 officers and men.

No. 3.

20 Staff and Departments, 132 Royal Artillery, 6 7-prs., 2 rocket troughs, 1,275 infantry, 320 cavalry, 2,566 Native Contingent, 346 conductors, drivers, and foreloopers, 1,507 oxen, 49 horses, 67 mules, 220 wagons, and 82 carts. Total, 4,709 officers and men.

No. 4.

25 Staff and Departments, 108 Royal Artillery, 6 7-prs. 2 rocket troughs, 1,502 infantry, 208 cavalry, 387 Native Contingent, 48 conductors, drivers, and foreloopers, 260 oxen, 20 horses, 123 mules, 41 wagons, and 5 carts. Total, 2,278 officers and men.

No. 5.

15 Staff and Departments, 1 Krupp gun, 2 6-pr. Armstrongs, 834 infantry, 553 cavalry, 338 Native Contingent, 25 conductors, drivers, and foreloopers, 150 oxen, 10 horses, 12 mules, 17 wagons, and 2 carts. Total, 1,565 officers and men.

Transport.

756 conductors, drivers, and foreloopers, 430 oxen, 110 horses, 40 mules, 285 wagons, and 10 carts.

Grand Total.

85 Staff and Departments, 263 Royal Artillery, 20 guns, 2 rocket tubes, 8 rocket troughs, 5,128 infantry, 1,193 cavalry, 315 mounted

natives, 9,035 Native Contingent, 1,910 conductors, drivers, and fore-loopers, 10,023 oxen, 803 horses, 398 mules, 977 wagons, and 56 carts. Total, 17,929 officers and men.

State of South African Field Force, end of May, 1879.

General Commanding	Lieutenant-General Lord Chelmsford, K.C.B.
Military Secretary............	Lieutenant-Colonel J. N. Crealock, 95th Regiment.
Aides-de-Camp	Captain Molyneux, 22nd Regiment. Lieutenant Frere, Rifle Brigade. Lieutenant Milne, R.N.
Extra Aide-de-Camp..........	Prince Louis Napoleon: Prince Imperial of France.
Deputy Adjutant and Quartermaster-Generals............	Colonel Bellairs, C.B., unattached. Lieutenant-Colonel C. J. East, h.p.,* late 57th Foot.
In charge of Intelligence Department	Honourable W. Drummond.
Assistant Adjutant and Quartermaster-General	Colonel Harrison, R.E.
Deputy Assistant Adjutant and Quartermaster-Generals	Major Grenfell, 60th Rifles. Lieutenant Carey, 98th Regiment. Captain Spalding, 104th Regiment.†
Commanding Royal Artillery ..	Colonel Reilly, C.B.‡
Brigade-Major	Captain Poole, R.A.
Commanding Royal Engineers.	
Commandant at Head-quarters	Captain E. Buller, Rifle Brigade.
Provost Marshal	Lieutenant Brewster, K.D. Gds.
Deputy Commissary-General ..	Commissary - General Strickland, C.B.
Principal Medical Officer	Surgeon-General Woolfryes, C.B.
Surgeon attached to Headquarters Staff	Surgeon-Major Scott.
Chief Staff Veterinary Surgeon	Inspecting Veterinary Surgeon T. P. Gudgin.
Principal Chaplain	Rev.

1st Division.

Major-General Commanding ..	Major-General H. H. Crealock.
Aides-de-Camp	Captain Byng, h.p., late Rifle Brigade. Captain Hutton, 60th Rifles.
Assistant Adjutant and Quartermaster-Generals............	Major Walker, 99th Regiment.
Deputy Assistant Adjutant and Quartermaster-Generals	Captain Cardew, 32nd Regiment. Captain Murray, 61st Regiment.

---

* Lieutenant-Colonel East did not join the army in the field till the 22nd June.

† Employed at base.

‡ Colonel Reilly met with an accident, and did not accompany the Headquarters when the army advanced.

Commanding Royal Artillery .. Lieutenant-Colonel F. T. H. Law, R.A.
Adjutant.................... Captain Cooke, R.A.
Commanding Royal Engineers Captain R. Blood, R.E.
Assistant Commissary-General R. C. Healy.
Principal Medical Officer....... Surgeon-Major T. Tarrant.
Chaplain.

1st Brigade.

Brigadier..................... Colonel Pearson, h.p., late 3rd Buffs.
Brigade-Major .... Captain MacGregor, 29th Regiment.
Orderly Officer .... Lieutenant Knight, 3rd Buffs.
Commissary.

Corps.	Strength.	Commanding officer.
2 | 3rd Regiment	8 companies	Lieutenant-Colonel Parnell
88th Regiment	6 ,,	Lieutenant-Colonel Lambert
99th Regiment	8 ,,	Lieutenant-Colonel Welman

2nd Brigade.

Brigadier .... Lieutenant-Colonel Clarke, 57th Regiment.
Brigade-Major .... Captain Hart, 31st Regiment.
Orderly Officer .... Lieutenant Towers Clark, 57th Regiment.

Commissary.

Corps.	Strength.	Commanding officer.
57th Regiment	8 companies	Major Tredennick
3 | 60th Rifles	7 ,,	Captain Tufnell
91st Highlanders	8 ,,	Major Bruce

Divisional Troops.

Corps.	Strength.	Commanding officer.
Naval Brigade and 3 guns	795	Commander Campbell
4th Batt. N.N.C.	789	Captain Barton
5th ,, N.N.C.	1,107	Commandant Nettleton
John Dunn's Scouts	112	Mr. J. Dunn
Mounted troops	564	Major Barrow
M | 6 R.A. (6 7-prs.)	160	Major Sandham
8 | 7 R.A. (2 7-prs.)	50	Major Ellaby
11 | 7 R.A. (2 7-prs.)	25	Lieutenant Lloyd
O | 6 R.A., Amn. Col.	75	Major Duncan
30th Co. Royal Engineers	85	Captain Blood

IInd Division.

Major-General Commanding ..	Major-General Newdigate.
Aides-de-Camp	Captain Lane, Rifle Brigade. Captain Sir W. Gordon Cumming, Scots Guards. Lieutenant Taafe, 17th Lancers.
Assistant Adjutant and Quartermaster-Generals	Major Robinson, Rifle Brigade. Major Gosset, 54th Regiment.
Deputy Assistant Adjutant and Quartermaster-General	Lieutenant-Colonel Montgomery, Scots Guards.
Commanding Royal Artillery ..	Lieutenant-Colonel Tatton Brown, R.A.
Adjutant..................	Captain J. Alleyne, R.A.
Commanding Royal Engineers..	Captain Anstey, R.E.*
Assistant Commissary-General.	
Principal Medical Officer	Surgeon-Major A. Semple.
Chaplain.	

1st Brigade.

Brigadier	Colonel Glyn, 24th Regiment.
Brigade-Major	Major Dalrymple, 88th Regiment.
Orderly Officer	Lieutenant Phipps, 1 | 24th Regt.
Commissary.	

Corps.	Strength.	Commanding officer.
2 | 21st Regiment.............	6 companies	Major Hazlerigg
58th Regiment	6 „	Major Whitehead

2nd Brigade.

Brigadier....................	Colonel Collingwood, 21st Regiment.
Brigade-Major	Captain Montague, 94th Regiment.
Orderly Officer	Captain Gordon, 2 | 21st Regiment.
Commissary.	

Corps.	Strength.	Commanding officer.
1 | 24th Regiment	7 companies	Major Tongue
94th Regiment...............	6 „	Lieutenant-Colonel Malthus

* Captain Anstey did not join the Division till the 4th June.

Divisional Troops.

Corps.	Strength.	Commanding officer.
N | 5 R.A. (6 7-prs.)	150	Lieutenant-Colonel Harness
N | 6 R.A. (6 9-prs.)	150	Major Le Grice
O | 6 R.A., Amn. Col............	68	Captain Alexander
2nd Company R.E.*............	55	Captain Courtney
Mounted troops†	210	
2nd Battalion N.N.C.	900	Major Bengough.
A.S. Corps	150	
A.M.D.	46	

The Cavalry Brigade.

(Attached to the IInd Division.)

Major-General Commanding .. Major-General Marshall.
Brigade-Major .... Captain H. Stewart, 3rd Dragoon Guards.
Aide-de-Camp .... Captain Viscount Downe, 2nd Life Guards.
Extra Aide-de-Camp .... Captain Heneage, R.E.

Regiment.	Officers and men.	Horses.	Commanding officer.
1st Dragoon Guards......	634	545	Colonel H. Alexander
17th Lancers...........	613	583	Colonel Drury-Lowe
Natives attached	108	110	

Brigadier-General Wood's Flying Column.

Brigadier-General Commanding Colonel Evelyn Wood, V.C., C.B.
Orderly Officer .... Lieutenant Lysons, 90th Regiment.
Principal Staff Officer .... Major Clery, h.p., 32nd Regiment.
For General Staff Duties ...... Captain Woodgate, 4th Regiment.
Commanding Royal Artillery .. Major E. Tremlett, R.A.
Adjutant.
Commanding Royal Engineers.. Major Moysey, R.E.
Commanding Mounted Troops.. Lieutenant-Colonel Buller.
Staff Officer .... Lord W. Beresford.
Orderly Officer .... Captain Prior, 80th Regiment.
Assistant Commissary-General.. Commissary E. Hughes.
Principal Medical Officer ...... Surgeon-Major Cuffe.
Chaplain.................... Rev. C. J. Coar.

* This company had formed part of the garrison of Etshowe.
† Bettington's Natal Horse and Shepstone's Basutos.

Corps.	Strength.	Commanding officer.
1 | 13th Regiment	617	Major England
80th Regiment	373	Major Tucker
90th Regiment	654	Major Rogers, V.C.
11 | 7 R.A. (4 7-prs.)	81	Major Tremlett
10 | 7 R.A. Gatlings............	64	Major Owen
5th Company R.E.	82	Captain Jones
Mounted Infantry..............	95	Captain Browne, 1 | 24th Regt.
Frontier Light Horse	209	Commandant D'Arcy
Transvaal Rangers..............	77	Commandant Raaf
Baker's Horse	202	Commandant Baker
Natal Native Horse	117	Captain Cochrane, 32nd Regiment
Natal Native Pioneers	104	Captain J. Nolan
Natal Light Horse..............	84	Commandant Whalley
Wood's Irregulars..............	485	Commandant L. White

Lines of Communication and Base.

ESTABLISHMENT of Staff, &c., about the end of May, 1879, previous to advance into Zululand.

		Station.
Inspector-General	Major-General Hon. H. Clifford, V.C., C.B., in command of the base, of the lines of communication between it and all the forces operating in Zululand, and o 1the troops, Imperial and Colonial, in the Colony of Natal	Pietermaritzburg
Aide-de-Camp	Lieutenant R. F. Westmacott, 77th Regiment	Pietermaritzburg
Assistant to Inspector-General	Captain W. R. Fox, R.A., Deputy Assistant Adjutant and Quartermaster-General	Pietermaritzburg

Staff Officers of Lines of Communication and Base.

Base and lines of communication from it to Lower Tugela and to Pietermaritzburg	Major Butler, C.B., h. p., late 67th Regiment, Assistant Quartermaster-General	Durban
Supernumerary Staff Officer at the base	Captain Brunker, 26th Regiment, special service	Durban
Senior Medical Officer at base	Surgeon-Major Wills	Durban
Senior Commissariat Officer at base	Deputy Commissary - General Morris	Durban
Senior Ordnance Store Officer at base	Commissary March	Durban
Railway Staff Officer........	Lieutenant-Colonel Tyrrell, C.E., late Madras Staff Corps	Durban
Commandant Remount Establishment	Major J. C. Russell, 12th Lancers	Pietermaritzburg
Principal Veterinary Surgeon	Inspecting Veterinary Surgeon T. P. Gudgin	Pietermaritzburg
Principal Medical Officer	Deputy Surgeon-General Holloway	Pietermaritzburg
Staff Paymaster............	Major W. C. Ball..............	Pietermaritzburg
Senior Commissariat Officer of Supplies	Deputy Commissary - General Palmer	Pietermaritzburg
Director of Transport	Commissary Elmes	Pietermaritzburg
Senior Ordnance Store Officer	Deputy Commissary - General Wright	Pietermaritzburg

Garrisons and Posts on the Line of Communication.

Garrisons, &c.	Corps.	Strength.	Commandants.	Staff Officers to Commandants.
Durban	58th Regiment Indian Corps	1 company 1 company	Major Huskisson, 56th Regiment	Capt. Kell, h.p.
Stanger	Various	About ½ company	Major Walker, 99th Regiment Capt. Jeffreys, 88th Regiment	None.
Lower Tugela Forts	Various	About 3 or 4 companies and Naval Brigade	Col. Walker, C.B., Scots Guards	None.
Pietermaritzburg	2 | 21st Regiment and General Depôt	2 companies Variable	Major Chamberlin, 2 | 24th Regiment	Lieut. Sutherland, 2 | 4th Regiment.
Greytown	94th Regiment	2 companies	Major Twentyman, 2 | 4th Regiment	None.
Krantz Kop, near Middle Drift, and various outposts	Natal Native Contingent	2 battalions		
Dundee	2 | 24th Regiment	4 companies	Lieut.-Col. Degacher	None.
Helpmakaar and Rorke's Drift	2 | 24th Regiment	4 companies	Major Black, 2 | 24th Regiment	None.
Ladysmith	58th Regiment	1 company	Capt. Somerset, R.B.	Lieut. Jopp, 58th Regiment.
Utrecht	2 | 4th Regiment	4 companies	Col. Bray, C.B., 2 | 4th Regiment	Major Middleton, 2 | 4th Regiment.
Newcastle		1 company		
Balte Spruit		1 company		
Luneberg		1 company		
Conference hill	King's Dragoon Guards 2 | 4th Regiment	2 squadrons 1 company	Col. Davies, Grenadier Guards	Capt. Hon. S. Cotton, Scots Guards.

Distribution of the Troops and Staff in South Africa, 26th July, 1879.

Commanding	His Excellency General Sir Garnet J. Wolseley, G.C.M.G., K.C.B.

Personal Staff.

Military Secretary...........	Brevet Lieutenant-Colonel Henry Brackenbury, R.A.
Aides-de-Camp	Brevet Major H. McCalmont, 7th Hussars. Captain E. L. Braithwaite, 71st H.L.I. Captain E. F. Lord Gifford, V.C., 57th Foot. Lieutenant A. G. Creagh, R.A.

General Staff.

Chief of the Staff	Brigadier-General G. Pomeroy Colley, C.B., C.M.G.
Orderly Officer...............	Lieutenant Hardy, Rifle Brigade.
Deputy Adjutant-General......	Brevet Colonel Bellairs, h.p., C.B., unattached.
Deputy Quartermaster-General .	Lieutenant-Colonel East, h.p., late 57th Regiment.
Deputy Assistant Adjutant and Quartermaster-General for Intelligence Duties	Captain Maurice, R.A.
Commanding Royal Artillery ..	Colonel Reilly, C.B., R.A.
Commanding Royal Engineers..	Lieutenant-Colonel Steward, R.E.
Commissary-General	Commissary-General Strickland, C.B.
Commissary-General Ordnance .	Deputy Commissary - General Wright.
Paymaster	Staff-Paymaster Morris (Hon. Major).
Principal Medical Officer......	Surgeon-General Woolfryes, C.B., M.D.
Principal Chaplain............	Reverend C. J. Coar, M.A.
Inspecting Veterinary Surgeon.	Inspecting Veterinary Surgeon T. P. Gudgin.

Lines of Communication and Base.

Inspector-General	Major-General the Hon. H. H. Clifford, V.C., C.B.
Aide-de-Camp	Lieutenant Westmacott, 77th Foot.
Assistant Adjutant and Quartermaster Generals	Major Butler, C.B., Durban. Major Webber, R.E., Landman's Drift. Lieutenant-Colonel Hale, R.E., Port Durnford.

Deputy Assistant Adjutant and Quartermaster-Generals	Captain W. R. Fox, R.A., with Inspector-General. Brevet Major Hon. H. J. L. Wood, 12th Lancers, Baker Russell's Column. Captain Yeatman Biggs, R.A., St. Paul's. Captain Patterson, 16th Foot, Port Durban.
Specially Employed	Brevet-Colonel Walker, C.B., Scots Guards, Fort Pearson. Captain Stewart, 3rd Dragoon Guards, Clarke's Column.
Commandant Remount Establishment	Major J. Russell, 12th Lancers.

Clarke's Column.

Commanding	Lieutenant-Colonel Clarke, 57th Foot.
Orderly Officer	Lieutenant Towers Clark, 57th Foot.
Principal Staff Officer.........	Captain Hart, 31st Foot.
Staff Officer..................	Lieutenant Harford, 99th Foot.
Commanding Mounted Troops..	Major (Local) Barrow, 19th Hussars.
Orderly Officer	Captain Hon. W. Elliott, 93rd Foot.
Senior Commissariat Officer....	Commissary Reeves.
Senior Medical Officer	Surgeon-Major Giraud, M.D.
Royal Artillery—Gatling Battery, and one Division N | 6	Major J. F. Owen, R.A.
Royal Engineers—1 Officer and 20 men	Captain Blood, R.E.
Imperial Infantry—57th Regt.	Major Tredennick.
" 3|60th Regt.	Major Tuffnell.
" 80th Regt. 5 Companies	Major Tucker.
2nd Squadron Mounted Infantry	Major Barrow.

COLONIAL TROOPS.

European.

1st Troop Natal Horse	Captain de Burgh.
Lonsdale's Horse, 2 Troops	Captain Lumley.

Native.

Jantzi's Horse................	Captain C. D. Hay.
Mafunzi's Horse..............	Captain Nourse.
Natal Native Contingent, 4th Battalion	Captain Barton, 7th Foot.
Native Pioneers	

Baker Russell's Column.

Commanding	Lieutenant-Colonel Baker Russell, C.B., 13th Hussars.
Orderly Officer	Captain Bushman, 9th Lancers.
Staff Officer	Captain Woodgate, 4th Foot.
Attached for Duty............	Captain Hon. R. A. J. Talbot, 1st Life Guards.
Commanding Mounted Troops..	
Senior Commissariat Officer....	Deputy Commissary Coates.
Senior Medical Officer	Surgeon-Major Cuffe.

Imperial Troops.

Cavalry, 1 squadron King's Dragoon Guards	
Royal Artillery, N | 5 Battery..	Lieutenant-Colonel Harness, R.A.
Royal Engineers, 2nd Company.	
94th Regiment	Lieutenant-Colonel Malthus.
1st Squadron Mounted Infantry.	Captain Browne, 1 | 24th Regiment.

COLONIAL CORPS.

European.

Lonsdale's Horse, 1 Troop	
Frontier Light Horse...........	Captain D'Arcy.
Transvaal Rangers............	Commandant Raaf.
Natal Mounted Police	Captain Mansell.

Native.

2nd Battalion Natal Native Contingent	Major Bengough, 77th Regiment.
Mounted Natives	

APPENDIX B.

THE ZULU WAR.—DESPATCH OF TROOPS TO NATAL AFTER RECEIPT OF INTELLIGENCE OF THE AFFAIR AT ISANDHLWANA.

(Fully armed and equipped, and provided with Camp Equipment.)

Regiment.	Officers.	Men.	Horses.	Wagons and other carriages.	Ship.	Port of embarkation of troops.	Date of embarkation.	Date on which left St. Vincent.	Date on which left Table Bay.	Date on which left Simon's Bay.	Date of disembarkation at Natal.	
From the United Kingdom:—												
Staff.. { Major-General Hon. H. H. Clifford, C.B., V.C. ...... Major-General Newdigate .. Brigade-Major .. Aide-de-Camp ..	4	..	5	..	Spain	Southampton..	27th Feb. ..	16th March	5th April ..	..	9th April	Major-General Clifford changed to "England" at Cape Town
Major-General Crealock, C.B. Brigade-Major .. Aide-de-Camp .. Major W. F. Butler, C.B. ..	4	..	4	..	Egypt..........	Southampton..	28th Feb. ..	16th March	1st April ..	5th April	9th April	
Major-General Marshall .... Brigade-Major .. Aide-de-Camp ..	3	..	6	..	England........	Southampton..	26th Feb. ..	12th March	2nd April ..	..	6th April	
Colonel Reilly, C.B. (Commanding Royal Artillery).. Brigade-Major ..	2	..	..	..	Russia	Portsmouth ..	26th Feb. ..	11th March	..	31st March ..	4th April	
1st Dragoon Guards { Head-qrs. ½ ..	14	311	270	..	Egypt..........	Southampton..	28th Feb. ..	16th March	1st April ..	5th April	9th April	
½	13	311	267	..	Spain	Southampton..	27th Feb. ..	16th March	5th April ..	..	9th April	
17th Lancers ...... { Head-qrs. ½ ..	15	302	263	..	England........	Southampton..	26th Feb. ..	12th March	2nd April ..	..	6th April	
½	13	292	264	..	France	Victoria Docks, London	24th Feb. ..	14th March	..	7th April	Arrived 11th April	
M. Battery, 6th Brigade, R.A. ...... (6 7-pr. guns)	5	168	92	16	Manora	Victoria Docks	21st Feb. ..	3rd March	..	18th March ..	22nd March	"Manora" also took out four Gatling guns with carriages and ammunition
N. Battery, 6th Brigade, R.A. ...... (6 9-pr. guns)	5	168	132	16	Olympus	Southampton..	24th Feb. ..	7th March	..	27th March ..	31st March	
Ammunition Column	5	162	..	19	Andean	Woolwich	11th March..	22nd March	..	10th April		
Royal Engineers, 30th Company......	6	196	46	6	Palmyra........	Portsmouth ..	27th Feb. ..	9th March	..	1st April	5th April	
Right Half C Troop, Royal Engineers..	5	172	109	13	Borussia........	Portsmouth ..	1st April ..	12th April*				
21st Foot, 2nd Battalion	25	906	7	..	City of Paris....	Queenstown ..	21st Feb. ..	5th March	..	{ 26th March in H.M.S. Tamar	} 31st March......	"City of Paris" ran aground entering Simon's Bay on 23rd March. Troops transferred to H.M.S. "Tamar"
58th "	30	903	5	..	Russia	Portsmouth ..	26th Feb. ..	11th March	..	31st March ..	4th April	
60th " 3rd Battn. { 6 companies	21	690	5	..	Dublin Castle ..	Gravesend	19th Feb. ..	26th Feb.*..	16th March	..	20th March	
2 "	9	209	..	..	Danube	Southampton..	27th Feb. ..	5th March*	27th March	..	1st April	
91st "	23	899	3	..	Pretoria........	Southampton..	19th Feb. ..	25th Feb.*..	13th March	..	17th March	
94th "	28	897	5	..	China..........	Southampton..	26th Feb. ..	9th March	..	29th March ..	2nd April	
Army Service Corps .... { (Nos. 3, 4, and 5 Companies)	6 and 4 conductors	198	150	28	City of Venice ..	Kingstown....	25th Feb. ..	7th March	25th March	..	30th March	
	4 and 2 conductors	217	230	140	Queen Margaret	Victoria Docks	22nd Feb. ..	7th March	22nd March	..	29th March	
Army Hospital Corps {	1	50	..	..	Palmyra........	Portsmouth ..	27th Feb. ..	9th March	..	1st April	5th April	
	1	20	..	..	Florence........	South-west	20th Feb. ..	6th March	2nd April ..	..	Arrived 6th April	

Army Medical Department	[illegible]	..	..	..	Distributed amongst vessels.							
Civilian Surgeons	7	..	..	..								
Veterinary Department	9	..	..	..								
Ordnance Store Department	4	..	..	..								
Commissariat and Transport Department	5	..	..	..								
Miscellaneous	36	22	..	..								
57th Foot	6	150	..	..	China	Southampton	26th Feb.	9th March	..	29th March	2nd April	
24th „ 1st Battalion	15	526	3	..	Clyde	Woolwich	1st March	13th March	..	7th April in H.M.S. Tamar	11th April	"Clyde" wrecked on Dyer's Island, about 70 miles from Simon's Bay, on 3rd April. Troops taken on in H.M.S. "Tamar."
N. Batt., 5th Brigade, R.A.	1	20	..	..	Manora	Victoria Docks	21st Feb.	3rd March	..	18th March	22nd March	
	1	68	..	..	Andean	Woolwich	11th March	22nd March	..	10th April		
11th „ 7th „ „	2	20	..	..	Olympus	Southampton	24th Feb.	7th March	..	27th March	31st March	
Army Service Corps (Ordnance Branch)	1	32	..	..	Manora	Victoria Docks	21st Feb.	3rd March	..	18th March	22nd March	
90th Foot	..	50	..	..	Nyanza	Southampton	10th April					
Drafts: 3rd „ 2nd Battalion	2	88	..	..	H.M.S. Orontes	Portsmouth	1st May					
13th „ 1st „	1	57	..	..		Queenstown	5th May	Arrived 13th May	..	31st May	4th June	
21st „ 2nd „	1	43	..	..								
24th „	2	51	..	..								
57th „	2	117	..	..								
58th „	1	45	..	..								
60th „ 3rd Battalion	2	100	..	..								
80th „	2	151	..	..								
88th „	2	116	..	..								
90th „	1	32	..	..								
91st „	1	49	..	..								
Total from United Kingdom	387	8,895	1,866	238								
From Ceylon:— 57th Regiment	21	788	2	..	H.M.S. Tamar	Ceylon	22nd Feb.	..	..	..	11th March	
From St. Helena:— No. 8 Battery, 7 Brigade, R.A.	3	52	..	..	H.M.S. Shah	St. Helena	12th Feb.	..	..	..	6th March	
88th Foot, 1 Company	2	109	..	..								
From Mauritius:— No. 10 Battery, 7th Brigade, R.A. (3 7-pr. guns)	2	52	..	..	Umvoti	Mauritius	12th March	..	..	..	26th March	
* 88th Foot, 1 Company	3	100	..	..								
Total from Colonies	31	1,101	2	..								
General total	418	9,996	1,868	238								

* Madeira.

Appendix C.

Action of the Inyezane, 22nd January, 1879.

Colonel C. K. Pearson, Commanding.

Staff.

Brevet Colonel Walker, C.B., Scots Guards.
Captain Macgregor, 29th Regiment.
Lieutenant Knight, 3rd Regiment.

Corps or Detachment.	Officers.	N.C.O. and men.	Officer in command.
Royal Artillery, 11 | 7 (2 7-prs.)..	1	22	Lieutenant Lloyd
Royal Engineers (No. 2 Company)	4	85	Captain Wynne
2nd Battn. 3rd Regiment (5 cos.)	11	400	Lieutenant-Colonel Parnell
99th Regiment (2 companies)	5	160	Lieutenant-Colonel Welman
Naval Brigade (2 7-prs., 1 Gatling, 1 rocket tube)	6	128	Commander Campbell, R.N.
No. 2 Squadron Mounted Infantry	5	115	Major Barrow
Natal Hussars..................	2	37	
Stanger Mounted Rifles	2	35	
Victoria Mounted Rifles	2	45	
2nd Regiment Natal Native Contingent	..	..	Major Graves. Capt. Hart, Staff Officer
1st Battalion	28	800	Major Graves
2nd Battalion......	27	800	Commandant Nettleton
No. 2 Company Natal Native Pioneers	2	60	Captain Beddoes
Total	95	2,687	

Casualties.

Corps or Department.	Killed.		Wounded.		Remarks.
	Officers.	N.C.O. and men.	Officers.	N.C.O. and men.	
2nd Batt. 3rd Regt.	..	2	..	5	Of these 1 man died of his wounds
Naval Brigade	..	..	..	7	Col. Pearson and Col. Parnell both had their horses shot under them
Mounted Infantry	..	..	..	2	
Native Contingent ..	Lt. J. L. Raines Lt. J. Platterer	6	Lt. H. Webb	1	
	2	8	1	15	

Isandhlwana, 22nd January, 1879.

Lieutenant-Colonel Durnford, R.E., Commanding.

Staff.

Lieutenant Cochrane, 32nd Regiment.
Captain G. Shepstone, Political Assistant.

Corps or Department.	Officers.	N.C.O. and men.	Officer in command.
Staff: Centre Column	3	9	
Royal Artillery, 2 7-pr. guns (N | 5)	2	70	Major Stuart Smith
Royal Artillery, 2 rocket tubes ..	1	9	Major Russell
Royal Engineers................	1	4	Lieut. McDowel
1st Battn. 24th Regt., 5 companies	16	403	Brevet Lieut.-Col. Pulleine
2nd Battn. 24th Regt., 1 company	5	178	Lieut. Pope
Army Service Corps	..	3	
Army Hospital Corps	1	10	
Army Medical Department	1	1	
Mounted Infantry..............	..	30	
Natal Mounted Police	..	33	
Natal Carbineers	2	27	Lieut. Scott
Newcastle Mounted Rifles	2	15	Captain Bradstreet
Buffalo Border Guard	1	8	Captain Smith
Sikali's Horse, 5 troops..........	5	257	
1st Battn. 1st Regt. Natal Native Contingent	6	240	
1st Battn. 3rd Regt. Natal Native Contingent	10	200	
2nd Battn. 3rd Regt. Natal Native Contingent	10	200	
No. 1 Company Natal Native Pioneer Corps	1	10	Captain Nolan
Total	67	1,707	

Casualties—Killed.

Corps or Department.	Officers.	N.C.O. and men.	Remarks.
Staff	Lt.-Col. Durnford	9	Including 1 civilian servant and 1 signalman, R.N.
	Capt. G. Shepstone		
Royal Artillery, N | 5....	Bt. Major Stuart Smith	61	
„ rocket batty.	Bt. Major Russell	6	
Royal Engineers	Lt. McDowel	4	
1st Battn. 24th Regiment	Lt.-Col. Pulleine	400	
	Capt. Degacher		
	Capt. Mostyn		
	Capt. Wardell		
	Capt. Younghusband		
	Lieut. and Adjt. Melvill		
	Lieut. Porteous		
Carried forward ..	12	480	

Casualties—Killed.

Corps or Department.	Officers.	N.C.O. and men.	Remarks.
Brought forward ..	12	480	
1st Battn. 24th Regiment	Lieut. Cavaye		
	Lieut. Anstey		
	Lieut. Coghill		
	Lieut. Daly		
	Lieut. Hodson		
	Lieut. Atkinson		
	2nd Lieut. Dyson		
	Paymaster White		
	Quartermaster Pullen		
2nd Battn. 24th Regiment	Lieut. Pope	178	
	Lieut. Austen		
	Lieut. Dyer		
	Sub.-Lieut. Griffiths		
	Quartermast. Bloomfield		
Army Service Corps	Nil	3	
Army Hospital Corps	Lieut. of Orderlies Hall	10	
Army Medical Department	Surg.-Major Shepherd..	1	Including 1 civilian servant
Mounted Infantry	Nil	13	Including 2 civilian servants
Natal Mounted Police....	Nil	26	
Natal Carbineers	Lieut. Scott	20	
	Quartermaster London		
Newcastle Mounted Rifles	Capt. Bradstreet	5	
	Quartermast. Hitchcock		
Buffalo Border Guard ..	Nil	3	
Sikali's Horse	Lieut. Roberts	—	
1st Batt. 1st Regt. N.N.C.	Lieut. Black	10	Europeans.
	Lieut. Lister		
1st Batt. 3rd Regt. N.N.C.	Capt. Krohn	29	Europeans
	Capt. Lonsdale		
	Lieut. Avery		
	Lieut. Halcraft		
	Lieut. Jamieson		
	Acting Surgeon Bull		
	Quartermast. McCormick		
	Interpreter Grant		
2nd Batt. 3rd Regt. N.N.C.	Capt. Erskine	28	Europeans.
	Capt. Barry		
	Capt. Murray		
	Lieut. Pritchard		
	Lieut. Young		
	Lieut. Gibson		
	Lt. the Hon. S. Vereker		
	Lieut. Rivers		
	Quartermast. Chambers		
Total	52	806	

The number of natives killed amounted to 471, including non-combatants.

RORKE'S DRIFT, 22ND JANUARY, 1879.

Lieutenant Chard, R.E., Commanding.

Regiment or Department.	Officers.	N.C.O. and men.	Remarks.
Staff	..	1	
Royal Artillery	..	4	3 of these were sick
Royal Engineers	1	1	
3rd Buffs	..	1	
1st Battn. 24th Regiment	..	11	5 of these were sick
2nd Battn. 24th Regiment	1	98	17 ditto (Lieut. Bromhead in command)
90th Regiment	..	1	Sick
Commissariat Department	3	1	
Army Medical Department	1	3	
Chaplain's Department	1		
Natal Mounted Police	..	3	Sick
Natal Native Contingent	1	6	6 men sick
Ferryman	..	1	
Total	8	131	

Casualties.

Regiment or Department.	Killed.		Wounded.		Remarks.
	Officers.	N.C.O. and men.	Officers.	N.C.O. and men.	
1 | 24th Regiment	..	3	..	2	1 man died of wounds
2 | 24th Regiment	..	8	..	5	1 man died of wounds
Commissariat Department	..	1	Mr. Dalton		
Natal Native Police	..	1			
Natal Native Contingent	..	2	..	2	
Total	..	15	1	9	

INTOMBI, 12TH MARCH, 1879.

Captain Moriarty, 80th Regiment, Commanding.
80th Regiment—1 company; 106 of all ranks.

Casualties.

Corps or Department.	Killed.		Wounded.		Remarks.
	Officers.	N.C.O. and men.	Officers.	N.C.O. and men.	
80th Regiment	Capt. Moriarty Civil Surgeon Cobbin	60	..	1	2 European conductors and 15 native drivers also perished
Total	2	60	..	1	

INHLOBANA, 28TH MARCH, 1879.

Brevet Colonel E. Wood, V.C., C.B., Commanding.

Staff.

Captain Hon. R. Campbell, Chief Staff Officer.
Lieutenant Lysons, Orderly Officer.
Mr. Lloyd, Political Assistant.

Lieutenant-Colonel Buller's Party—Captain Gardner, Staff Officer.

Corps or Department.	Officers and men.	Officer in command.
Royal Artillery, Rocket Party	7	Major Tremlett
Dutch Burghers	32	Mr. Piet Uys
Frontier Light Horse	156	Capt. Barton
Transvaal Rangers	71	Commandant Raaf
Border Horse	53	Commandant Weatherley
Baker's Horse	79	Lieut. Wilson
nd Battalion Wood's Irregulars	277	Major Leet, 13th Regt.
Total	675	

Lieutenant-Colonel Russell's party.

Corps or Department.	Officers and men.	Officer in command.
Royal Artillery, Rocket Party	10	Lieut. Bigge, R.A.
Mounted Infantry	80	Capt. Browne, 24th Regt.
Basutos	70	Capt. Cochrane, 32nd Regt.
Kaffrarian Rifles	40	Commandant Schermbrucker
1st Battalion Wood's Irregulars	240	Commandant Loraine White
Uhamu's People	200	Lieut. Williams, 58th Regt.
Total	640	

Inhlobana—Casualties.

Corps or Department.	Killed.		Wounded.		Remarks.
	Officers.	N.C.O. and men.	Officers.	N.C.O. and men.	
Frontier Light Horse	Capt. Barton, Coldstream Gds. Lt. Von Stietencron Lieut. Williams	26	Capt. Brusseau	2	
Burgher Force..	Mr. Piet Uys				
Transvaal Rangers	Capt. P. R. Hamilton	6	..	2	
Border Horse ..	Lt.-Col. Weatherley Adjt. Lys Lieut. Poole Sub.-Lt. Weatherley Sub.-Lt. Parminter	39	..	1	Trooper Grandier, who afterwards rejoined, is not included
Baker's Horse ..	..	8	..	1	
Staff	Captain Hon. R. Campbell Mr. Lloyd				
Wood's Irregulars	Capt. Potter* .... Lieut. Dunscombe	..	..	..	*Missing Number killed uncertain
Mounted Infantry	..	..	..	1	
Uhamu's People	Lt. Williams, 58th	..	..	..	Number killed uncertain, probably about 80
Total....	15	79	1	7	

Captain Barton's remains were identified and buried on the 28th May, 1880, by a small party sent from the Ityotyosi River by Major-General Sir E. Wood, V.C., K.C.B., who had returned to South Africa in attendance on the Empress Eugènie. It appears that Captain Barton descended safely to the open country north of the Inhlobana mountain and was endeavouring to make his way back towards Kambula, but that having taken a dismounted man up behind him he was overtaken near the Manzana River by some Zulus on horseback, who were pursuing him and the other fugitives from the Ityenteka Nek. On finding escape impossible, it seems that Captain Barton and his companion dismounted and separated. The latter being unarmed was killed almost immediately, and the Zulus then turned on Captain Barton, whose only weapon was a revolver, which was out of order, and missed fire three times. Being thus defenceless and unable to keep his enemies at a distance, he soon fell shot from behind, and was then assegaied by the Zulu who fourteen months afterwards guided the party to the spot where his remains were found undisturbed.

Kambula, 29th March, 1879.

Brevet Colonel E. Wood, V.C., C.B., Commanding.

Staff.

Captain Maude, 90th Regiment.
Captain Woodgate, 4th Regiment.
Lieutenant Lysons, 90th Regiment.

Corps or Department.	Officers and men.	Officer in command.
Royal Artillery	110	Major Tremlett
Royal Engineers	11	
1 | 13th Regiment	527	Lieut.-Colonel Gilbert
90th Regiment	711	Major Rogers
Mounted Infantry	99	The whole of the mounted troops acted together under the orders of Lieut.-Colonel Buller
Frontier Light Horse	165	
Transvaal Rangers	135	
Baker's Horse	99	
Kaffrarian Rifles	40	
Dutch Burghers	41	
Border Horse	16	
Mounted Basutos	74	
Wood's Irregulars	58	Major Leet
Total	2,086	Including 88 sick in hospital

Casualties.

Corps or Department.	Killed.		Wounded.		Remarks.
	Officers.	N.C.O. and men.	Officers.	N.C.O. and men.	
Royal Artillery	..	..	Lieut. Nicholson*	1*	* Died of wounds
1 | 13th Regiment	..	6	Capt. Cox Capt. Persse	19	2 of these died of their wounds
90th Regiment	..	8	Major Hackett Lieut. Smith Lieut. Bright*	26 ..	5 of these died of their wounds * Died of wounds
Frontier Light Horse	..	2	..	2	
Mounted Infantry	..	1	Capt. Gardner	4	
Transvaal Rangers	..	..	Lieut. White*	1	* Died of wounds
Baker's Horse	..	..	..	1	
Kaffrarian Rifles	..	..	..	1	
Dutch Burghers	..	..	..	1	
Mounted Basutos	..	..	..	1	
Contractor's Agent (civilian)	..	1			
Total	..	18	8	57	

GINGINHLOVO, 2ND APRIL, 1879.

Lieutenant-General Lord Chelmsford, K.C.B., Commanding.

Staff.

Military Secretary	Lieutenant-Colonel J. N. Crealock, 95th Regiment.
Aides-de-Camp	Captain W. C. F. Molyneux, 22nd Regiment. Lieutenant A. Milne, R.N.
Senior Medical Officer	Surgeon-Major Tarrant.
Senior Commissariat Officer....	Assistant Commissary Walton.
Intelligence Department	Hon. W. Drummond. Mr. J. Dunn.

Corps or Department.	Officers and men.	Officer in command.
1st Brigade. Lieut.-Col. Law, R.A., Commanding Staff: Capt. Hart, 31st Regt.		
Naval Brigade	350	
91st Highlanders	850	Major Bruce
The Buffs (2 companies).............	140	Major Walker, 99th Regt.
99th Regiment (5 companies)	430	
4th Battalion N.N.C.	800	Capt. Barton, 7th Regt.
Artillery :— 2 9-pr. guns 2 24-pr. rocket tubes 1 Gatling gun		
Commissariat Department		
Transport Department		
Medical Department		

Total 1st Brigade: British troops and Naval Brigade, 1.770; Native Contingent, 800. Grand total, 2,570.

Corps or Department.	Officers and men.	Officer in command.
2nd Brigade. Lieut.-Col. Pemberton, 60th Rifles, Commanding Staff: Capt. Buller, Rifle Brigade		
Naval Brigade	190	
Royal Marines	100	
57th Foot	640	Lieut.-Col. Clarke
60th Rifles (6 companies)	540	Lieut.-Col. Northey
5th Battalion N.N.C.	1,200	Commandt. Nettleton
Artillery, Commissariat, Transport		
Medical Department		
2 24-pr. rocket tubes		
1 Gatling gun		

Total 2nd Brigade: British troops, including Naval Brigade and Marines, 1,470: Natal Native Contingent, 1,200. Grand total, 2,670.

Corps or Department.	Officers and men.	Officer in command.
Divisional Troops.		
Major Barrow, 19th Hussars, Commanding.		
Staff: Captain Courtenay, 20th Hussars.		
Mounted Infantry	70	
Volunteers	50	
Mounted Natives	130	
Non-commissioned Officers........	30	
Native Foot Scouts	150	

Total: British troops and Volunteers and N.C.O's., 150; Mounted natives, 130; Foot scouts, 150. Grand total, 430.

Grand Total of Fighting Men engaged at Ginginhlovo, 2nd April, 1879.

1st Brigade	2,570	Including 800 natives
2nd Brigade	2,670	" 1,200 "
Divisional Troops................	430	" 280 "
Grand total	5,670	Including 2,280 natives

Casualties—Ginginhlovo.

Corps or Department.	Killed.		Wounded.		Remarks.
	Officers.	N.C.O. and men.	Officers.	N.C.O. and men.	
Staff............	..	..	Lt.-Col. Crealock		
2 | 3rd Regiment	..	..	..	1	
57th Regiment ..	..	..	Capt. Hinxman	3	
3 | 60th Rifles ..	..	1	Lt.-Col. Northey* ..	5	* Died of wounds
91st Regiment ..	..	1	..	8	
99th Regiment ..	..	2	Lt. J. C. J. Johnson*	4	* Died of wounds
Mounted Infantry	..	..	Major Barrow......	2	
Royal Navy	..	..	Sen. Surg. Longfield	6	
Native Contingent	..	5	..	17	2 of these died of wounds
Total	..	9	6	46	

Ulundi, 4th July, 1879.

Liieutenant-General Lord Chelmsford, K.C.B., Commanding.

Staff.

Military Secretary............	Lieutenant-Colonel J. N. Crealock, 95th Regiment.
Aides-de-Camp	Captain Molyneux, 22nd Regiment. Lieutenant Milne, R.N.
Deputy Quartermaster-General	Lieutenant-Colonel East, h.p., late 57th Regiment.
In charge of Intelligence Department	Hon. W. Drummond.
Commanding R.A.	Lieutenant-Colonel Tatton Brown, R.A.
Commanding R.E.	

Corps or Department.	Officers.	N.C.O. and men.	Horses.	Officer in command.
IInd Division.				
Major-Gen. Newdigate, Commanding.				
Staff:				
Captain Lane, A.D.C.....	6	37	12	
Capt. Sir W. Gordon-Cumming				
Major Robinson, A.A.G.				
Major Gosset, 54th Regt., A.Q.M.G.				
Lieut.-Col. Montgomery, D.A.Q.M.G.				
1st Dragoon Guards	2	24	26	Col. Drury-Lowe
17th Lancers	21	239	285	
Royal Artillery	12	249	140	(8 guns). Lt.-Col. Harness
Royal Engineers				
Infantry Brigade.				
Lieut.-Colonel Glyn, Commanding.				
Staff:				
Major Dalrymple, 88th, Brigade-Major	3	11		
Lieut. Liebenrood, 58th Regt.				
Lieut. Phipps, 24th Regt.				
2 | 21st Regiment	11	205	6	Major Hazlerigg
58th Regiment..........	19	407	8	Lt.-Col. Whitehead
94th Regiment..........	21	616	10	Lt.-Col. Malthus
2nd N.N.C.	19	385	25	Major Bengough
Shepstone's Basutos	10	108	124	Capt. Shepstone
Bettington's Horse	1	12	14	
Army Medical Dept.	8	18	9	
Natives attached........	—	47		

Total: 132 officers, 1,752 N.C.O's. and men, 540 natives, 659 horses, 39 camp followers, 8 guns.

Corps or Department.	Officers.	N.C.O. and men.	Horses.	Officer in command.
Flying Column.				
Brig.-Gen. Sir E. Wood.. Commanding.				
Staff:				
Orderly Officer, Lieut. Lysons, 90th Regt.				
Principal Staff Officer, Major Clery, h.p.				
For General Staff duties, Capt. Woodgate, 4th Regt.	5	10	21	
Royal Artillery	7	89	79	(4 guns and 2 Gatlings). Major Tremlett
Royal Engineers	5	62	11	Major G. J. Moysey
1 | 13th Regiment	24	587	9	Major E. L. England
80th Regiment..........	11	357	3	Major C. Tucker
90th Regiment..........	22	688	5	Major R. M. Rogers, V.C.
Wood's Irregulars	6	330	26	Commandt. Loraine White
Natal Pioneers..........	4	46	4	Capt. J. Nolan
Mounted Infantry	4	64	76	Capt. Browne, 24th Regt.
Transvaal Rangers	5	62	72	Commandt. Raaf
Frontier Light Horse	10	96	121	Commandt. D'Arcy
Baker's Horse	6	86	100	Commandt. Baker
Natal Light Horse	3	54	61	Commandt. Whalley
Natal Native Horse......	3	89	92	Capt. Cochrane, 32nd Regt.
Army Hospital Corps....	6	3	2	
Natives attached	..	44		
Army Staff Corps	1	1	3	

Total: 122 officers, 2,159 N.C.O's. and men, 465 natives, 685 horses, 108 camp followers, 4 guns, and 2 Gatlings.

Casualties—Ulundi.

Corps or Department.	Killed.		Wounded.		Remarks.
	Officers.	N.C.O. and men.	Officers.	N.C.O. and men.	
Staff............	Hon. W. Drummond.*	..	Lieut. Milne, R.N.	..	* Missing; body found afterwards
IInd Division.					
Staff............	..	..	Lieut. and Capt. Hon. S. Cotton Lt. A. B. Phipps Lieut. Liebenrood		
17th Lancers	Capt. Wyatt-Edgell	1	Col. Drury-Lowe Lieut. James Lieut. Jenkins	4	
Royal Artillery ..	..	..	Lieut. Davidson .	1	
2 | 21st Regiment	..	..	Major Winsloe ..	10	
1 | 24th Regiment	..	..	..	1	
58th Regiment ..	..	1	Major Bond	10	
94th Regiment ..	..	2	Lieut. Brooke ..	12	
2nd N.N.C.......	..	..	Lieut. Lukin .. Lieut. Moncrieff .	4	
Shepstone's Horse	..	1	..	3	
Hospital Bearers .	..	..	..	1	
Total—Staff and IInd Division	2	5	13	46	
Wood's Flying Column.					
Royal Artillery, 10 | 7	..	..	..	2	
Royal Artillery, 11 | 7	..	1	..	..	
Royal Engineers..	..	..	..	1	
1 | 13th Regiment	..	2	Lieut. Pardoe*..	9	* Lieut. Pardoe died of his wounds on 14th July
80th Regiment ..	..	1	..	5	
90th Regiment ..	..	..	..	1	
Wood's Irregulars	..	..	Comdt. White .. Capt. S. S. Horber Lieut. J. Cowdell		
Natal N. Horse ..	..	1	..	2	
Natal Pioneers ..	..	..	Lieut. Hickley Lieut. Andrews		
Baker's Horse ..	..	..	..	1	
Mounted Basutos	..	..	..	2	
Total—Wood's Flying Column	..	5	6	23	
Grand Total ..	2	10	19	69	

CASUALTIES in Minor Actions during the Campaign.

Date.	Column or Detachment.	Place.	Killed.		Wounded.	
			Officers.	N.C.O. and men.	Officers.	N.C.O. and men.
12th Jan. ...	Centre Column ...	Bashee River ...	...	2*	1	13*
18th Jan. ...	Wood's Column ...	On March.........	...	...	...	2*
20th Jan. ...	" "	" "	...	...	...	2
24th Jan. ...	" "	Zungen Nek ...	...	...	...	5*
15th Feb. ...	Lt.-Col. Buller's Party	Intombi River...	...	3*	...	3*
"	Col. Rowlands' Column	Tolaka Mountain	...	...	...	6*
21st Feb. ...	Capt. Harvey's Party	Eloya Mountain	...	...	...	2*
17th March	Right Column......	Etshowe	...	1	...	...
1st June......	II Division	Ityotyosi	The Prince Imperial	3	...	...
5th June ...	II Division and Flying Column	Ezunganyan Hill	Lieut. Frith, 17th Lancers	...	...	2
1st July......	II Division	Fort Evelyn......	Lieut. Scott Douglas, 2 | 21st	1	...	...
3rd July......	Flying Column ...	White Umvolosi	...	3	...	4
		Total	3	13	1	39

*Natives.

SUMMARY of Losses in Action.

Place.	Killed.			Wounded.		
	Officers.	N.C.O. and men.	Natives.*	Officers.	N.C.O. and men.	Natives.*
Inyezane........	2	8	4	1	15	..
Isandhlwana	52	806	471	..	..	..
Rorke's Drift	..	15	..	1	9	..
Intombi	2	60	15	..	1	..
Inhlobana	15	79	100	1	7	..
Kambula........	..	18	..	8	57	..
Gingihlovo	..	4	5	6	39	17
Ulundi..........	2	10	3	19	69	10
Minor actions....	3	7	6	1	9	30
Total	76	1,007	604	37	206	57

* Returns incomplete.

In the period between the 11th January, 1879, and the 15th Oct., 1879, 17 officers and 330 men died of diseases consequent on the operations in Zululand.

During the year 1879, 99 officers and 1,286 non-commissioned officers and men were invalided from the command for causes incidental to the campaign.

APPENDIX D.

VOLUNTEER and other Corps called out during the Zulu War of 1879.

Names.	Raised.	Disbanded.	Strength.		Remarks.
			Men.	Horses.	
Alexandra Mounted Rifles	Nov., 1878	Aug., 1879	20	27	At first employed with No. 1 Column; afterwards with the IInd Division.
Buffalo Border Guard	Ditto	July, 1879	38	38	At first with No. 3 Column; afterwards in Natal.
Durban Mounted Rifles	Ditto	Ditto	64	72	At first with No. 1 Column; afterwards with the Ist Division.
Natal Carabineers	Ditto	Aug., 1879	25	35	At first with No. 3 Column; afterwards in Natal.
Natal Hussars	Ditto	July, 1879	38	46	At first with No. 1 Column; afterwards with the Ist Division.
Natal Mounted Police	Ditto	Sept., 1879	80	83	At first with No. 3 Column; afterwards in Natal; a portion joined Col. Baker Russell's Column.
Newcastle Mounted Rifles	Ditto	July, 1879	16	16	At first with No. 3 Column.
Stanger Mounted Rifles	Ditto	Ditto	40	40	No. 1 Column and Ist Division.
Victoria Mounted Rifles	Ditto	Ditto	51	51	No. 1 Column and Ist Division.
Amangwani Scouts	April, 1879	Aug., 1879	37	..	Attached to Cavalry.
Amatonga (or Amaboma)	Feb. and Mar., 1879	Ditto	71	71	Attached to 17th Lancers.
Baker's Horse	Ditto	Ditto	236	224	Served with Wood's Flying Column.
Border Horse [Weatherley's]	..	..	61	108	" "
Burgher Force [Piet Uys']	..	..	45	..	With General Wood. Not regularly engaged.
Dunn's Scouts	Jan., 1879	Sept., 1879	244	..	Served with Ist Division.
Fereira's Horse	..	..	115	114	Raised by Colonial Government; served with Wood's Column.

Frontier Light Horse	1877	..	216	278	With General Wood's Column; afterwards to Baker Russell's Column; name changed to Natal Light Horse.
Jantzi's Native Horse	Feb. and Mar., 1879	Sept., 1879	68	83	At first with No. 2 Column; then with the Ist Division; afterwards with Clarke's Column.
Kaffrarian Rifles [Schermbrucker]	Feb., 1879	June, 1879	42	42	With General Wood.
Lonsdale's Mounted Rifles	Feb. and Mar., 1879	Aug. and Sept., 1879.	236	234	Raised principally at Cape Town; served with Ist Division; afterwards with Clarke's Column (two troops, and with Baker Russell's Column (one troop).
Mafunzi's Mounted Natives	Ditto	Sept., 1879	73	80	With Ist Division and Clarke's Column.
Natal Horse, No. 1 Troop [de Burgh].	Feb., 1879	Ditto	48	55	Composed of N.C.O.'s of 3rd N.N.C.; with Ist Division and Clarke's Column.
„ No. 2 Troop [Cooke]	Ditto	July, 1879	50	18	Composed of N.C.O.'s of 3rd N.N.C.; with Ist Division.
„ No. 3 Troop [Bettington]	Ditto	Oct., 1879	60	67	Composed of N.C.O.'s of 3rd N.N.C.; with IInd Division.
Natal Light Horse	Mar., 1879	Ditto	138	161	Originally a troop of Frontier Light Horse; served with Baker Russell's Column.
Natal Native Horse [Cochrane]	Feb. and Mar., 1879	July, 1879	129	159	At first with No. 2 Column; afterwards with Wood's Column.
Natal Native Pioneers, No. 1 Company [Nolan.]	Nov. and Dec., 1878	Oct., 1879	80	..	Served with No. 3 Column; afterwards with Wood's Column.
„ „ No. 2 Company [Beddoes.]	Ditto	Ditto	104	..	Served with No. 1 Column.
„ „ No. 3 Company [Allen.]	Ditto	Ditto	89	..	Served with No. 2 Column.
Native Zulu Carriers	July, 1879	Sept., 1879	2,000	..	Carried stores between Port Durnford and St. Pauls.
Shepstone's Native Horse	Feb. and Mar., 1879	Ditto	180	212	Served with IInd Division and Baker Russell's Column.
Transvaal Rangers [Raaf's]	April, 1879	..	138	168	Served with Wood's Flying Column; afterwards with Baker Russell's Column.
Wood's Irregulars	Dec., 1878	July, 1879	460	10	With Wood's Column.

Natal Native Contingent.

Original Title.		Commanding Officer.	New Title.	Commanding Officer.	Raised.	Disbanded.	Strength.	Remarks.
1st Regt. Colonel Durnford	1st Batt.	Comdt. Montgomery .	1st Batt. .	Comdt. Montgomery .	Nov. and Dec., 1878	Sept., 1879	960	Remained at Krans Kop; a detachment was at Isandhlwana.
	2nd Batt.	Major Bengough	2nd Batt. .	Major Bengough	Ditto	Ditto	1,066	Served with the IInd Division; three companies left in posts on line of advance, remainder went on to Ulundi.
	3rd Batt.	Captain Cherry......	3rd Batt. .	Captain Cherry......	Ditto	Ditto	879	Remained at Krans Kop.
2nd Regt. Major Graves	1st Batt.	Major Graves	4th Batt. .	Captain Barton......	Ditto	Ditto	1,134	Served with No. 1 Column; Ist Division and Clarke's Column.
	2nd Batt.	Comdt. Nettleton...	5th Batt. .	Comdt. Nettleton....	Ditto	Ditto	887	Served with No. 1 Column and Ist Division; afterwards at Forts Crealock and Chelmsford, and Port Durnford.
3rd Regt. Comdt. Lonsdale	1st Batt.	Comdt. Brown	..	..	Ditto	..	..	These two battalions served with No. 3 Column, but after Isandhlwana they ceased to exist. The European N.C.O.'s formed the Natal Horse.
	2nd Batt.	Comdt. Cooper	..	..	Ditto			

Note.—When these troops were first raised, 10 per cent. of the rank and file were armed with fire-arms. Afterwards they were armed nearly entirely with fire-arms, the 4th Battalion receiving Martini-Henrys, and the 3rd Battalion Sniders and muzzle-loaders.

Appendix E.

Transport in South Africa.

The principal means of transport employed in connection with the Zulu War was the bullock wagon commonly used throughout South Africa. This is a ponderous vehicle, carrying from three to eight thousand pounds, and drawn by a team of from ten to eighteen oxen, yoked in pairs to a long chain or "Trek-tow," attached to the pole or "Dissel-boom." Two natives accompany each team, a "driver," and a "leader" or "fore looper." These men have charge of the cattle, and on the march the "fore looper" walks in front of the leading pair of oxen, while the "driver" uses the whip and attends to the brake when necessary.

The usual dimensions of an ox-wagon are as follows:—length of body, 18′; diameter of hind wheel, 5′ 2″; of fore wheel 3′ 10″; extreme width of track, 5′ 10″. The fore wheels do not lock under, and the centre of gravity is low. The ox in draught occupies a space of 9′ 6″, so that the road space required for a wagon whose total length is 20′, drawn by 16 oxen is $20 + 8 \times 9\frac{1}{2} = 96' = 32$ yards, or allowing for intervals 40 yards, but in practice it was found that with bad driving each wagon took up about 60 yards of road.

Besides the ox-wagons, a considerable number of mule-wagons were employed, which carried 2,000 lbs. Their dimensions were as follows:—length of body, 12′ 6″; diameter of hind wheels, 4′ 7″; of fore wheel, 3′ 2″; extreme width of track, 5′ 6″. The fore wheels of these wagons lock under, and taking the length of the vehicle at 14′, the road space required when drawn by eight mules is $14 + 12 \times 4 = 62' = 21$ yards.

The daily ration for mules was 5 lbs. grain and 10 lbs. hay, which had to be carried in the wagons.

With ox-wagons there was not this loss of transporting power, but their rate of progress was much slower, as draught or "trek" oxen will not keep in good condition unless they have abundant time for grazing. Twelve to fifteen miles a day is the utmost that should be required of them, and they should not be kept in the yoke for more than three or four hours at a time.

The wagons and carts required for transport during the Zulu War were obtained both by purchase and by hire. The following table shows the numbers, and the prices paid:—

TRANSPORT in South Africa. 1879.

Description.		Greatest Number on Establishment at any time.	Highest Price Paid.	Average Price Paid.	Rate of Wages and Hire.	Remarks.
			£ s. d	£ s. d.		
Horses		748	40 0 0	27 0 0		
Mules	Colonial	4,246	30 0 0	23 0 0		
	American	387				
Oxen	Government	13,329	20 0 0	17 0 0		
	Hired	13,823	..	..	..	Hire included with wagons.
Carriages	Horse and mule, of sorts	641	..	..	..	Of various descriptions. Price from £35 to £150.
	Ox wagons, Government	836	140 0 0	100 0 0	..	Complete with stores.
	Ox wagons, hired	934	..	..	90 0 0	Per month with span. Lowest £60 per month. Also by cwt., according to distance.
	Ox carts, Government	93	48 0 0			
	Ox carts, hired	8	..	..	35 0 0	Per month with span.
Ox drivers.	Government paid	788	..	..	5 0 0 3 10 0	When in Zululand, per month. Not in Zululand, ,,
	Hired transport	880	..	..	Paid by owners and contractors.	Rationed by Government.
Ox leaders.	Government paid	755	..	..	2 10 0 1 10 0	When in Zululand, per month. Not in Zululand, ,,
	Hired transport	882	..	..	Paid by owners and contractors.	Rationed by Government.
Mule drivers and leaders, Government paid		775	..	..	3s. to 5s.	Per day.

PLAN OF CAMP OF IIND DIVISION

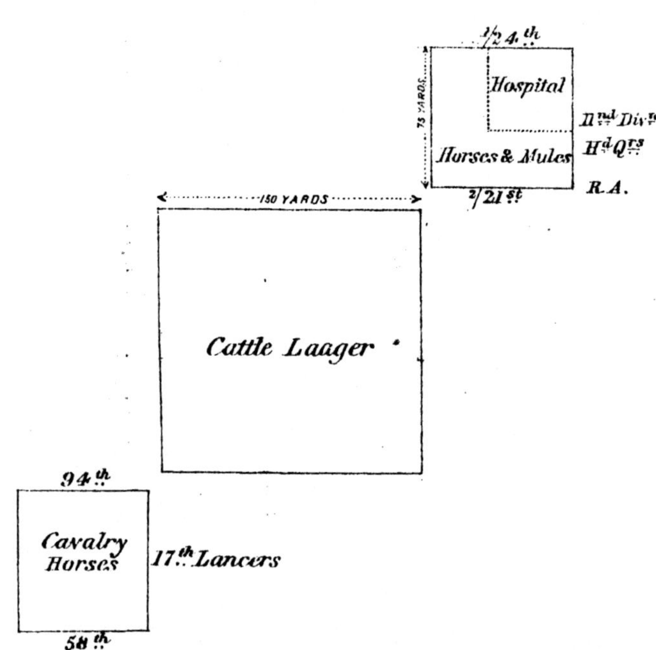

To face page 173.

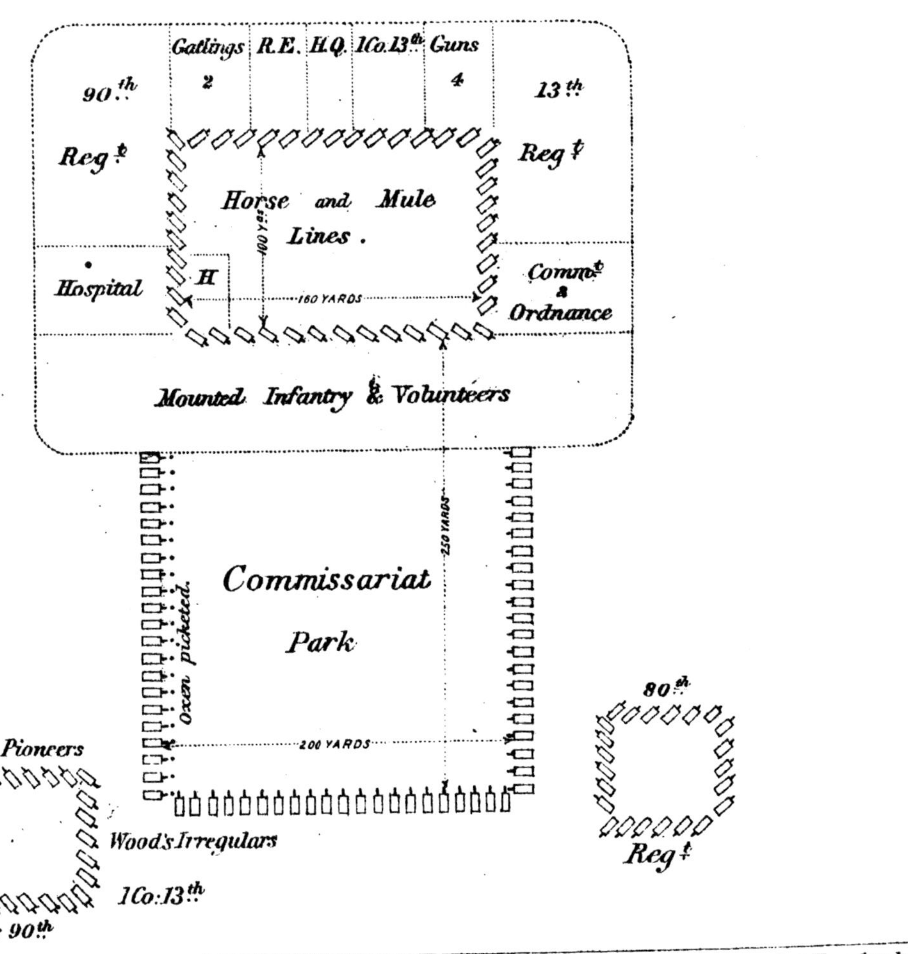

Zincographed at the Intelligence Dept Horse Guards. March 1881

The Dutch residents in South Africa when travelling in small parties had always been in the habit of parking their wagons at night, so as to make a wagon or square enclosure called a "laager." Their oxen were usually placed within this enclosure, which, in case of attack by the natives, formed a defensible post.

A similar plan was adopted by the British troops when advancing to the relief of Etshowe, and also during the march to Ulundi. Various forms of laager were tried, the systems generally adopted by the IInd Division and by the Flying Column being shown on the accompanying sketches.

Appendix F.

Approximate Summary of Cost of the Zulu War of 1879.

	£	£
1. Army: Net cost over normal expenditure 1st August, 1878, to 30th September, 1879	4,095,528	
Further net cost calculated after deducting credits in aid	300,000	
		4,395,528
2. Cost of naval transport		700,000
3. Stationery		2,500
4. Treasury chest: Cost of raising and moving funds		39,845
5. Colonial Government of Natal: War expenditure to 30th September, 1879 ..	56,225	
" actual further payments to 31st December, 1879	20,039	
Extra cost of telegraphs	9,722	
		85,086
6. Colonial Government of Transvaal: War expenditure	1,263	
Value of material taken for use of Imperial troops	5,201	
		6,464
		£5.230,323

Intelligence Dep^t. N°. 19.

TO JOIN

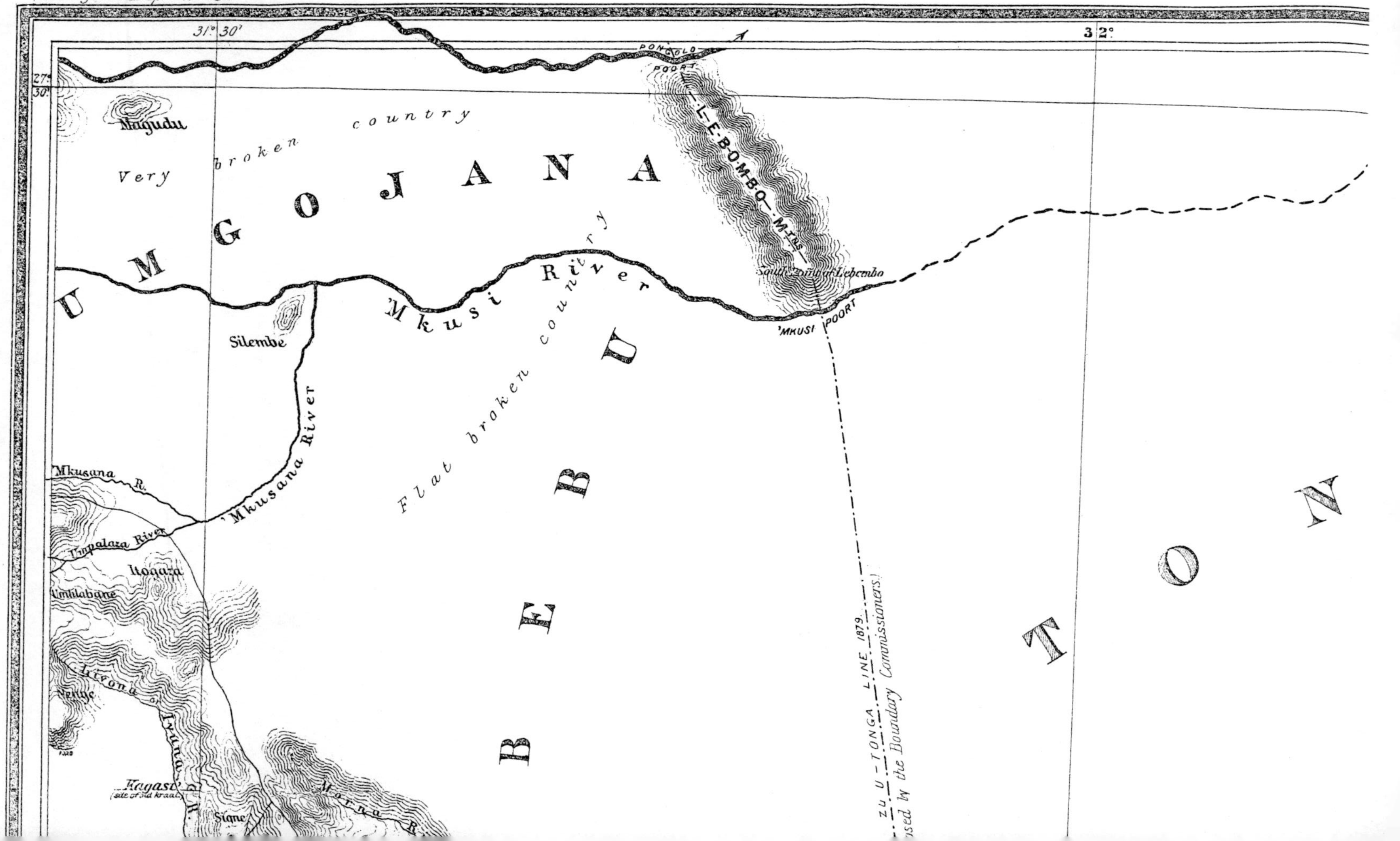

31° 30'

32°

27°
30'

PONGOLO POORT

LEBOMBO MTNS

South end of Lebombo

'MKUSI POORT

Magudu

Very broken country

UMGOJANA

Silembe

'Mkusi River

Flat broken country

UBEBE

TONGA

'Mkusana River

'Mkusana R.

Umpalaza River

Itogara

Umhlabane

Livona

Nenge

Iyuna R.

Hagasti (site of old kraal)

Signe

Morna R.

ZU U-TONGA LINE 1879.

(...osed by the Boundary Commissioners.)

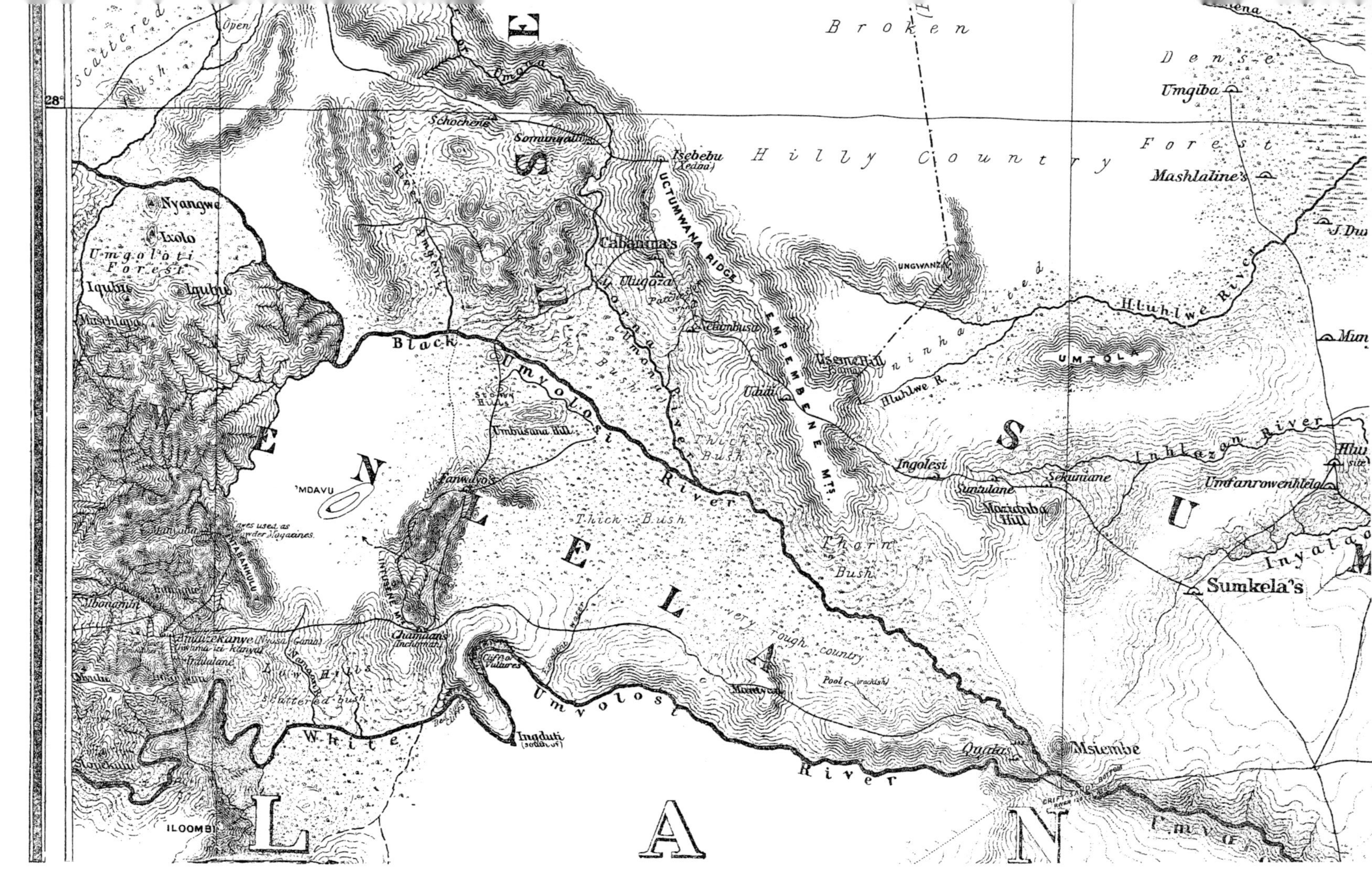

Broken Hilly Country
Dense Forest
Umgiba
Mashlaline's
Scattered Bush
Open
28°
Umona
Schochene
Somunqali
Isebebu (Xedna)
UCTUMWANA RIDGE
Cabanina's
Uluqaza
Patches
Nyangwe
Ixolo
Umgoloti Forest
Iqubu
Iqubu
UNGWANZI
Hluhlwe River
Hluhlwe R.
Uninhabited
UMTOLA
EMPEMBENE MTS.
Black Umvolosi River
Thick Bush
Thorn Bush
Umbusana Hill
Stony Hills
'MDAVU
Ingolesi
Sekumane
Inhlazon River
Umfanrowenhlela
Sumkela's
Inyalao
Very rough country
Pool (brackish)
Thick Bush
INTABANKULU
Chamanas
INTUSENE MT
Ingduti
Umvolosi
White Umvolosi River
Low Hills
Scattered Bush
Msiembe
Quadas
ILOOMBI
Manyeba
Imduzekanye
Mbonamin
Umvoti
Z U L U L A N D

ESKOMANA
Hills
Umsanduse River
Nunywine
T
ESKOMANE
'MDAVU
W
A
Thorn
Bush
Nonqudu Hills
Umlandela
28°
30'
Inseleni R.
Undulating
Eskorto
MAKUSANA RANGE
Impule River
Indama
Udisa-lu-ise
Ambaba (Imbabake) R.
Patches of Thorn
SKASA-AMA-BOVELA SLANGASA RANGE
Ntembeni
Umgitywa
NTONDWENI
DRIFT VERY BAD
Inseleni River
M
L
A
N
Umhlatuz River
Marjian
Empangwene M.S.
Umzinyati L.
Umkazaan
O'Neill Peak
Ingoto R.?
Ondine
Pouw Hill
Kwambonambi
Lagoon
Umhlatuz River
Richards Bay
UNGOYA
MOUNTAINS
Umlalaz Plain

Conical Hill
Maquamba's
Mejia's
Inyezane
One Tree Hill
Napoleon
Laager
Umlalaz River
Fort Durnford
Inyezane
Inyezone River
Fᵗ Chelmsford
Siyai R.
Open
Level &
Marshy
Umisia Hill
Gingindlovo
Inyezane River
High Hills
High steep Hills
Foot track to Etschowe
Dense Bush
Mahlilwan & Sachonyana's Kraals
Amatikulu R.
Fᵗ Crealock
Beacon Hill
Amatikulu River
Old Mouth Amatikulu R.
Inyoni River
Scattered Bush
Laagers
Inyoni R.
Walker's Laager
Sᵗ Andrews
Tenedos
Fᵗ Pearson
Tugela River
29°
31° 30'
32°

References.

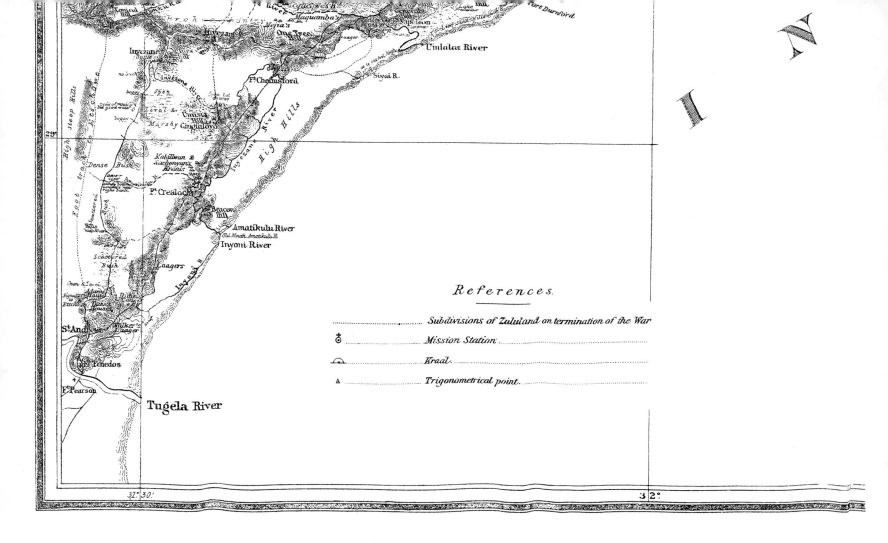

Subdivisions of Zululand on termination of the War

Mission Station

Kraal

Trigonometrical point

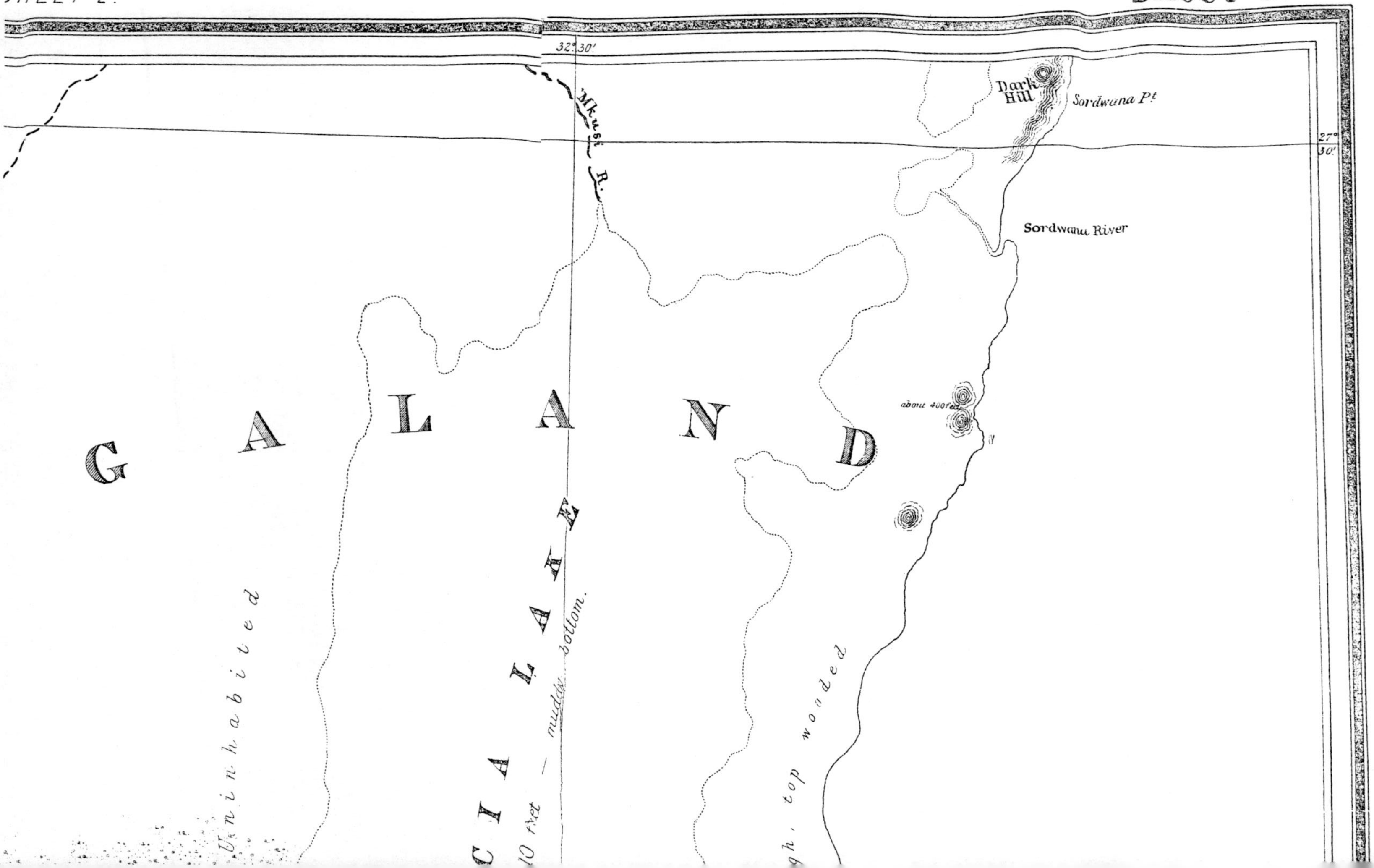

SHEET 2.

Sheet 1.

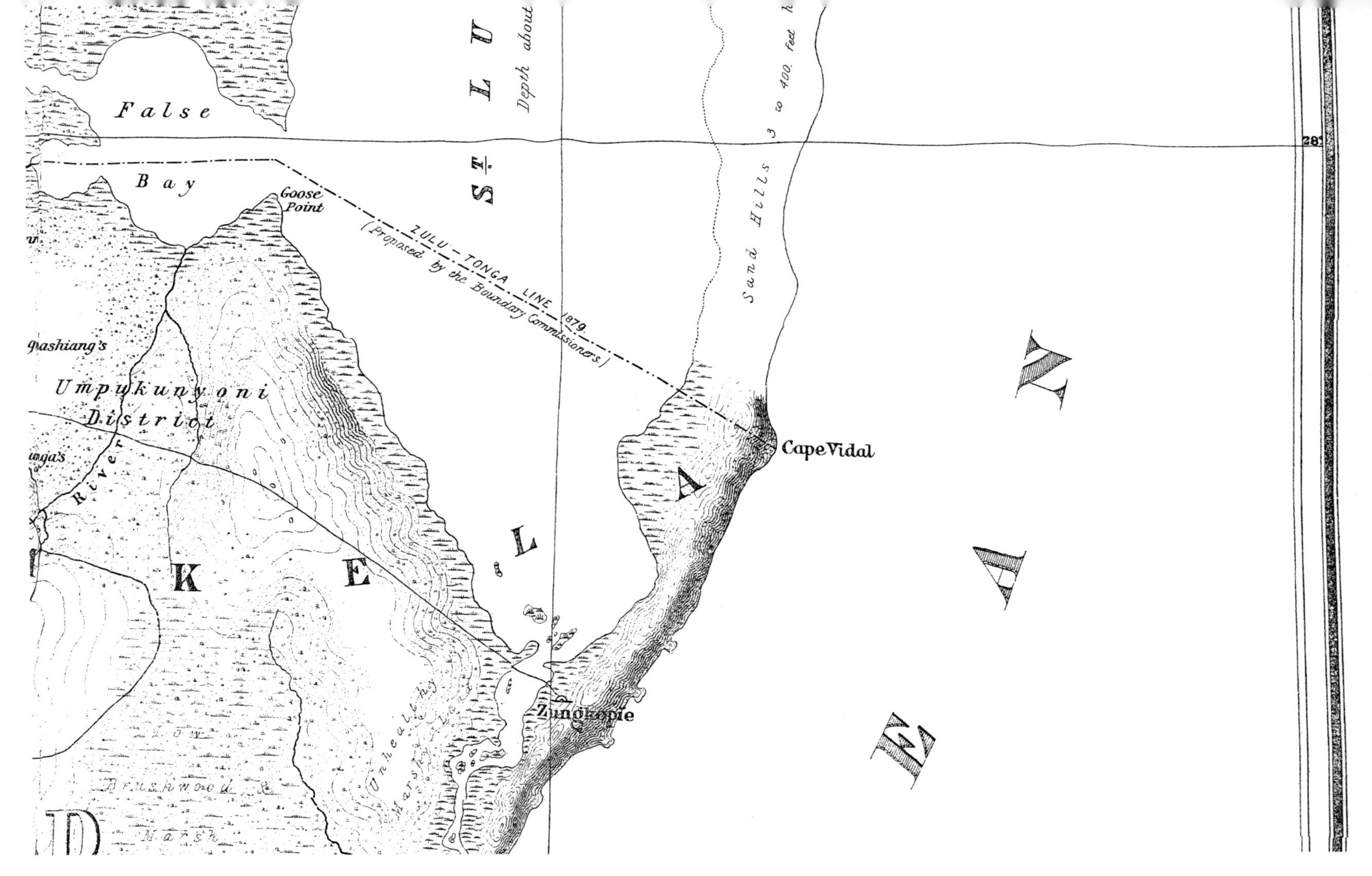

False
Bay
Depth about
Sand Hills 3 to 400. feet h
Goose Point
ZULU – TONGA LINE 1879.
(Proposed by the Boundary Commissioners.)
Cape Vidal
Zungkopie
Umpukunyoni District
River
Unhealthy Marshy Land
Brushwood
Marsh

St Lucia Bay
Sugar Loaf
Nsoba
L. Dani
Two sand patches
Cape St Lucia
Sharp Peak
Cone with patch
Sand Hill
Sandy beach wi breakers
flat bushy and marshy
Black Bluff
29°
30'
OCEAN
INDIAN
ELA
MAP

29°

OF

Compiled at the **Intelligence Dept Horse Guards**, from the **Military Trigonometrical Surveys** and the various **Topographical Sketches** made by **Officers** during the **Campaign** of

1879.

Scale $\frac{1}{253,440}$ or 4 Miles to 1 Inch.

5 4 3 2 1 0 5 10 15 20 25 30 MILES.

In 2 Sheets.

32°30'

Compiled & Lith.d at the Intelligence Dep.t War Office May 1881.

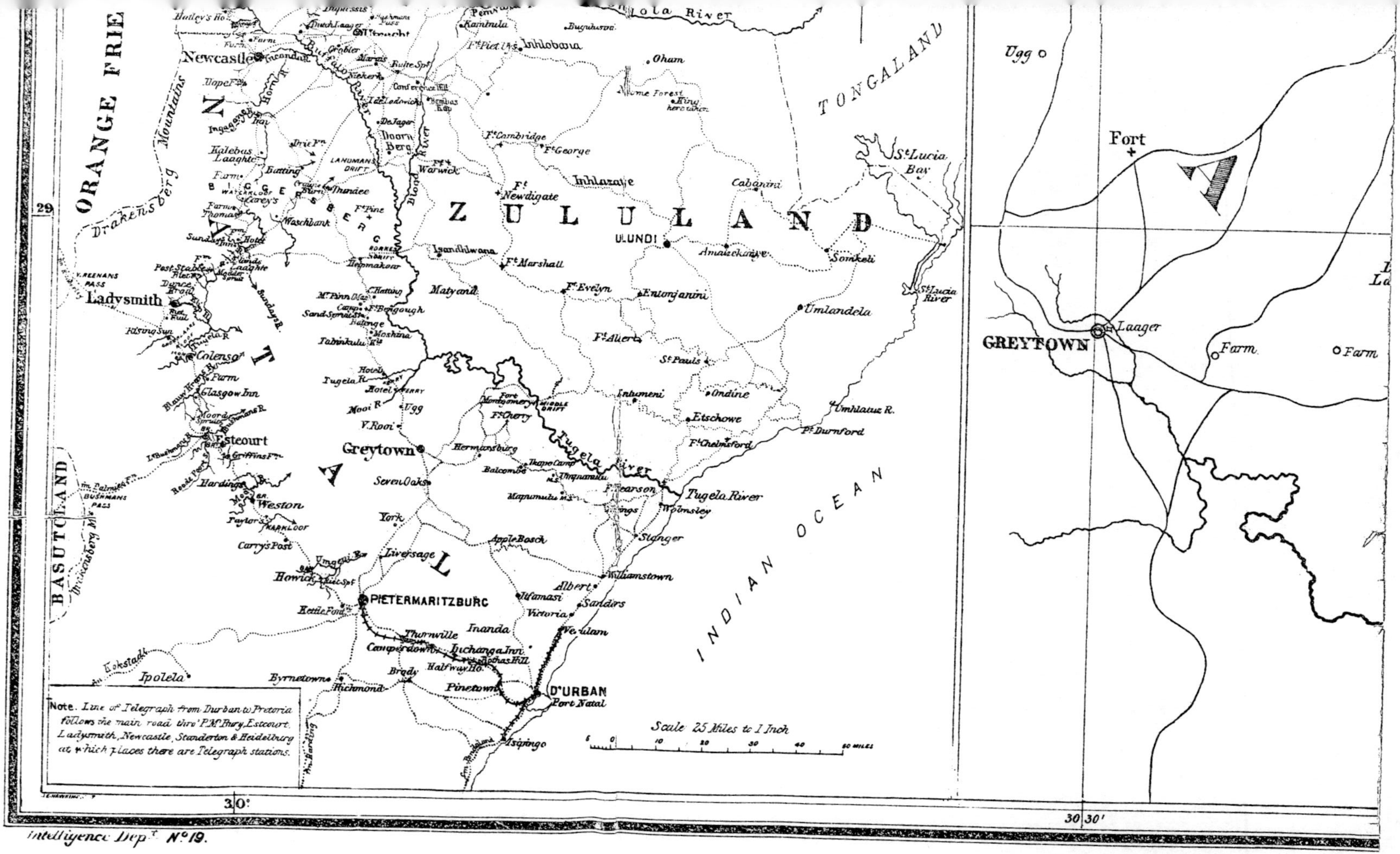

ORANGE FRIE

BASUTOLAND

NATAL

ZULULAND

TONGALAND

INDIAN OCEAN

Drakensberg Mountains

Newcastle

Ladysmith

Colenso

Estcourt

Greytown

PIETERMARITZBURG

D'URBAN

Port Natal

ULUNDI

Isandhlwana

Tugela River

Blood River

St. Lucia Bay

Note. Line of Telegraph from Durban to Pretoria follows the main road thro' P.M. Burg, Estcourt, Ladysmith, Newcastle, Standerton & Heidelburg at which places there are Telegraph stations.

Scale 25 Miles to 1 Inch

29

30°

30 30'

GREYTOWN

Laager

Fort

Ugg

Farm

Farm

Intelligence Dept. No. 19.

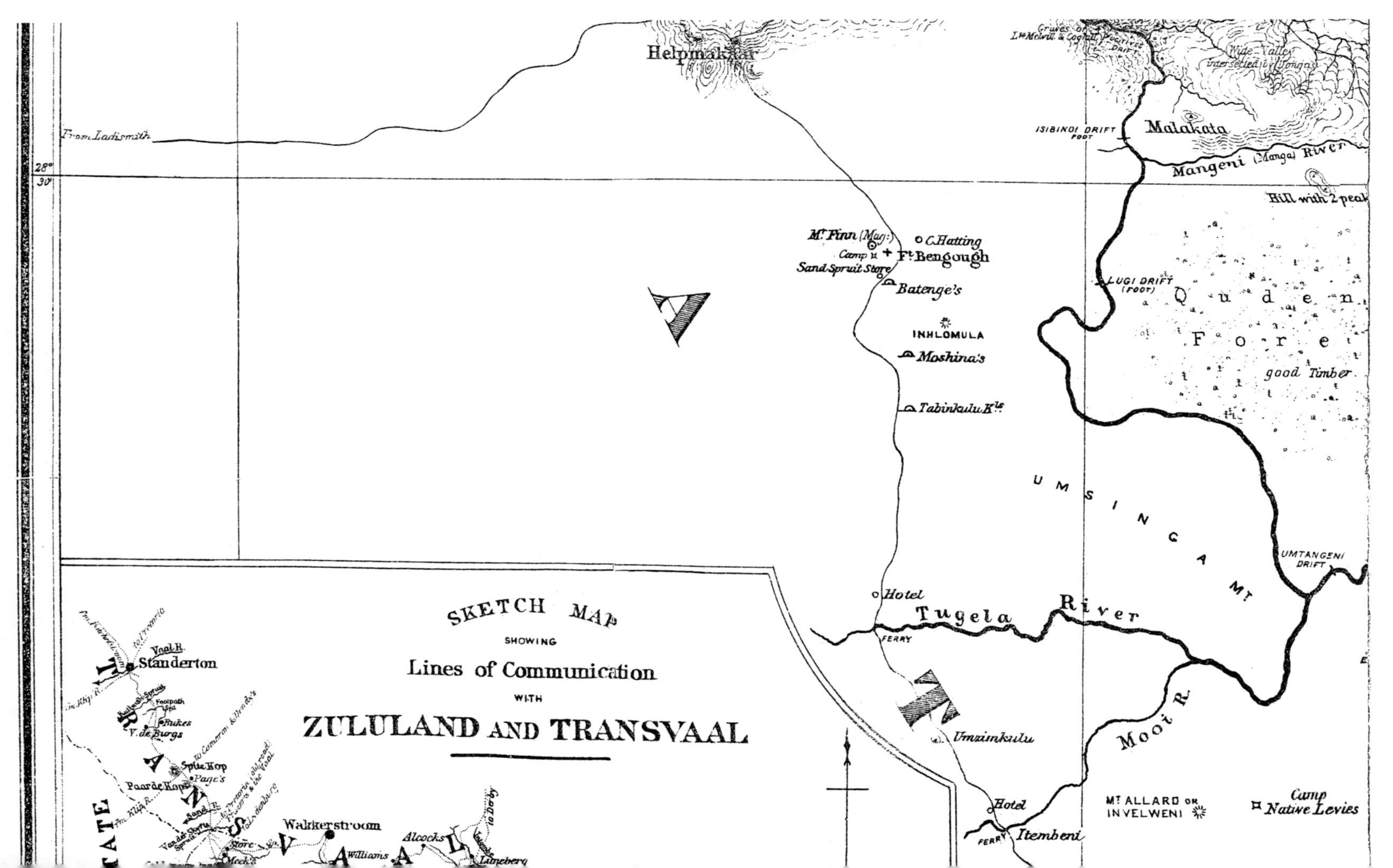
SKETCH MAP
SHOWING
Lines of Communication
WITH
ZULULAND AND TRANSVAAL
From Ladismith
28°
30'
Helpmakaar
Graves of Lt. Melvill & Coghill
Fugitives Drift
Wide Valley intersected by Dongas
Isibinoi Drift Foot
Malakata
Mangeni (Manga) River
Hill with 2 peak
Mr. Finn (Mag:)
C. Hatting
Camp
Ft. Bengough
Sand Spruit Store
Batenge's
INHLOMULA
Moshina's
Tabinkulu K.ls
Lugi Drift (Foot)
Quden Forest
good Timber
UMSINGA MT
Umtangeni Drift
Hotel
Tugela River
Ferry
Umzinkulu
Hotel
Ferry
Itembeni
Mooi R.
Mt. ALLARD OR INVELWENI
Camp Native Levies
TRANSVAAL
STATE
Vaal R.
Standerton
to Pretoria
Fm. Klip R.
Footpath
Bukes
V. de Burgs
to Cameron & Dendy's
Spitz Kop
Page's
Paarde Kop
Sand R.
to Pretoria (old road)
Lydenburg
Van de Sputs Spruit
Store
Meek's
Walkerstroom
Williams
Alcocks
to Derby
Luneberg

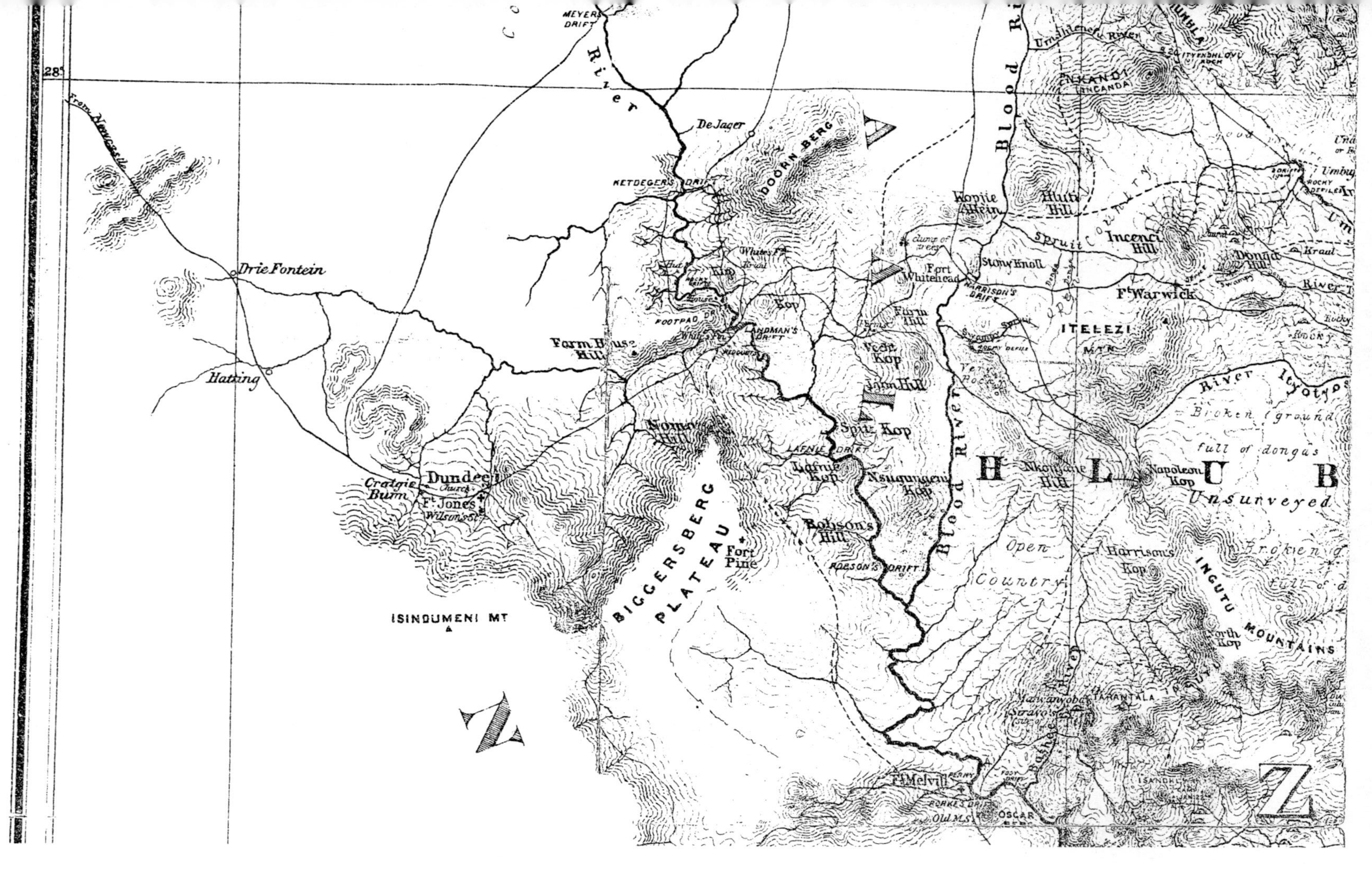

28°
From Newcastle
Drie Fontein
Hatting
Dundee
Craigie Burn
Church
Ft. Jones
Wilson's St.
ISINDUMENI MT
BIGGERSBERG PLATEAU
Fort Pine
Farm House Hill
MEYERS DRIFT
River
De Jager
KETDEGERS DRIFT
DOORN BERG
FOOTPAD DT
LANDMAN'S DRIFT
Kop
Vecht Kop
Farm Hill
Spitz Kop
Robson's Hill
ROBSON'S DRIFT
Nsuqungeni Kop
Fort Whitehead
Stony Knoll
HARRISON'S DRIFT
Kopjie Allein
Hutt Hill
Spruit
Incenci Hill
F.t Warwick
ITELEZI MTN
Blood River
Open Country
Harrisons Kop
INGUTU MOUNTAINS
Napoleon Kop
Unsurveyed
Broken ground full of dongas
Dongo Hill
Kraal
NKANDI
INCANDA
Umhlatusi River
ROCKY DEFILE
Ft. Melvill
FERRY
RORKES DRIFT
Old M.S.
OSCAR
TARANTALA
Bashee River
ISANDHLWANA
Z
Z
H L U B

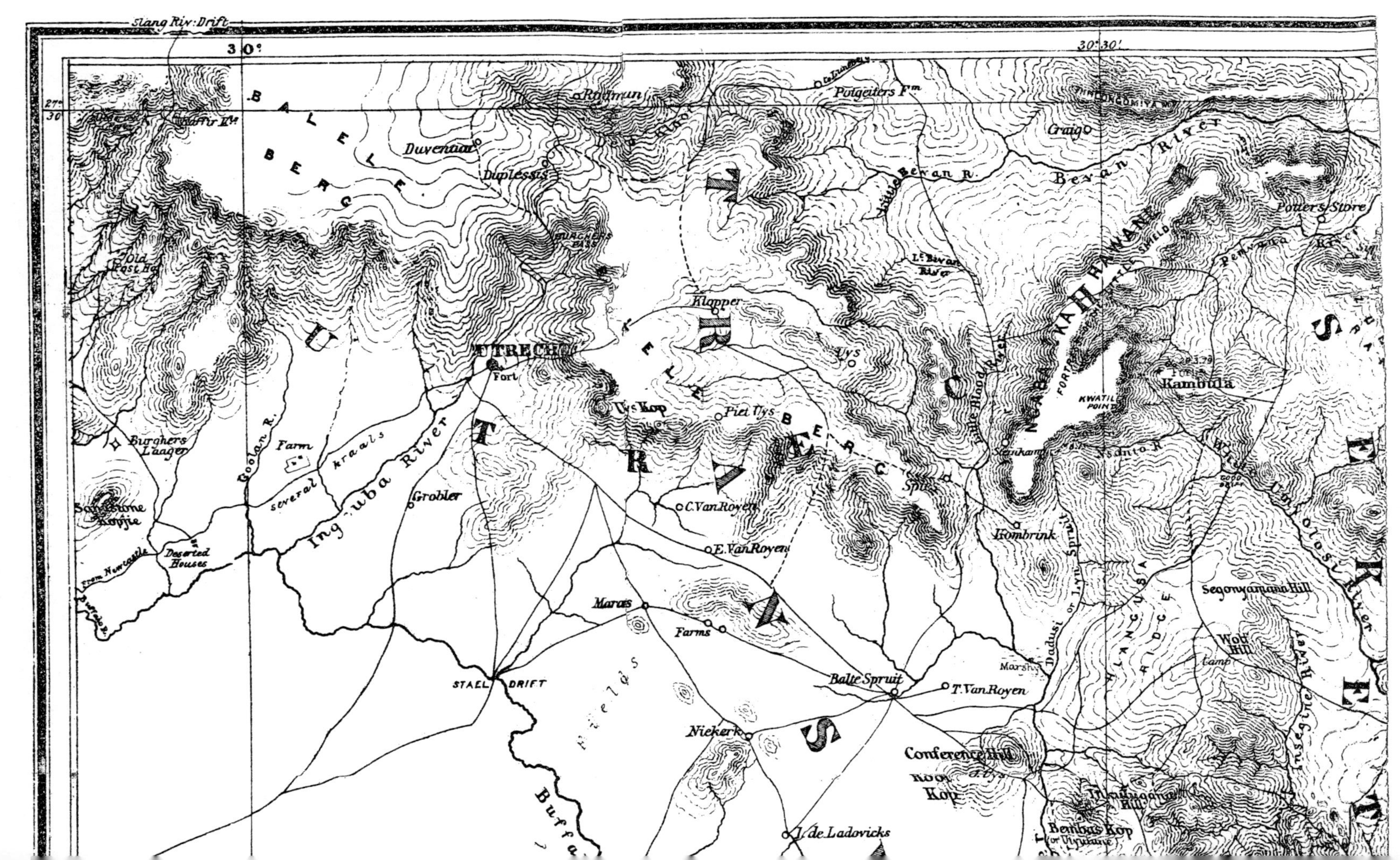

Slang Riv: Drift
30°
30° 30'
BALELE BERG
Duvenaar
Duplessis
Potgeiters Fm
Craig
Bevan River
Little Bevan R.
Potters Store
Burghers Pass
Old Post Rd
Burghers Laager
Goolan R.
Farm
several kraals
Inguba River
Grobler
Utrecht
Fort
Klopper
Uys Kop
Piet Uys
Uys
C. Van Royen
E. Van Royen
Marais
Farms
Stael Drift
Niekerk
Balte Spruit
T. Van Royen
Conference Hill
Kop
de Ladovicks
Deserted Houses
from Newcastle
Kombrink
Dadusi or Lyn Spruit
Marshy
Little Blood River
Kwatil Point
Kambula
Hlangusa Ridge
Segonyanana Hill
Wolf Hill
Camp
Insegine River
Bembas Kop
Buffalo
Transvaal

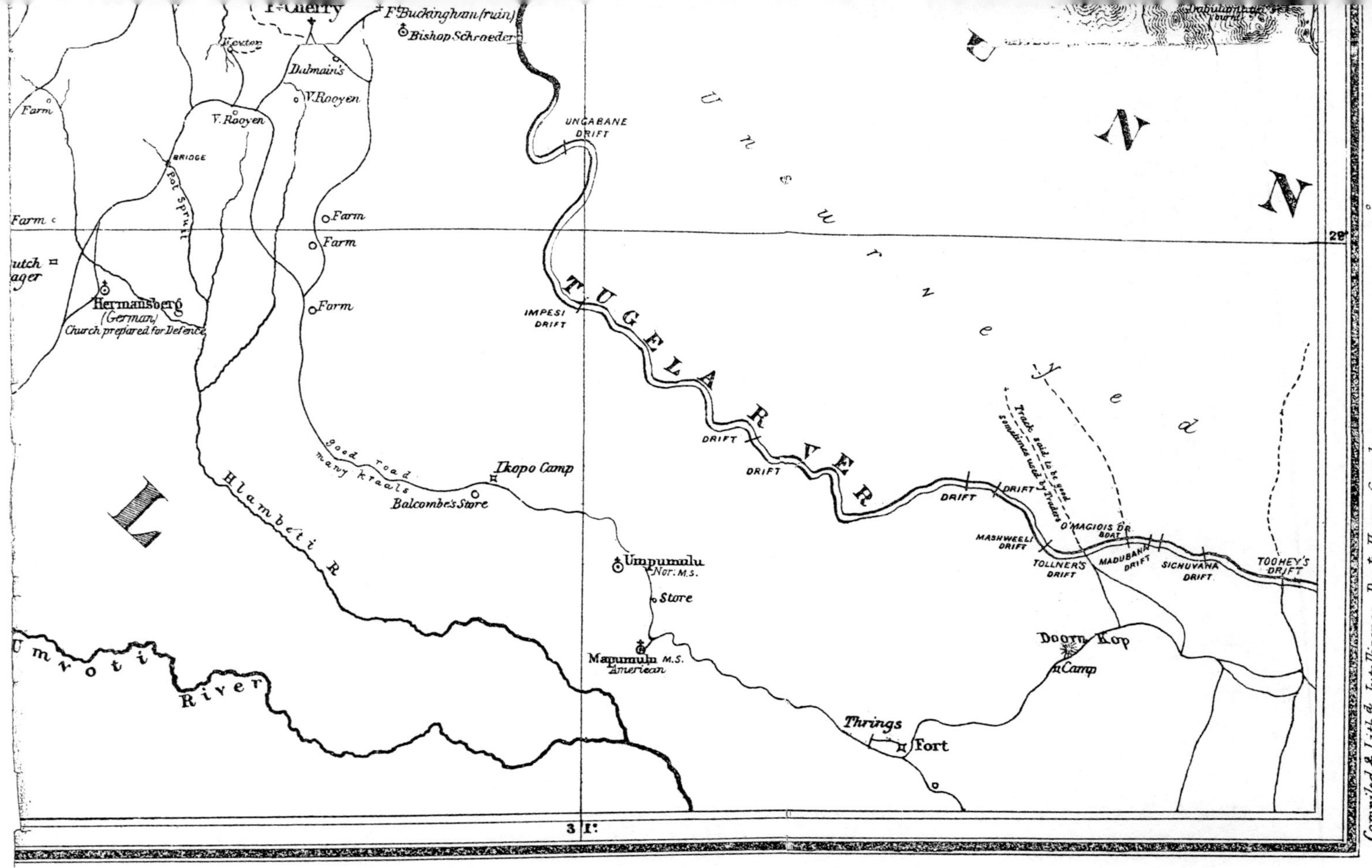

Compiled & Lith.d Intelligence Dep.t Horse Guards
March, 1881.

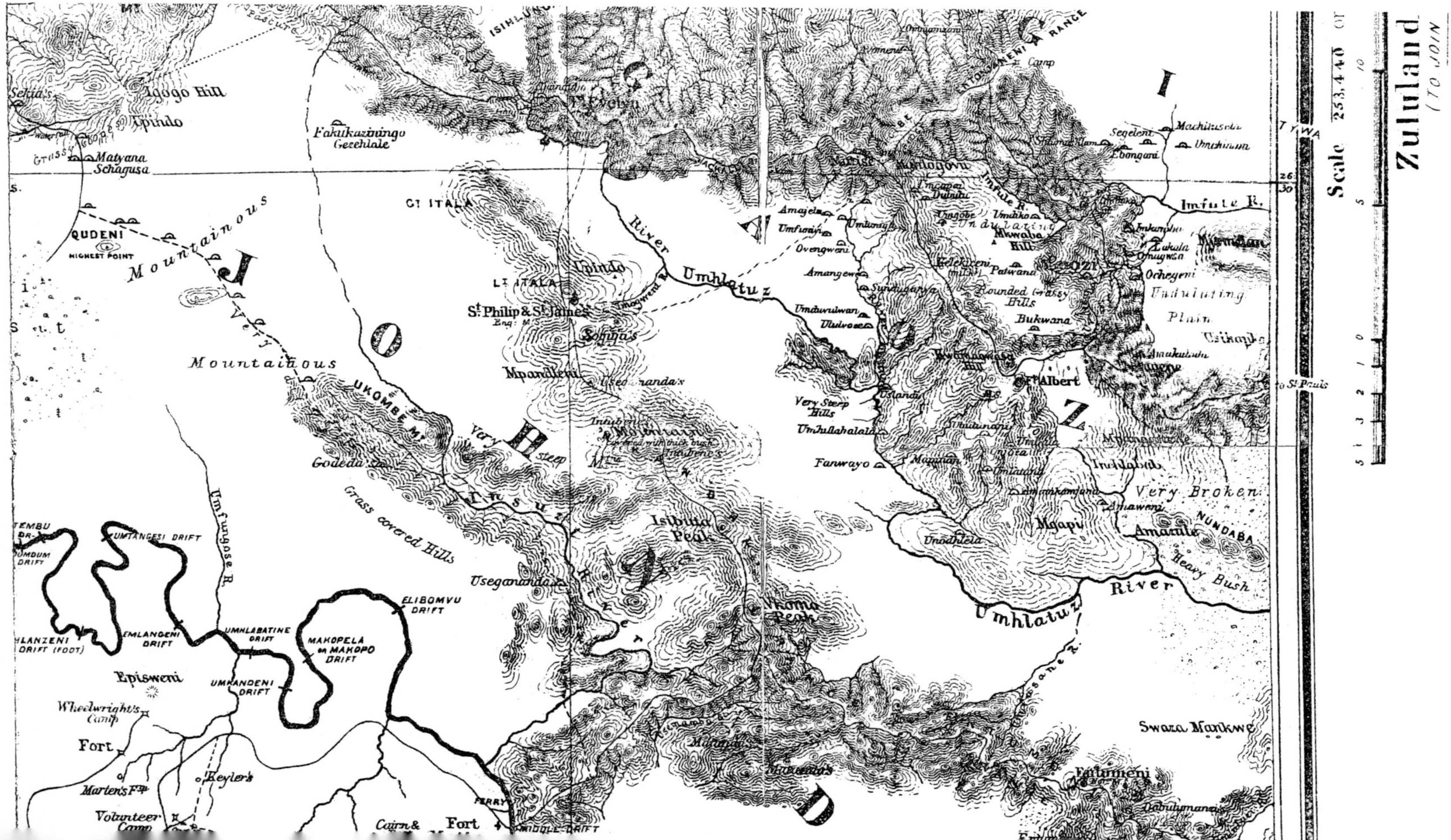

Sekia's
Igogo Hill
Ipindo
Matyana
Schagusa
Fakukazimingo
Gezehlale
QUDENI
HIGHEST POINT
Mountainous
Very
Mountainous
Gt. ITALA
Lt. ITALA
St. Philip & St. James
Mpandleni
UKOMBE Mt.
Godeda
Grass covered Hills
Useganandas
River
Umhlatuz
Isibula Peak
Nkoma Peak
Very Steep Hills
Fanwayo
St. Albert
Undulating
Plain
Rounded Grassy Hills
Bukwana
Imfule R.
Machitusela
Segeleni
Ebongani
Very Broken
NUNDABA
Amanule
Heavy Bush
Mqapi
Unodhlela
Umhlatuz
River
Swaza Mankwe
TEMBU DR.
UMTANGESI DRIFT
UMDUM DRIFT
HLANZENI DRIFT (FOOT)
EMLANGENI DRIFT
UMHLABATINE DRIFT
UMKANDENI DRIFT
MAKOPELA or MAKOPO DRIFT
ELIBOMVU DRIFT
Umfugose R.
Episweni
Wheelwright's Camp
Fort
Keyler's
Marten's Fm.
Volunteer Camp
Cairn &
Fort
FERRY
MIDDLE DRIFT
Scale 1/253,440 or
5 4 3 2 1 0 5 10
Zululand
(TO JOIN

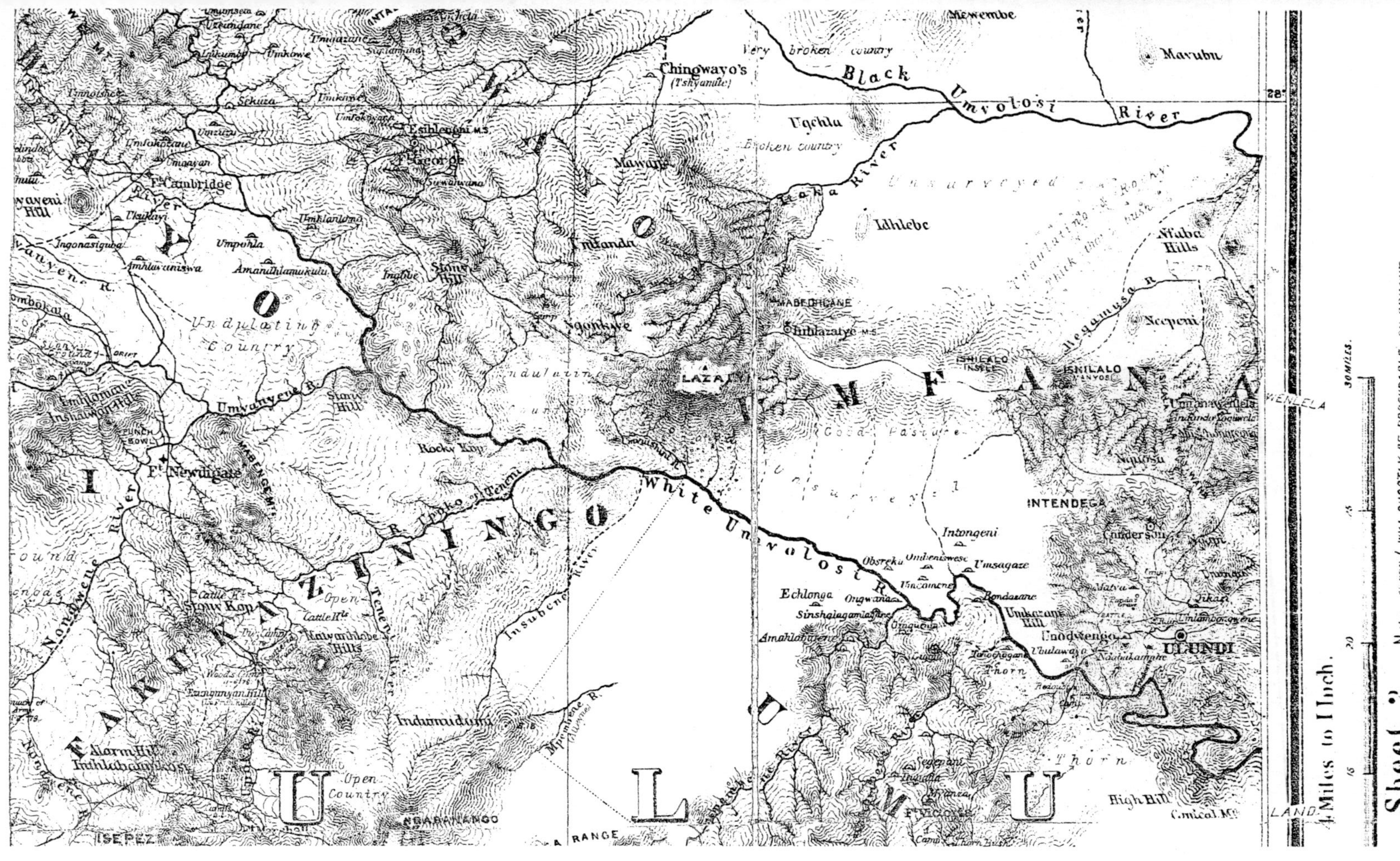

4 Miles to 1 Inch.

15 20 25 30 MILES.

Sheet 2.

Note, SHEET I WILL SHORTLY BE PROCURABLE, ON PAYMINT IN THE USUAL MANNER.

SHEET (1)

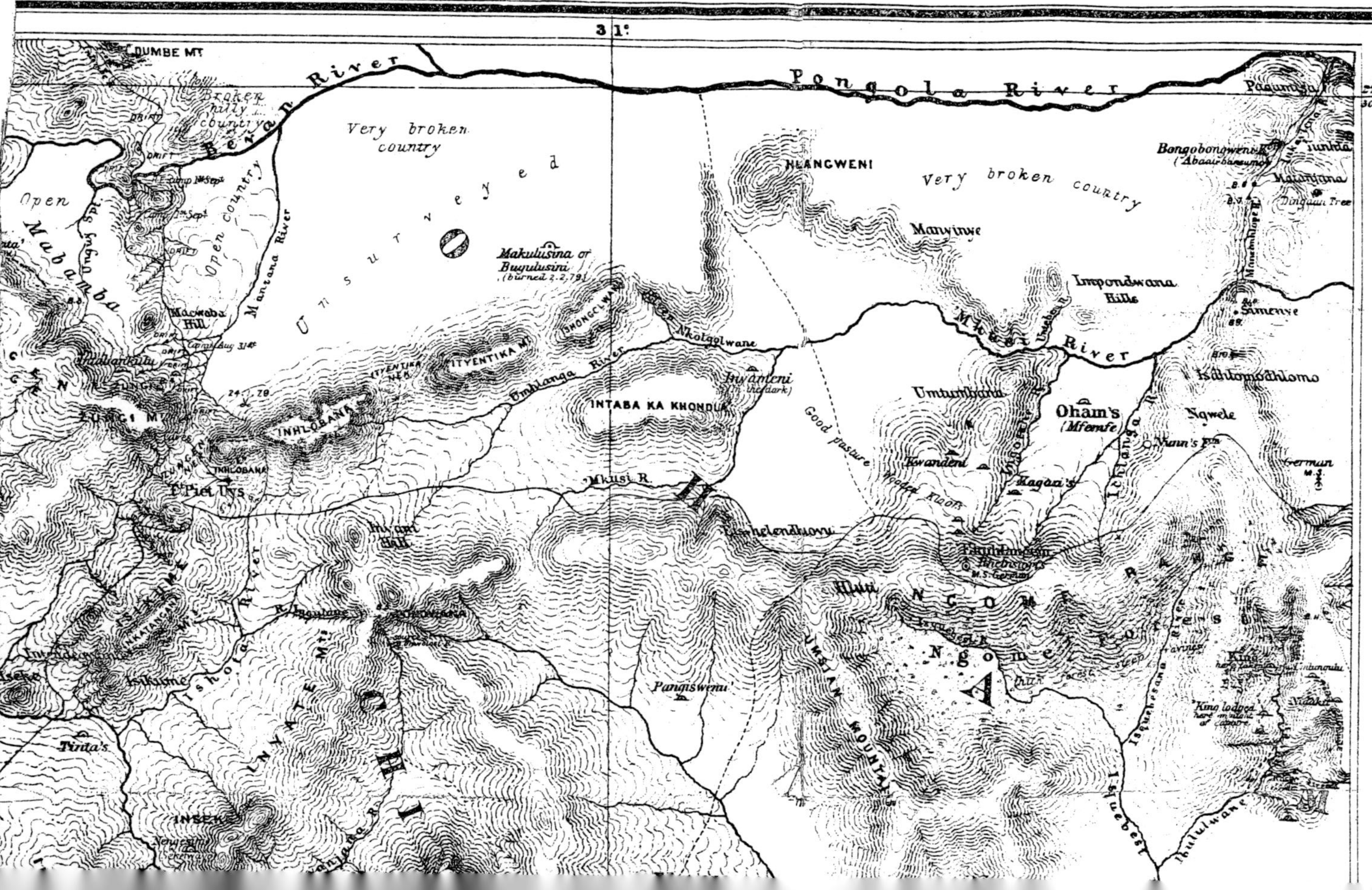

31°
COUMBE MT
Pongola River
Bevan River
Broken hilly country
Very broken country
Open country
Open
Unsurveyed
Manzana River
Makulusina or Buyulusini (burned 2.2.79)
Macwaba Hill
ITYENTIKA M.
ITYENTIKA NEK
SHONGCLWANA
INHLOBANA
INTABA KA KHONDLA
Umhlanga River
Nkotgolwane
Mkusi R.
Ft. Piet Uys
HLANGWENI
Very broken country
Manyinye
Impondwana Hills
Mkusi River
Umtumbana
Ohām's (Mfemfe)
Kwandeni
Kagaa's
Nqwede
German
Bongobongweni
Makunyana
Dingaan Tree
Simenye
Good pasture
Pangisweni
UMSIAN MOUNTAINS
NGOME RANGE
Ngome Forest
Iskhume
Ishota River
INSEKE
Tinta's
Isquebesana River
Ihululwane
I. Isquebesi
King lodged here at time of capture
Open
Unguy Spt.
Mabamba

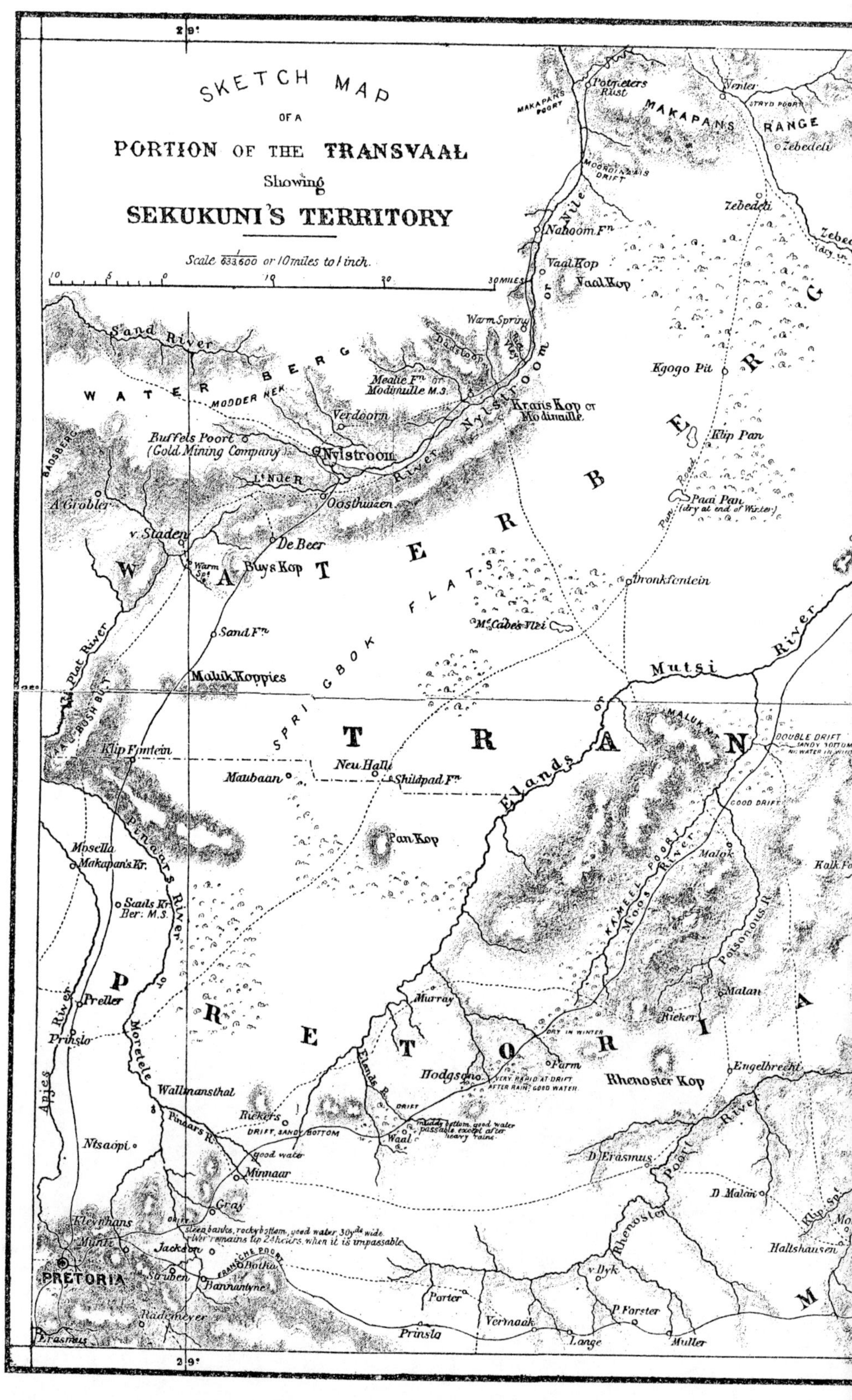
SKETCH MAP
OF A
PORTION OF THE TRANSVAAL
Showing
SEKUKUNI'S TERRITORY
Scale 1/633,600 or 10 miles to 1 inch.
29°
WATER BERG
Sand River
MODDER NEK
Nylstroom
Nylstroom River
Buffels Poort
(Gold Mining Company)
Verdoorn
Mealie Fn
Modimulle M.S.
Krans Kop or Modimulle
Warm Spring
Nahoom Fn
Vaal Kop
Nile
Potgieters Rust
MAKAPANS POORT
MAKAPANS RANGE
Venter
Zebedeli
Kgogo Pit
Klip Pan
Paai Pan (dry at end of Winter)
Oosthuizen
De Beer
A Grobler
v. Staden
Buys Kop
SPRINGBOK FLATS
Sand Fn
Malak Koppies
Dronkfontein
Mc Cabe's Vlei
Mutsi River
Elands River
Klip Fontein
Maubaan
Neu Halle
Shildpad Fn
Pan Kop
Plat River
Pinaars River
Moretele River
Mosella
Makapan's Kr.
Scads Kr Ber: M.S.
Preller
Prinslo
Apies River
Wallmansthal
Ntsaopi
Rieker's
Minnaar
Gray
Kleynhans
Muntz
Jackson
PRETORIA
Struben
Bannantyne
Botha
FRANSCHE POORT
Rademeyer
Erasmus
Porter
Prinslo
Vermaak
Lange
P. Forster
Muller
v. Dyk
Rhenoster
D. Erasmus
Poort River
D. Malan
Hallshausen
Murray
Hodgson
Farm
Waal
Elands R.
Rhenoster Kop
Engelbrecht
Rieker
Malan
Malok
KAMEEL POORT
Moos River
Poisonous R.
MALUK MT
DOUBLE DRIFT
GOOD DRIFT
Kalk Fo
PRETORIA
WATERBERG
DRY IN WINTER
VERY RAPID AT DRIFT AFTER RAIN; GOOD WATER
DRIFT, SANDY BOTTOM
good water
muddy bottom, good water passable except after heavy rains
steep banks, rocky bottom, good water, 30yds wide. River remains up 24 hours, when it is impassable

II.

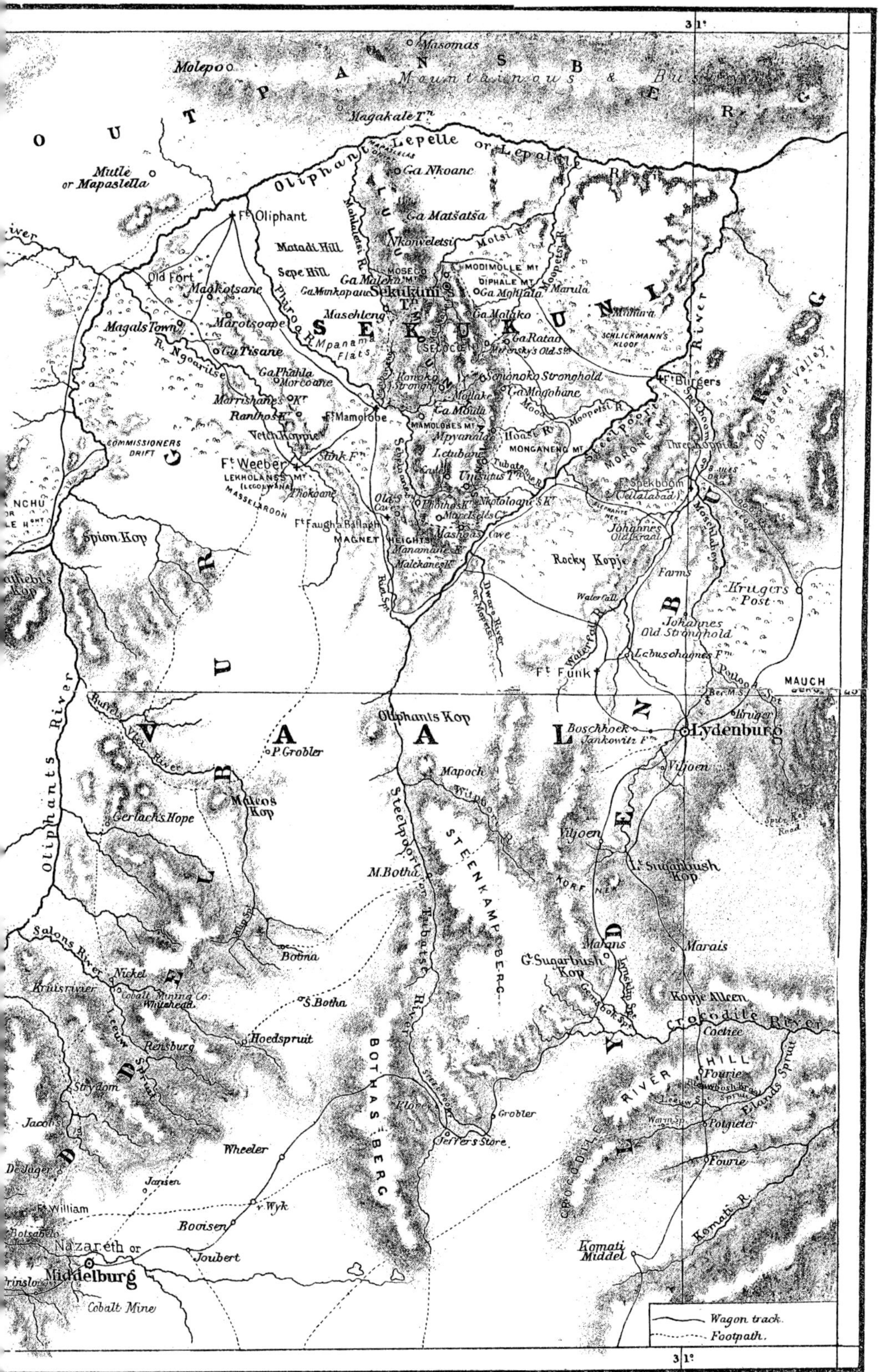

Compiled & Lithd. at the Intelligence Branch Qr. Mr. Genls. Dept., Horse Guards.
March 1881.

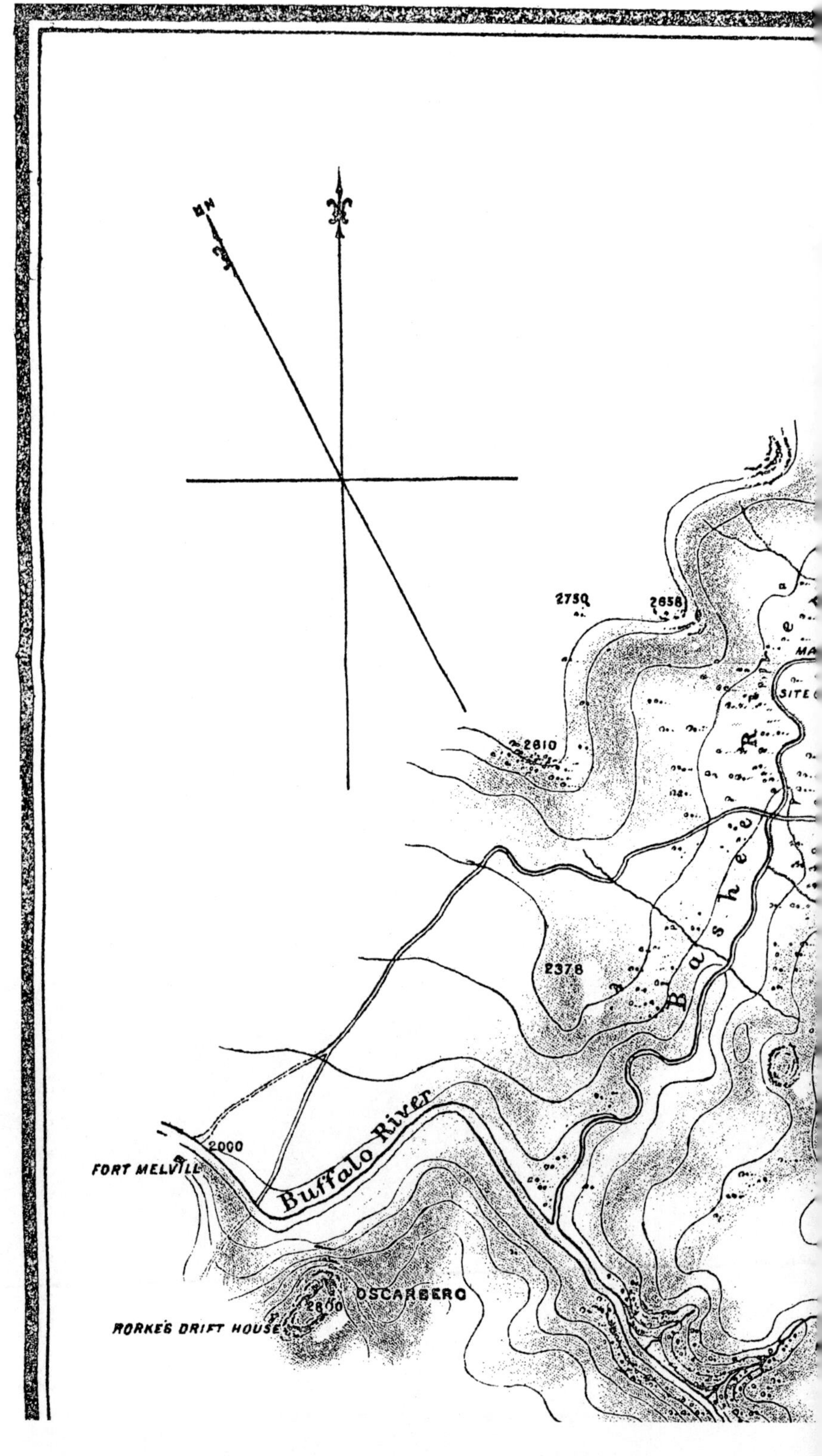

MN
2750
2658
2810
2378
Buffalo River
2000
FORT MELVILL
OSCARBERG
RORKE'S DRIFT HOUSE

NGUTU M^T
S I R A Y O
NYOBASO KRAAL
SIRAYOS KRAALS
2768
3400
TARANTALA M^T
N G U T
3334
3160
2890
2500
2920
2945
2875
2610
2650
2400
ISANDHLWANA HILL
2820
2280
2570
k
1950
2250
2530
2364

MILITAR
of
COUNTRY AROU

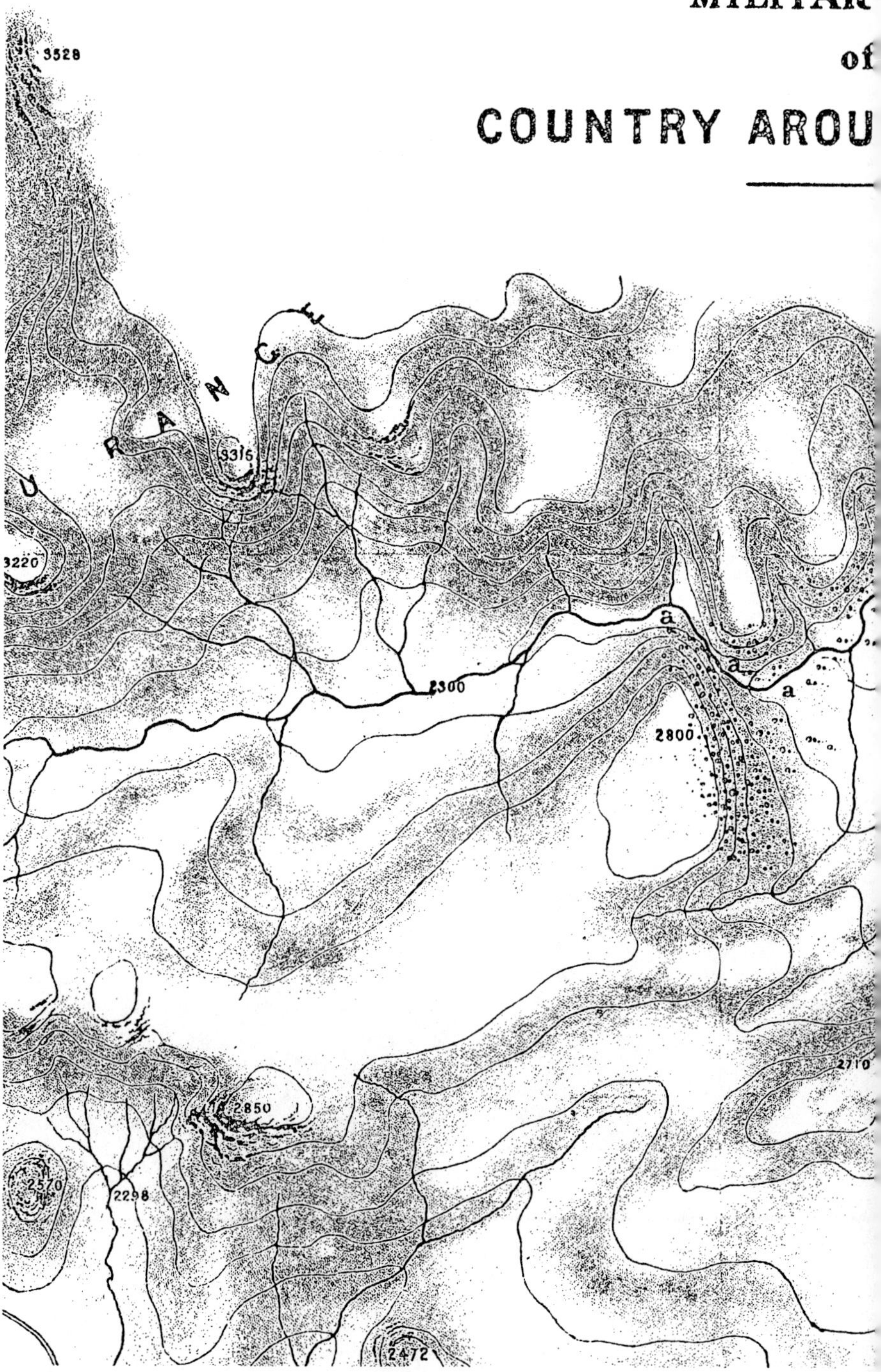

3528
U R A N G E
3315
3220
2300
a
a
a
2800
2710
2850
2570
2298
2472

III.

SURVEY

e

D ISANDHLWANA

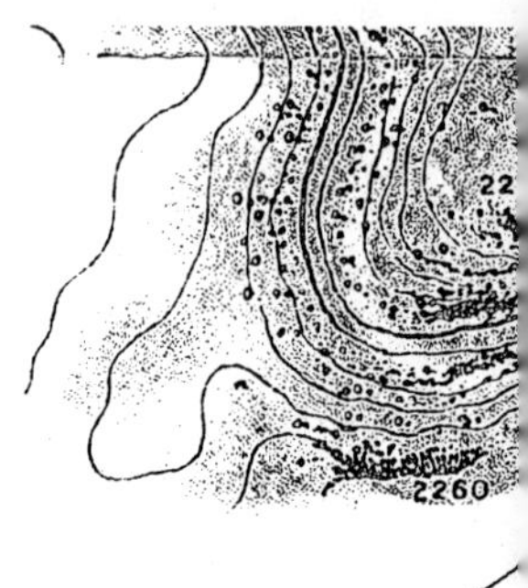

REFERENCES

a. a. *Valley in which the Zulu army bivouacke*
of Jany. 21st-22nd
b. b. *Site of Major Dartnell's bivouack on the*
c. + *Graves of Lieut^s. Melville and Coghill.*

Surveyed with Theodolite and Prismati
Contours 100 feet vertical intervals. Da
as 2000 at Rorke's Drift Ponts.

d.d. *Ridge on which Lord Chelmsford halted*
e. *Ridge on which L^t. Col: Harness halted.*
fff. *New camping ground.*
g.g. *Scene of Dartnell's skirmish.*
h. *Lonsdale met about this spot.*
i. i. *Low ground where Lord Chelmsford halted*
await Col: Glyn's arrival.
k. *Ground where the Battery came into action : 7*

C. Penrose Lieut R.E. del^t.

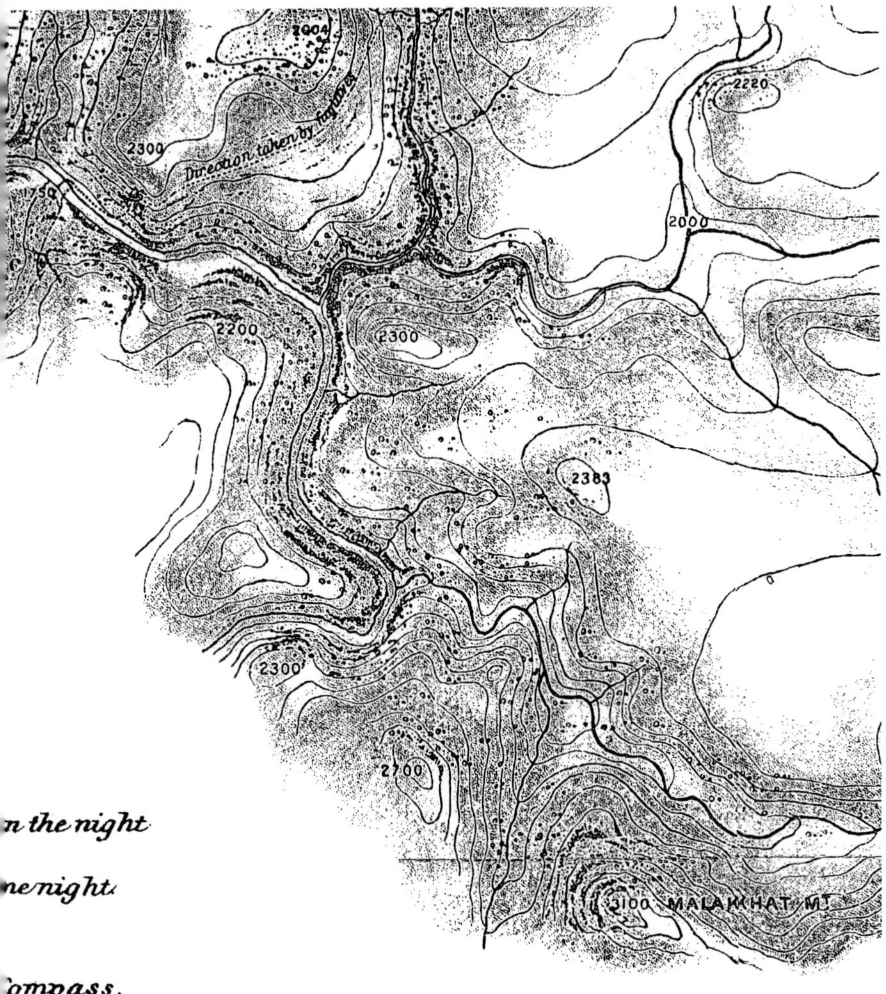

n the night

ne night

'ompass.

n level taken

breakfast.

Scale $\frac{1}{63360}$ or One Inc

P.M.

1 ¾ ½ ¼ 0 1 2

Surveyed by Captain Anstey R.E. ar

ːh to a Mile.

3 4 5 Miles

ːd Lieut. Penrose R.E.

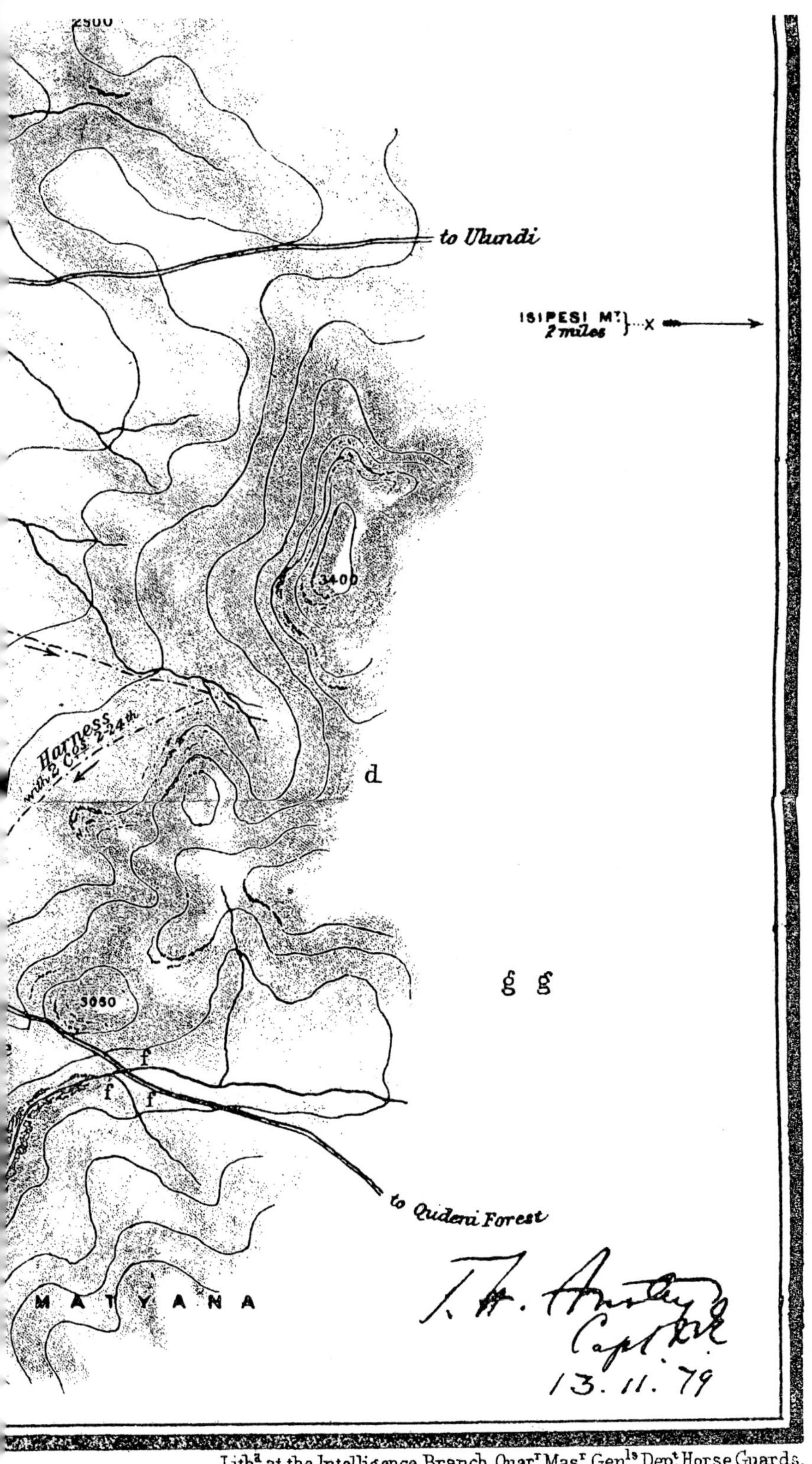

Lith^d. at the Intelligence Branch, Quar^r. Mas^r. Gen^ls. Dep^t. Horse Guards.
March, 1881.

REFERENCES.

The Contours are numbered with reference
Datum Level of 2000 feet: Rorke's Drift ha
arbitrarily fixed at this level, and all contou
referable to it. The main points on this Plan
taken from the Triangulation made by Capt. A
and Lieut. Porter R.E.

○ *Burnt Kraals.*

E. *Left bank of Spruit strewn with Cartridge-c*

F. *Cartridge-cases lying thickly behind the boul*

♂. *Vedette.*

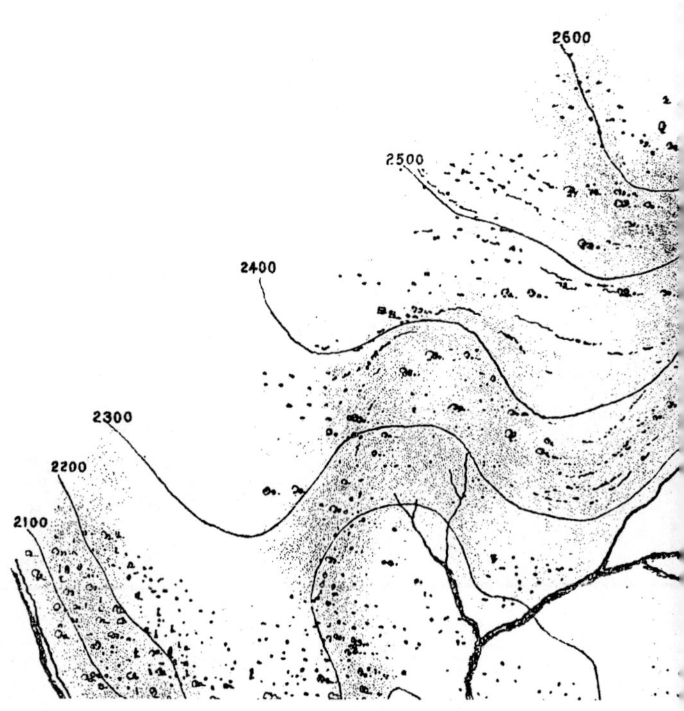

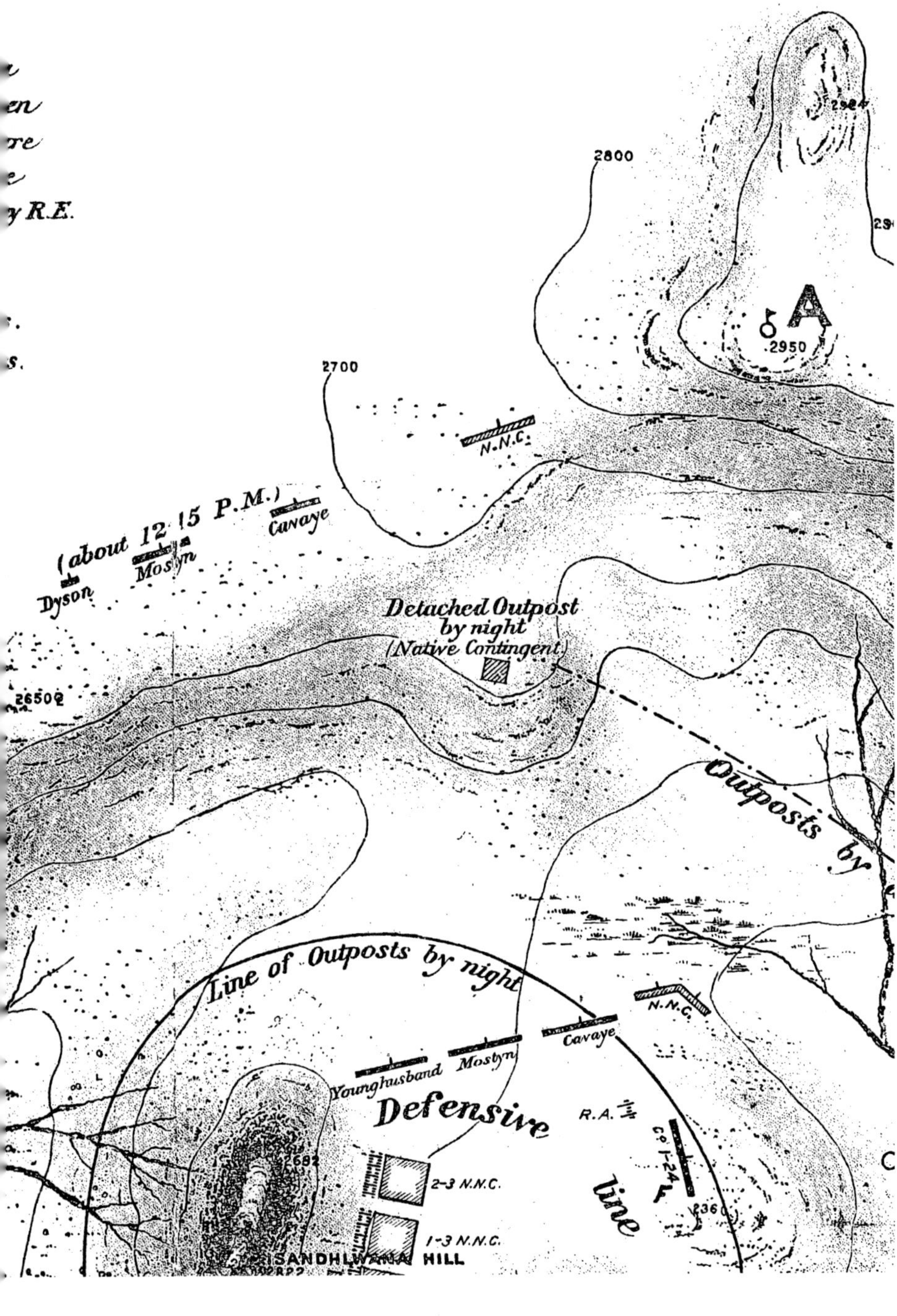

en
re
y R.E.
s.

A
2950
2800
2700
N.N.C.
(about 12.15 P.M.)
Cavaye
Mostyn
Dyson
Detached Outpost
by night
(Native Contingent)
2650
Outposts by
Line of Outposts by night
N.N.C.
Cavaye
Mostyn
Younghusband
Defensive
line
R.A.
Co 1-24
2-3 N.N.C.
1-3 N.N.C.
SANDHLWANA HILL

MILIT

BATTLE-FIEL

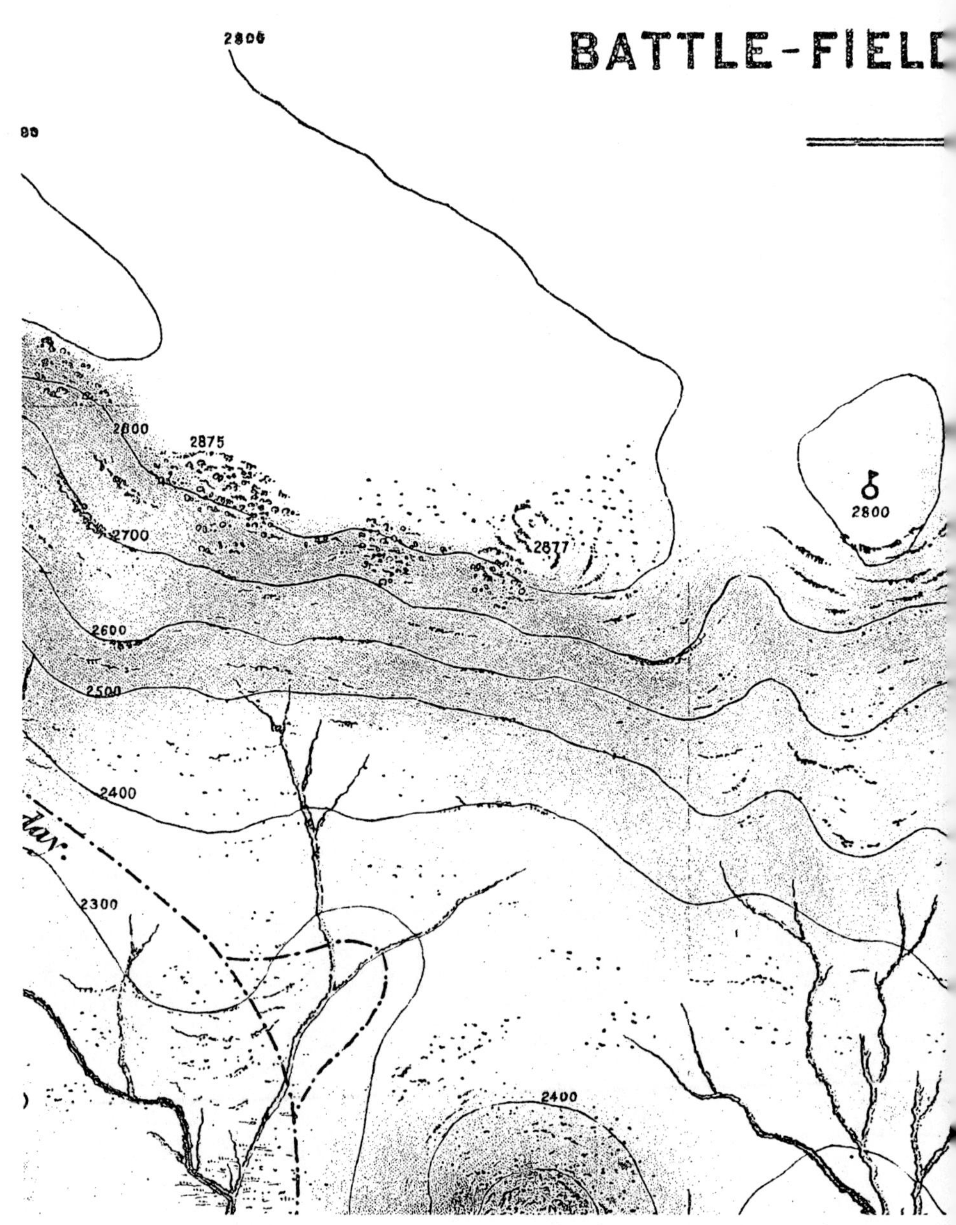

IV.

RY SURVEY

of the

OF ISANDHLWANA

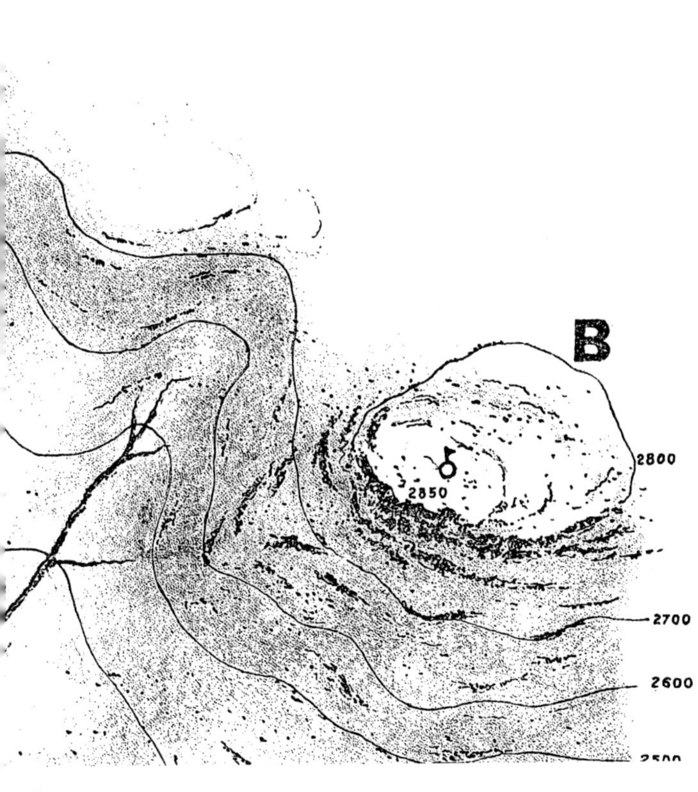

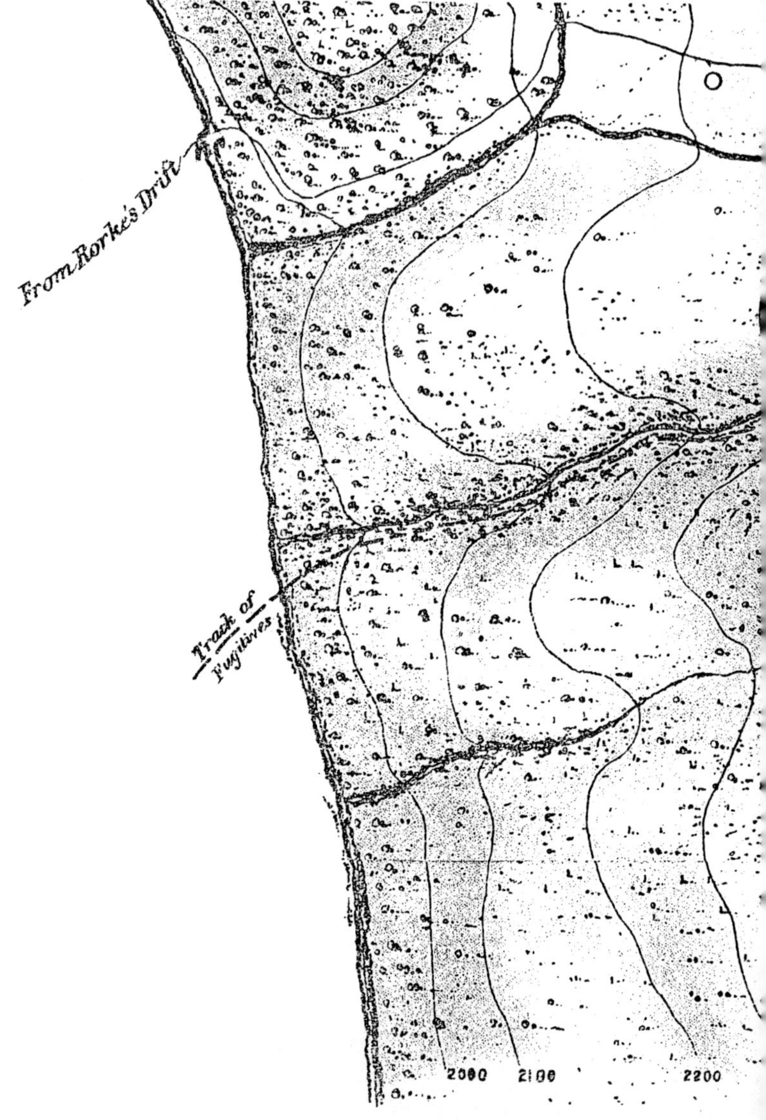

Contours at 100 feet vertical intervals.

C. Penrose Lieut R.E. delt

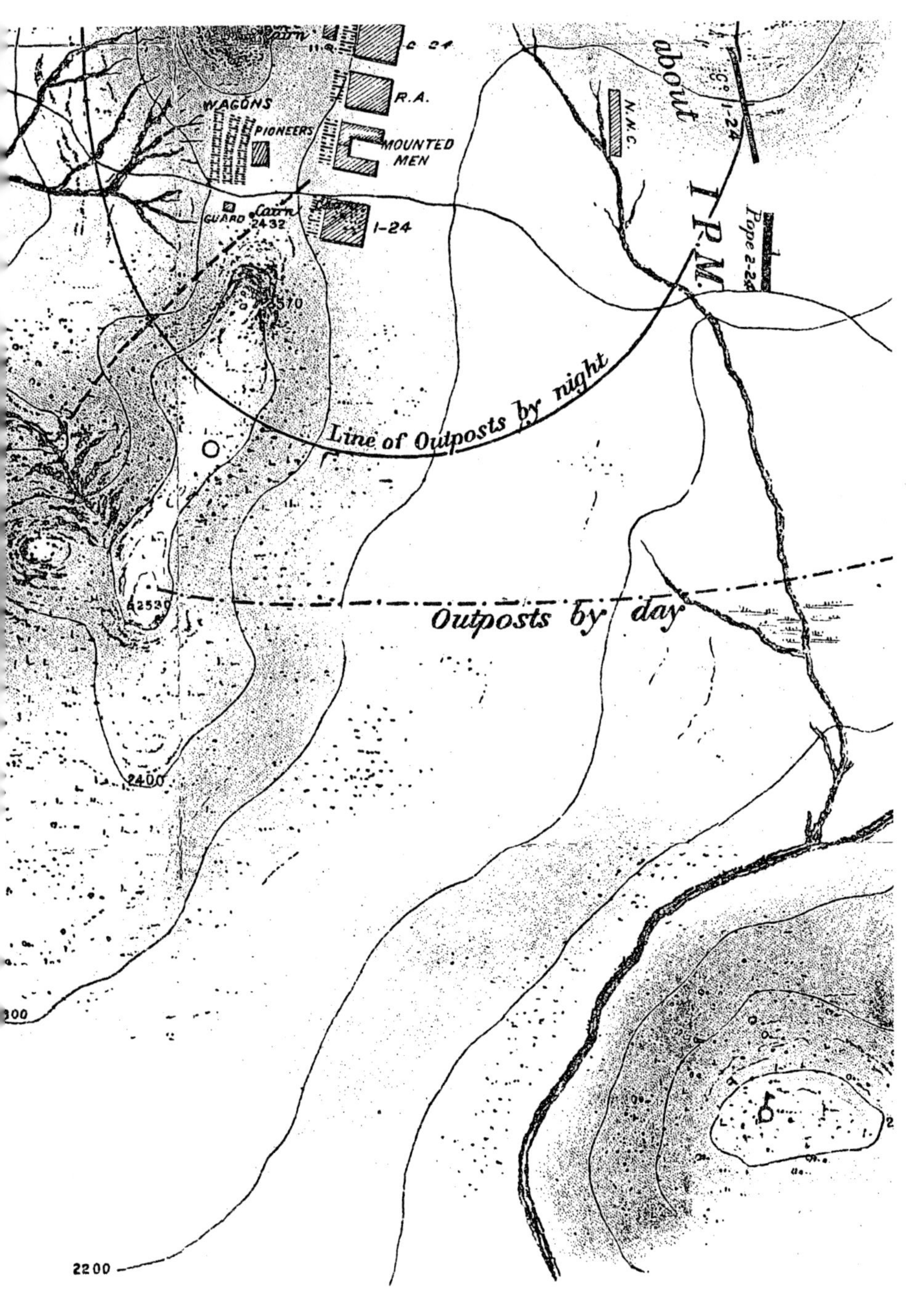

Cairn
C 24
R.A.
WAGONS
PIONEERS
MOUNTED
MEN
GUARD
Cairn
2432
1-24
2570
N.N.C.
about
Co 1-24
I.P.M.
Pope 2-24
Line of Outposts by night
Outposts by day
2520
2400
2200

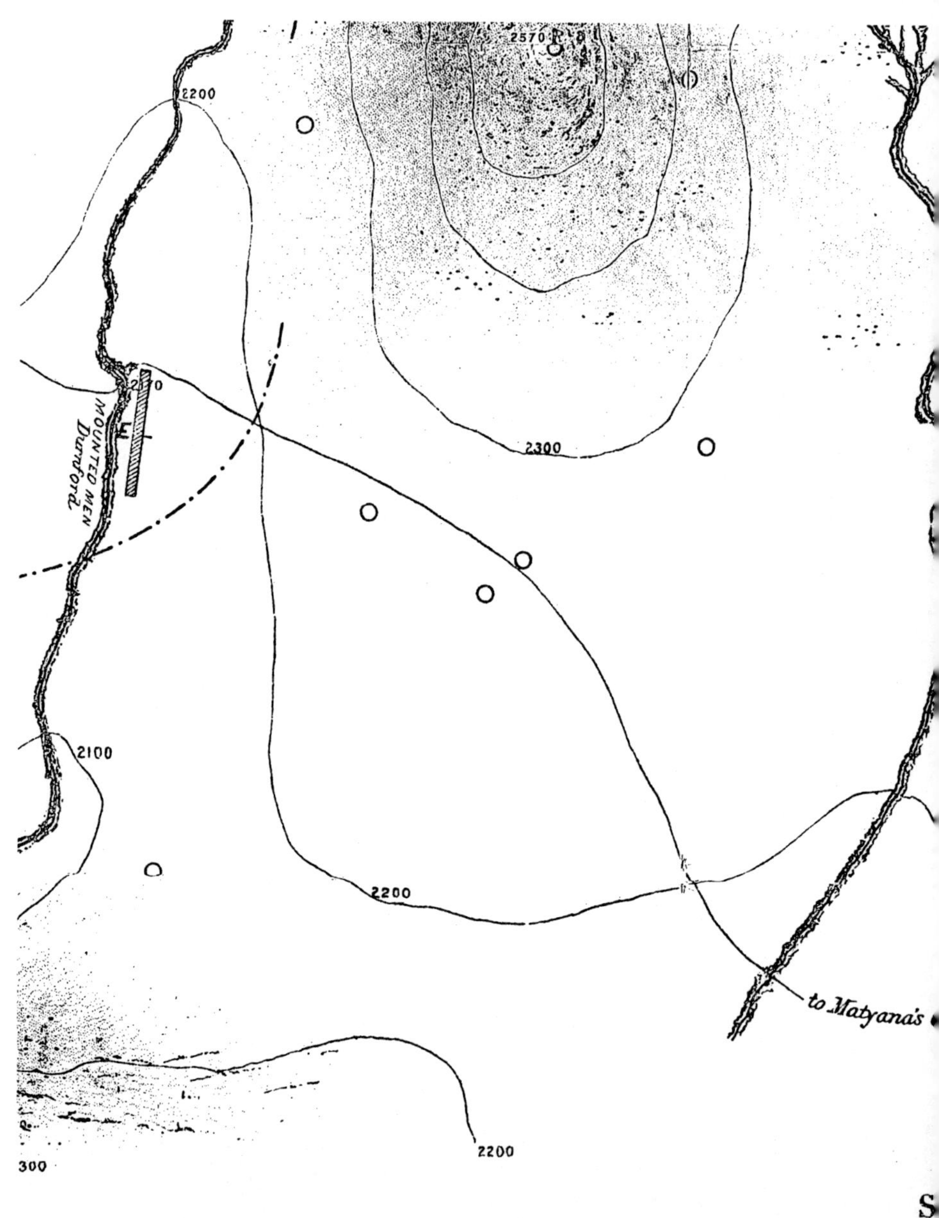
2570
2200
2170
MOUNTED MEN
Durnford
2300
2100
2200
to Matyana's
2200
300
S
Yards 100 50 0 100 200 300 400

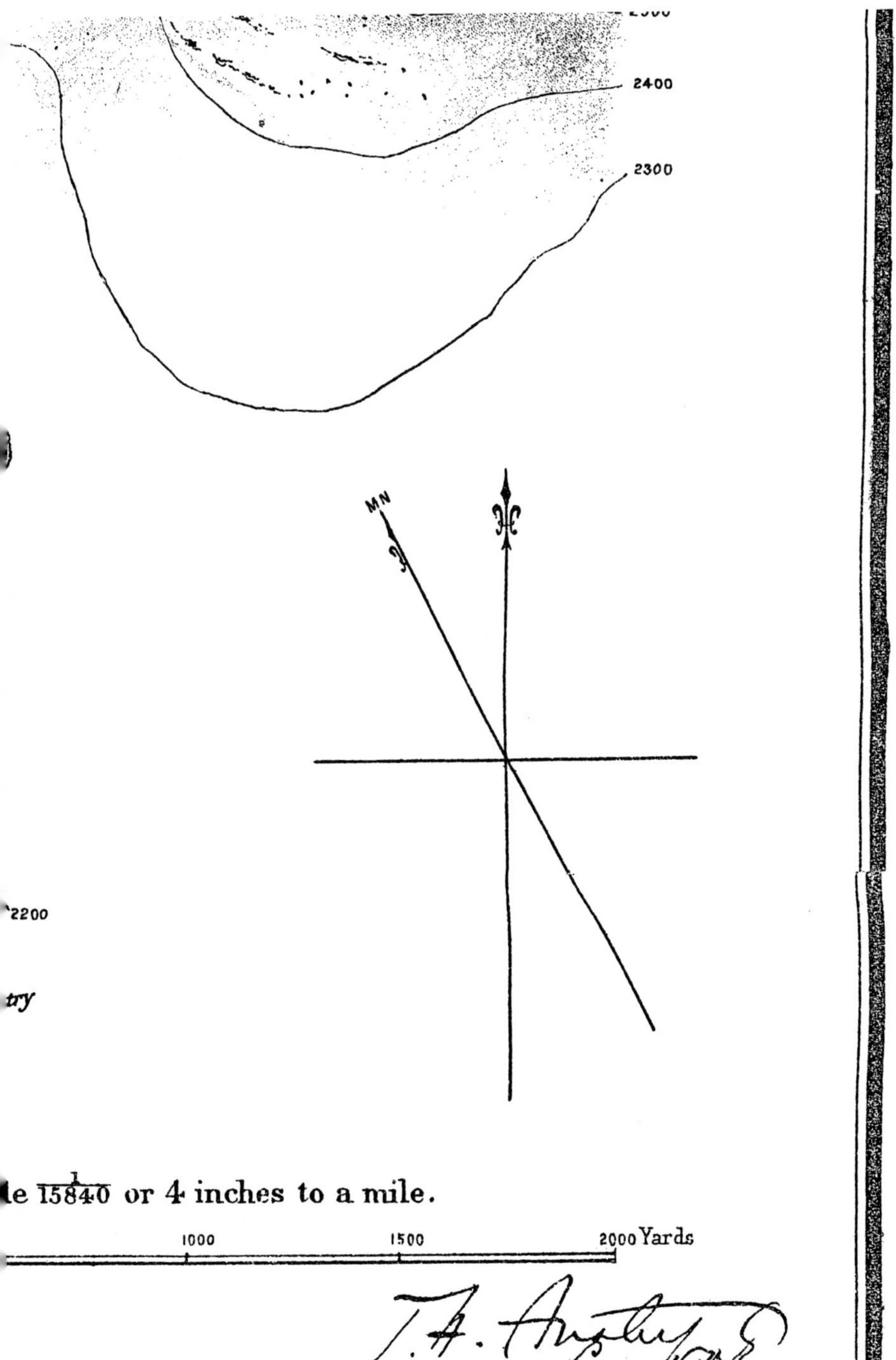

Lith.^d at the Intelligence Branch, Quar.^r Mas.^r Gen.^ls Dep.^t Horse Guards.
March, 1881.

General Profile.

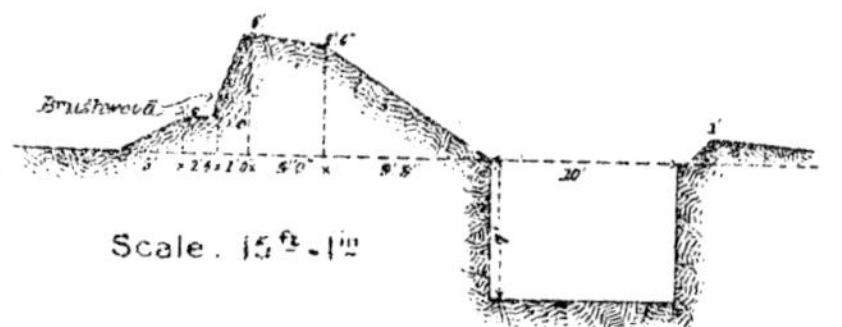

Section through Drawbridge

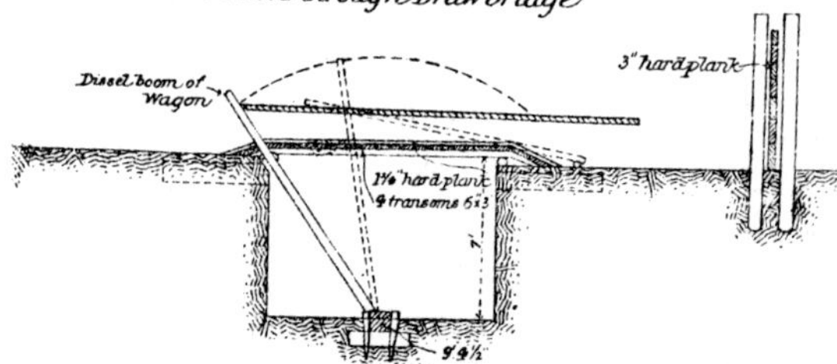

Scale. 10 ft = 1 in.

Profile of Faces A.F. – F.E. – at Point near F.

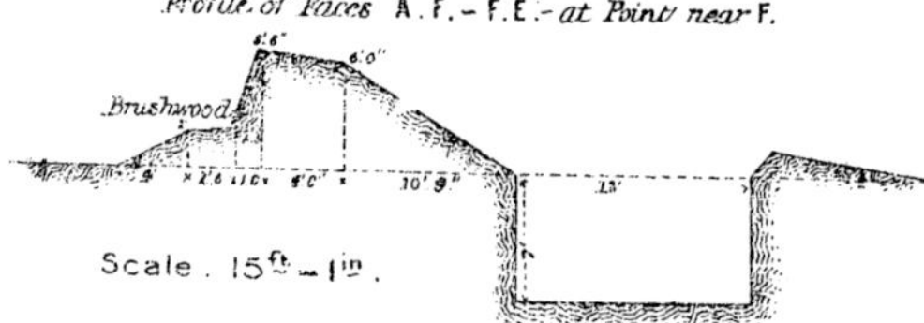

Section at A. shewing Gun Blindage

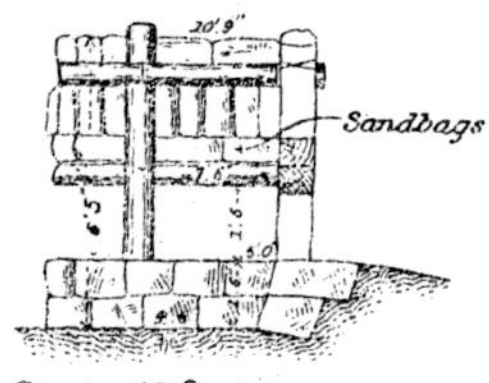

Sectional Elev^n of Drawbridge

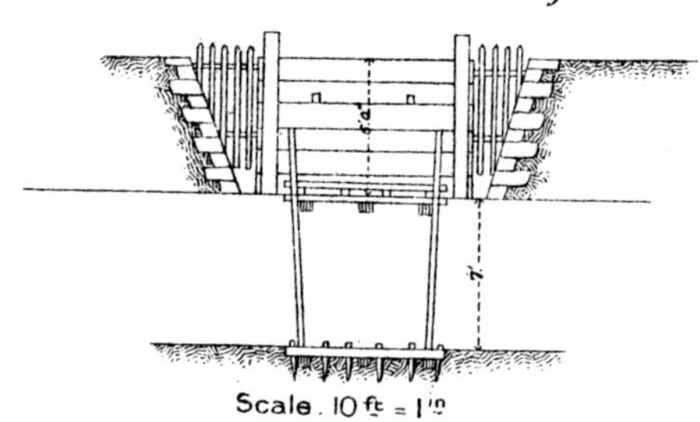

Section & Elev^n of Drain at Y.Z

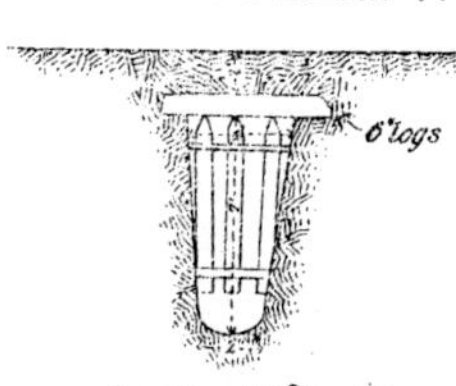

Section at M.N.

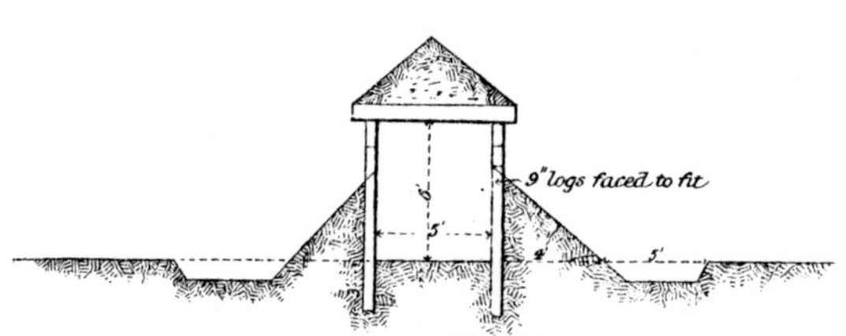

Scale. 10 ft = 1 in.

Sectional Elev^n of Stockade

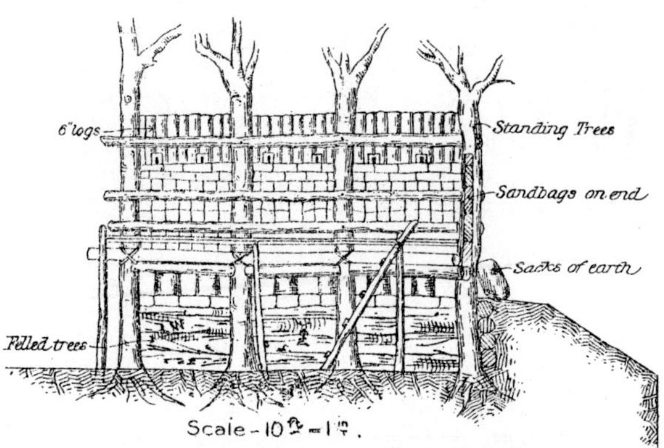

Scale for Plan. 1/260

Scale of 1050 — 50 — 100 — 150 — 200 — 250 — 300 feet

PLAN OF FORT AT ETSHOWE. V.
ZULULAND.

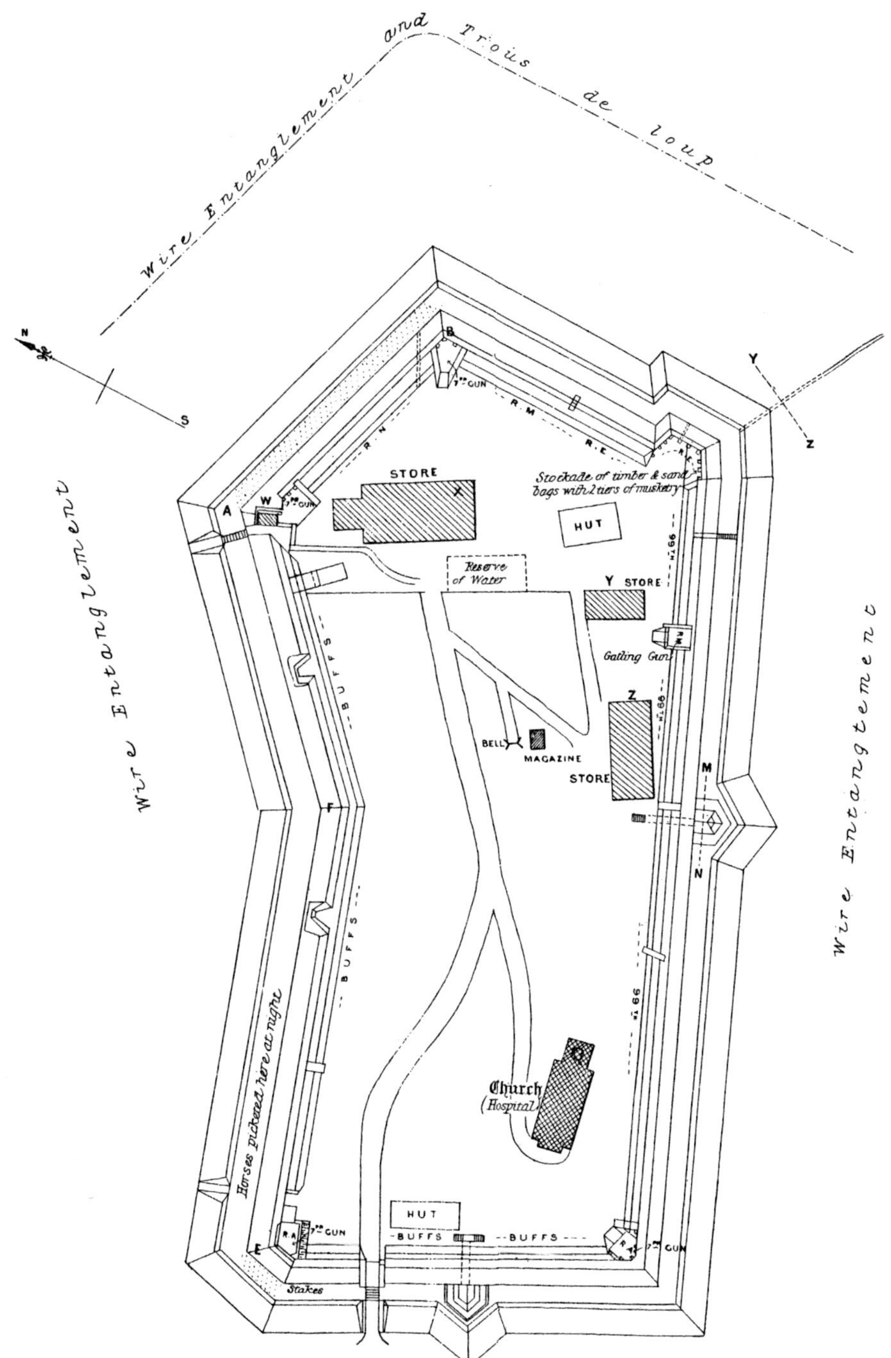

Traced from plans drawn by Lieuts Main & Willock R.E.

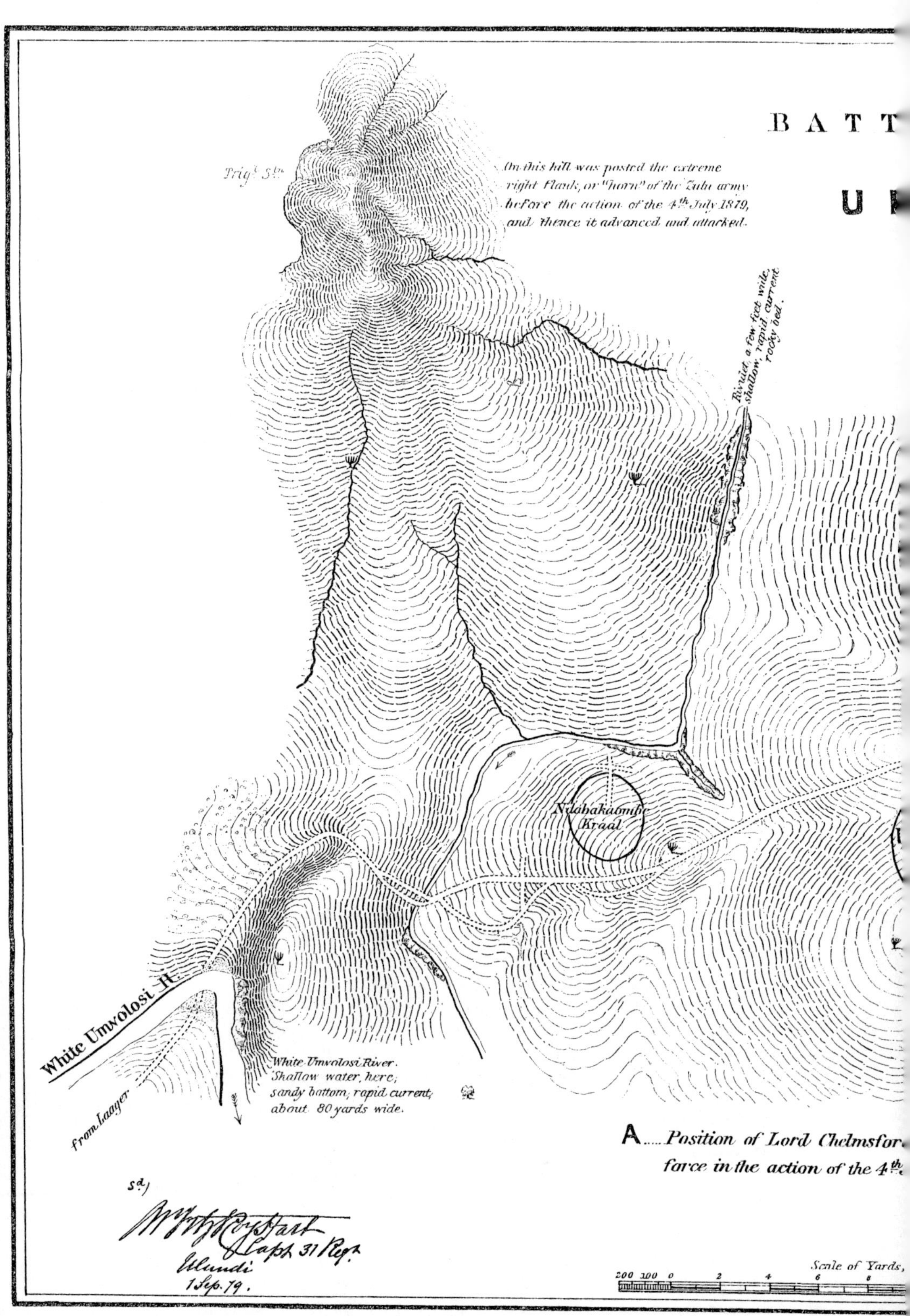
B A T T
U
Trig¹ St.ⁿ
On this hill was posted the extreme right Flank, or "horn" of the Zulu army before the action of the 4th July 1879, and thence it advanced and attacked.
Rivulet, a few feet wide, shallow, rapid current rocky bed.
Ndabakaombe Kraal
White Umvolosi R.
White Umvolosi River. Shallow water, here; sandy bottom; rapid current; about 80 yards wide.
from Laager
A.....Position of Lord Chelmsfor
force in the action of the 4th
Sd.)
W. Wyly Coyhart
Capt. 31 Regt.
Ulundi
1 Sep. 79.
Scale of Yards,
200 100 0 2 4 6 8

VI.

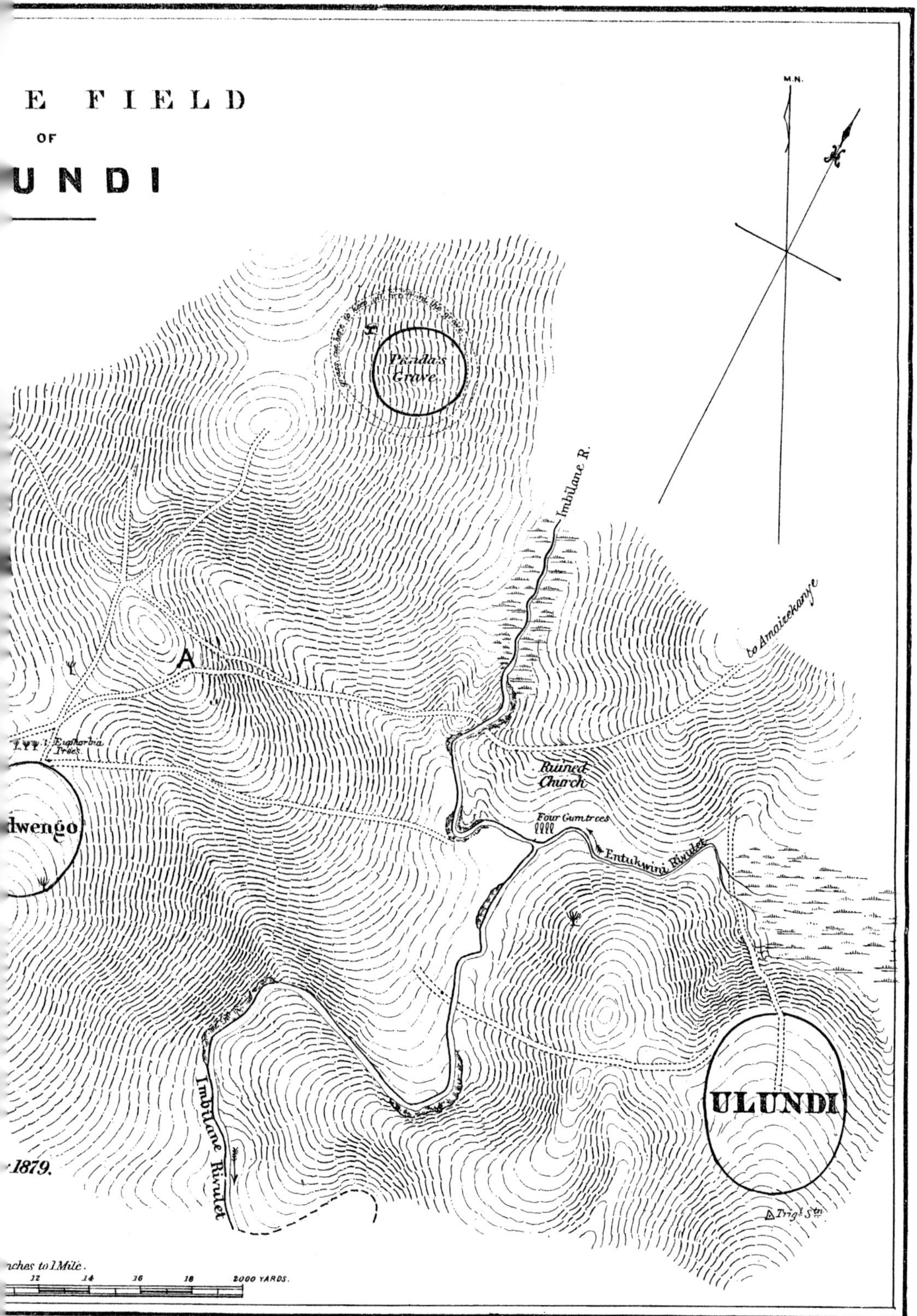

E FIELD
OF
UNDI
M.N.
Panda's Grave.
Imbilane R.
to Amaizekanye
A
Euphorbia Trees.
Ruined Church
Four Gumtrees
Entukwini Rivulet
dwengo
ULUNDI
Imbilane Rivulet
1879.
Trig! Stn
nches to 1 Mile.
12
14
16
18
2000 YARDS.

Printed in the United Kingdom
by Lightning Source UK Ltd.
117678UKS00001B/166-168